PRAISE FOR *ULTIMATE WILDERNESS GEAR*

"Whether you are going on a two-hour hike or a two-week deployment, Craig puts the *sense* back into *common sense* when it comes to outdoor gear. This is a must-read for both the weekend outdoorsperson and the seasoned adventurer."

—**Mike Poynter**, EMT-P, Former FBI Tactical Paramedic and Flight Paramedic

"Craig has a firm understanding of the principles, skills and equipment needed for man-tracking endeavors and backcountry operations. Knowing what you are doing is important, as is knowing what equipment you need to carry. Craig has an unmatched understanding of both. His equipment recommendations will keep you on track."

—**Cornelius B. Nash**, Former U.S. Army Major, Joint Task Force-North (JTF-N) and Senior Military Tracking Instructor with Enhanced Tracking Applications

PRAISE FOR *EXTREME WILDERNESS SURVIVAL*

"Craig has written one of the most densely packed manuals of survival common sense I've ever read. Clearly cultivated from countless hours in the field, this information can save your life. Read it. Memorize it. Use it!"

—**Creek Stewart**, Survival Instructor, Author and TV Host

"Craig Caudill has masterfully captured the art of extreme survival. The everyday Joe or Joan can fully understand and learn from this book!"

—**EJ Snyder**, Extreme Survivalist, 25-Year Army Combat Vet, Host of *Dual Survival*

"Essential reading for the outdoors enthusiast. From tenderfoot to special forces, Craig's expertise covers all bases."

—**Tim Farmer**, Outdoorsman and Host of *Tim Farmer's Country Kitchen*

"Craig Caudill knows from hard-won experience what works and what doesn't. If I were in a true survival situation, I can't think of another instructor I'd want by my side."

—**Jim Cobb**, Author of *Prepper's Long-Term Survival Guide*

"Craig Caudill's *Extreme Wilderness Survival* is a great intro to all things survival and tactical for the extremes, covering not only the fundamentals of survival but also new subjects traditionally reserved only for the military. It is sure to get everyone thinking about some new aspects of the overall survival situation they may encounter."

—**Mykel Hawke**, U.S. Army Special Forces Combat Veteran, Author and Host of *Lost Survivors*

ULTIMATE WILDERNESS GEAR

EVERYTHING YOU NEED TO KNOW TO CHOOSE & USE THE BEST OUTDOOR EQUIPMENT

CRAIG CAUDILL

AUTHOR OF *EXTREME WILDERNESS SURVIVAL*,
CHIEF INSTRUCTOR AT NATURE RELIANCE SCHOOL

PAGE STREET
PUBLISHING CO.

PAGE STREET
PUBLISHING CO.

Copyright © 2018 by Craig Caudill

First published in 2018 by
Page Street Publishing Co.
27 Congress Street, Suite 105
Salem, MA 01970
www.pagestreetpublishing.com

Distributed by Macmillan, sales in Canada by The Canadian Manda Group.

22 21 20 19 18   1 2 3 4 5

ISBN-13: 978-1-62414-552-0
ISBN-10: 1-62414-552-3

Library of Congress Control Number: 2017963200

Cover and book design by Page Street Publishing Co.
Photography by Jennifer Caudill

Printed and bound in China

TO MY CHILDREN, LILY AND ZANE.

IF I COULD COUNT THE TIMES YOU HAVE BROUGHT ME JOY, IT WOULD OUTNUMBER THE TREES IN THE WILDERNESS.

CONTENTS

INTRODUCTION

In every walk with nature, one receives far more than he or she seeks.

—John Muir

Let's get right to it. You want to spend more time in the wilderness. You should. Countless studies have proven that spending time outside is beneficial to the enrichment and development of a better you. If you picked up this book for one of the following reasons, you have done yourself a great favor:

- You are new to being outdoors and don't know where to begin when it comes to buying gear.

- You are an experienced outdoorsperson, but you like learning about and using ideas from someone else with different experiences.

- You are a "buy once, cry once" type of person, meaning you don't want to fall victim to slick marketing or sales pitches and would rather learn how to make the right decisions for gear purchases.

- You are a gear nut, and you like all things related to gear.

You have picked up the right book, because this one can do all that and a lot more. I have had an incredible range of experiences in the outdoors over my near-50-year life-span. From backpacking through mixed hardwood forests in my home state of Kentucky to fishing in Alaska, I have seen—and used—a lot of gear. I have spent solo time in a wilderness "living off the land" with nothing more than a knife, and I have spent copious amounts of time in campgrounds with my family when we took along the proverbial kitchen sink.

I have spent the better part of the last decade teaching others how to safely make their way in the outdoors. This means I have seen thousands of students who have brought with them nearly every piece of gear available. I have worked with people who have never spent a night outside and members of the Special Forces with the most technologically advanced gear in the world. I have watched as gear pieces have exceeded expectations for some and failed miserably for others. Therefore, I have a broad knowledge of gear founded on my diverse experiences as well as my observations of what has and has not worked for others. I want you to have that knowledge, and that is why I wrote this book.

Author (right) and friend hiking the Sheltowee Trace in Kentucky, circa 1989.

This book is not a sales flyer for certain brands. It is a guide to help you learn how to make sound decisions on gear. However, with that said, I will give you my recommendations for gear and brands from time to time when they have proven to exceed my expectations. This is the book I wish I had had many years ago. My experiences and knowledge have been achieved through valuable hard work. I have loved every second of it. This book is a compilation of my experiences (good and bad), the students I have taught and an exhaustive amount of research.

You need to spend more time in the wilderness. It is good for you. This book will assist you in avoiding the pitfalls of poor gear choices and reward you with knowledge that only comes from decades of experience, making your time in nature that much more enjoyable.

As I say in all of my Nature Reliance School programs, "Come on, join in and let's learn together!"

Craig Caudill

CHAPTER 1

THE FUNDAMENTALS OF ACQUIRING GEAR

AND UNDERSTANDING YOUR NEEDS

Why do you go away? So that you can come back. So that you can see the place you came from with new eyes and extra colors. And the people there see you differently, too. Coming back to where you started is not the same as never leaving.

—Terry Pratchett, *A Hat Full of Sky*

I WILL NEVER FORGET MY FIRST BACKPACKING TRIP WHEN I WAS EIGHTEEN.
Until that point in my life, I had spent a great deal of time participating in period-correct reenacting. I spent much of my childhood learning the skills of a prerevolutionary scout. That means I spent a considerable amount of time living off the land so to speak. This included trekking, hunting, fishing and more. My dad and I often stayed in period-correct shelters like tepees and lean-tos. These were situations in which I had an established base camp and would venture out in search of resources that I needed (or just to play in the woods). Often, though, I came back to camp and ate what my dad brought to eat. I had a fair amount of security waiting back at the camp.

Backpacking is not like that at all. A friend and I got the crazy idea to go backpacking over spring break. Spring break in Kentucky is nothing like sunnier spring break destinations. Often it is cold and snowy. Regardless of this fact, however, I wore the work boots that I donned while working on the family farm, carried an ancient canvas Boy Scout pack my dad had lying around, and ate canned spaghetti and chili mac. My sleeping bag was 100 percent cotton and I had an old canvas military-style tent that felt like it weighed 300 pounds (135 kg). I was tough enough to make three days and two nights on the trail, but I was not comfortable at any point during the trip. My sleeping bag got wet, my feet stayed wet the whole time and cold canned chili mac is not the best breakfast when you can't get a fire built to warm it.

Fortunately, no unexpected challenges came up that put me into survival mode for any reason. It was snowing and moderately cold. Had I experienced something drastically unexpected (such as a broken ankle), I would have most likely succumbed to hypothermia. In short, it was a small slice of heaven being out there like that.

I was hooked. The refreshing distance from civilization, the smells, the quietness—they were part of me immediately. There is something right about carrying your own needs on your back into the wilderness. It made me want to spend more time in the wilderness on backpacking trips. That trip was the catalyst for many future adventures and the book you now have in your hand. Experience is often hard-won. The gear that I use is a testament to that mind-set. I am very excited to share many of my life experiences with you so you can save a lot of money and gain valuable insight. There are certain truths that remain constant no matter what your purpose in going outside is. I want to share those truths with you here, as well as consider how some very accomplished outdoorsmen in history

MIND-SET, SKILLS AND TACTICS

HOW TO CHOOSE GEAR THAT LASTS AND WORKS

In my first book, *Extreme Wilderness Survival*, I grouped the important aspects of safety and survival into four categories: (1) mind-set, (2) skills, (3) tactics and (4) gear. This order of categories is instantly recognizable to many who understand the role that each of these plays in any wilderness adventure, not just a survival-related event. They give us an order of priorities to follow, starting with mind-set, when we are trying to stay safe. You will note that gear is last on the list. Although it is last, it is at the forefront of bridging the gap between our normal lives at home and the wilderness. However, each of those other three priorities has its own merits for consideration. For that reason, I am including them in this first chapter so we can organize experiences with gear selection and use.

I can summarize this whole book in the following five words: You need to do you. There is no cookie-cutter answer to purchasing gear. That is why I have dedicated this whole book to the subject. It will save you countless hours and dollars on gear. I am going to provide you with the basis of acquiring gear, for *you*. This means I will be helping you make intelligent decisions on what works and what does not in a multitude of geographical areas. I want you to be able to make informed decisions on gear for serious wilderness use. We can all learn from the experience of others, and you can learn from mine. Throughout this book, I am going to cover a collection of topics to help you prepare for your first, or next, wilderness adventure. As with all that I do, I want to spend more time outside in a safe manner. Ultimately, the goal is for you to make informed decisions and not purchase gear because of emotional reactions or slick marketing.

MIND-SET: HOW TO GET THE MOST BANG FOR YOUR BUCK

Many outdoor gear purchases, whether they be online or in a retail store, tend to be more of an impulse buy than anything else. That is unfortunate because a slick sales pitch or an otherwise-attractive marketing method could lead you to buy a piece that is not suited for you. This serves to either attack your wallet and leave you not having the funds to get other usable products or to lead you to a piece of gear that underperforms for your needs.

This book will help you change that cycle of disappointment and frustration. I want to put you in a position where you can make informed decisions and get the gear you need. There are several different facets to this mind-set that I want you to make sure you understand as we move forward through this book:

- You should acquire gear that will take care of your needs in both expected and unexpected circumstances. This means you need to have gear that you can rely on during difficult times. I have spent a lifetime using gear outdoors in wonderful and not-so-wonderful circumstances and will tell you what works and what doesn't.

- The most expensive gear is not always the best gear. You can easily acquire gear that won't break the bank. That doesn't mean we should consider only price. Some gear is worth spending extra money on.

- You should know the specifications of the gear you are buying so it meets your needs. Knowing the details about your gear will also help you not fall victim to the marketing that draws us all in at times.

Developing your mind-set will ensure safety and years of fun outdoor adventuring.

- You should determine your purpose in going to the wilderness. Are you a backpacker, day hiker, car camper or maybe even a glamper? Different gear will meet different needs.

- You should determine whether you prefer trekking solo or sharing the wilderness with others. Your answer will determine whether you will be taking care of everything yourself or possibly sharing the load of items with members of a group.

I am also very cognizant that we may be at very different stages of life. The gear that I comfortably carried as a college-age, physically fit backpacker is not what I carry today at nearly 50 years old. Back then, I was all about putting miles under my feet and carrying little to eat. Now I am more of a "stop and smell the roses" type of person, mainly because I am naturally curious to what nature can teach me. You will find yourself like me; you will most likely have different reasons for being outside at various times or stages of life. I will help you find the gear that will suit you in many of these situations.

SKILLS: HOW TO ASSEMBLE AND CARRY YOUR GEAR

I am widely known as a survival expert. While that may be true, I prefer to focus my attention on *safety* instead. The way I see it, if you plan your trip with contingencies for trouble, you can avoid most mishaps in the backcountry. That is what I consider being safe. Wilderness adventure in the backcountry is all about taking care of your needs and some of your wants. I plan my gear setup so that in case something unexpected occurs, I have certain things that stay attached to my body and the rest goes in my pack. It serves us well to understand what our needs are from a safety perspective. I covered the Rule of Three (see sidebar on page 15) in my first book. It is common knowledge and gives us a great way of determining what gear is high priority.

As I prepare to pack and get my gear ready, I always consider the Rule of Three and how to maintain it. I want to cover these individually so you can see how to pack properly. Personal safety will be covered in Chapter 3. In Chapters 4 and 5 we will look at the multitude of options to help you maintain your core body temperature. Chapter 6 will delve into the gear and methods that will keep you hydrated. Chapter 7 will help take care of that rumbling in your tummy so you can eat like royalty in the backcountry.

In a nutshell, your water bottle can leak and you will survive, but if your body leaks blood or oxygen you will not live for more than a few short minutes. I want to use this understanding to prompt you to take care of your personal safety. Taking care of blood flow and oxygen in your body is best left to preemptive planning and risk analysis.

RULE OF THREE

1. **THREE MINUTES FOR AIR AND BLOOD.** You cannot live more than three minutes without oxygen and blood flow continuing in your body. This means you will need items to take care of your personal safety.

2. **THREE HOURS FOR CORE BODY TEMPERATURE.** You cannot live more than three hours without maintaining your core body temperature. This means you will need gear that will keep you warm, such as clothing, shelter and fire-making supplies.

3. **THREE DAYS FOR HYDRATION.** You cannot live more than three days without maintaining or obtaining hydration for your body. You will need to either carry water or procure and clean water from your environment.

4. **THREE WEEKS FOR FOOD.** You cannot live more than three weeks without the energy you derive from eating food. You will need to carry energy in the form of meals and snacks and use them intelligently.

5. **THREE MONTHS FOR COMPANIONSHIP.** It is incredibly important to work with others whenever possible rather than going alone. I include this thought because it does play out in long-term survival needs, but it also true for short-term adventuring. Going outdoors with others can keep you safer and better able to handle stressful situations.

You should consider what sort of things may cause you harm and be prepared for them. One example is knowing what sort of wildlife may harm you and how to prevent it from doing so. This was highlighted for me many years ago while on a fishing trip to Alaska. Alaska is known as America's last frontier for good reason. It is rugged and has little human encroachment in many areas. These areas are often home to wildlife that is at the top of the food chain. I was wade fishing during my first trip there and came to a distinct turn in the Kenai River. The turn caused the water to get so deep that it was not wadable and I had to cross a very short neck of land to get back to the river. The small trees and growth were thick and inhospitable, and I felt like I was in a physical fight with nature. But the best was yet to come.

When I popped out the other side of the vegetation, I stumbled onto the sand of the riverbank. I looked down at my feet and instantly recognized the freshly laid track of a grizzly bear. There were water droplets and splashes in and around the track; this meant the bear was still in the area and very close. That grizzly had the same idea I had, which was to grab some salmon from that beautiful river. At the exact moment I saw the track, I realized I was wholly unprepared for an encounter with a bear. I had no bear spray, firearm or even a first aid kit. To put it mildly, I was young and dumb.

Compare that to the story of my friend who lived in Alaska for eighteen years. He cleared trails for the United States Department of Agriculture's Natural Resources Conservation Service and he regularly made his way into the bush to perform his duties. Carrying his needs on his back was part of daily life, not just a fun trip for adventure. On one such trip he was awoken by a friend yelling that a bear was in the area. When

◄ (Left) Skills development is your excuse to spend more time outside doing what you enjoy.

he stuck his head out of his bivy tent, a female grizzly was literally standing over him. She was snapping her teeth and stomping her front feet on either side of his head, both of which are signs of a very agitated bear. Since my friend kept his bear spray right next to him, he grabbed it and sprayed the grizzly fully in the face. She momentarily stood there looking at him, tried to shake it off, then ran off into the bush. It was then that he discovered two cubs in the tree above his tent. They had wandered into his campsite and went up the tree when they were alarmed by his scent or presence. Momma grizzly had done her best to protect her young. My friend used bear spray just once in eighteen years, but it most likely saved his life. He was better prepared for the backcountry than I had been on my fishing trip.

Your best strategy for taking care of blood flow and oxygen needs is one of avoidance. Avoid the issues that will cause you to die. Seems simple, right? Evidently, not really. I have trained countless search-and-rescue (SAR) volunteers who share stories of how people very rarely consider dangers. Preplanning may seem too safe, that you are not being "wild" enough. To an extent that is true, but I am suggesting that you simply develop a plan and carry the gear that will help take care of you when the inevitable surprise comes. This will allow you to spend more time outside being "wild" and returning safely so you can do it again and again. During your preplanning of any wilderness trip, you should consider the risks. They come in four categories.

Wilderness adventure can be both beautiful and dangerous.

1. **WILDLIFE.** What wildlife is in the area you plan on visiting? You should have a plan of avoidance, but if a situation arises that makes avoidance impossible, the right gear will help. This should include deterrent spray, firearms (where legal) and a first aid kit (see Chapter 3 for details on these items).

2. **WEATHER.** While planning, you should check the weather and plan accordingly.

3. **GEOGRAPHY.** Is there a chance for avalanches or rock slides? Are there holes to fall into or fast rapids to get swept away with? Know the area you'll be traveling through and have plans for things that may not go well.

4. **PEOPLE.** Adrenaline junkies can get you in a position that results in a mechanical injury, such as a broken collarbone or a twisted ankle. I am a fan of wilderness experiences that include a measure of danger, but they should be undertaken with plans and contingencies in place if problems occur.

You should have certain gear that stays attached to your body should issues arise. We will cover the details of each of these throughout the book.

In all things safety and survival, I am a proponent of avoidance and awareness strategies so you can enjoy wilderness travel and adventure time and time again. To cover those first three minutes mentioned on page 15, I think everyone should always carry a map, compass and first aid kit. I include a map and compass here because with those items and the skill to use them you can avoid getting lost. Getting lost and stressed is the primary reason people fall victim to outdoor problems. With land-navigation skills utilizing a map and a compass, you can avoid these problems. The map and the compass will allow you to keep track of where you have been and where you are going so you do not get lost.

The first aid kit should be in your pack in case you need it. When I say *first aid kit*, you may be thinking of the big and bulky kits typically found in the big-box stores. Thankfully, first aid kits do not need to be so bulky. That is why I have included a section in Chapter 3 specifically covering medical gear.

Your core body temperature is vital to your morale and comfort in the wilderness. You should pack clothes that allow you to layer (see Chapter 4) and a pack that allows you to stow them away for easy grab-and-go use (Chapter 8). You don't want to find yourself in a surprise snowstorm or rainstorm, digging your gear out of the bottom of your pack. You should also have a basic shelter that it is easy to get to in case you are incapacitated and need protection in a hurry.

With all that said, let me summarize for you. You need the following attached to you: a first aid kit, land-navigation supplies and layered clothing.

While those are the basics that should be on you (or close to you) at all times, I would also like to add the following items, not because you *need* them to stay alive but because they have multiple uses for your safety and survival. I cover each of these in-depth in later chapters:

- **KNIFE.** A knife is the epitome of a multiuse item. You should have one on your belt or in your pocket or both.
- **CORDAGE.** Cordage is one of the most difficult things to replicate in the wilderness while under stress. You should always have some on you. Wear a paracord bracelet, have extra on your knife sheath or carry some in your pocket.

- **BRIGHTLY COLORED BANDANA.** This piece of cloth has dozens of uses, the least of which is as a signaling device. It can also be used as a nice insulator when you grab the handle of a hot cup of coffee in the morning or as a cooling rag on your neck.
- **WHISTLE.** If it is needed, a whistle can be another signaling device for your rescue as well as a warning to bears that you are in the area.

I get the opportunity to teach and train with many first responders including SAR teams. Much of what I have shared thus far is based on my conversations with them. Items like the ones I just mentioned are tools that SAR teams have noticed people could have used to avoid needing rescue. SAR teams are good at what they do, but they would rather you go to the wilderness, have fun, return safely and not need their services. If you do need their assistance, those things will make it easier for them to find you.

TACTICS: WORKING WITH OTHERS TO SHARE THE LOAD

Going solo into the wilderness is good for you in many ways. You can rid yourself of inner turmoil. I have done it numerous times and it has been rewarding. However, many great authors and philosophers have gone solo into the wilderness and come out agreeing with Christopher McCandless, who said that "happiness is only real when shared." That has been my experience as well. Going into a wilderness with others and sharing in the fun is just that: fun. There are several other reasons that come to mind that should encourage you to go out with others often:

Working with others makes your wilderness experience safer and more enjoyable.

- **MORALE.** It is easy to get tired, hungry and down on yourself. If someone is with you, they can provide encouragement and boost your morale.

- **LOAD SHARING (SEE BELOW).** Other people can literally share some of the load. You can also trade gear if a person in your party is "not feeling it." For example, there is no need for both people in a party of two to carry their own tent. Share the load and ease the burden.

- **SAFETY.** There is a lot of decision-making that happens in the backcountry. Which fork to take, where to set up your shelter, how to clean water and the list goes on. With a companion, you can discuss the options, get a different viewpoint and arrive at conclusions. This will help you to make sounder decisions.

DON'T BE A PACK MULE, SHARE THE LOAD

When it comes to gear, others can share the load so you do not have to carry it all. There are several items that can easily be shared in a group because there is no need for everyone to carry the same gear:

1. **WATER FILTER.** When filling up water bottles and pack bladders, a good water filtration pump is easy for everyone to share. However, I am an advocate of everyone in the group having a personal filter straw because of survival needs and ease of use.

2. **STOVE.** A stove can work for two or three people in a group if that group is high-functioning. If the members of the group do not get along well, this could prove to be an issue at mealtime. I do recommend everyone carry their own fuel and that someone carry a pocket-style stove as a backup.

3. **KITCHEN GOODIES.** Spices, spatulas, pans and more can easily be shared much like the stove.

4. **TOILETRIES.** No, I am not suggesting you share a toothbrush, but you can certainly share a tube of toothpaste, hand soap and toilet paper or wipes.

5. **TENT AND POLES.** A good way to share the load for your shelter is to divide up the tent, poles, rainfly and footprint among the group evenly.

6. **HONEY.** If you want to surprise your friends on or off the trail, take along some honey packets to share. Honey can be used as an addition to coffee or tea, a nice little burst of energy or a spread on oats at breakfast. This is one nice way to boost the morale of yourself and others in your group.

HISTORICAL GIANTS

KNOWLEDGE WEIGHS NOTHING

I think it serves us well to consider those in history, as well as some who are alive and well today, to see what they carried with them. There are similar items that can be found in various kits throughout history. Some of these individuals ventured into the wilderness and stayed safe with these supplies for weeks and months at a time. We would do well to heed their mind-set on gear. These individuals are giants in my estimation because they have offered us a wonderful look at self-sufficiency.

ÖTZI (CIRCA 3300 BCE)

Our friend Ötzi's body was found in 1991 in the Ötztal Alps along the Austrian-Italian border. I say *friend* because the evidence suggests that this man was very self-sufficient and had the knowledge and tools necessary to live in a harsh time and environment. It is estimated that he lived around 3300 BCE. When his body was discovered, his clothes and supplies were preserved quite well due to being frozen in ice. This gives us some insight into how this man made his way in a very inhospitable location.

His clothing was made of various animal skins with the hide on for insulation. One interesting tidbit about his outerwear is that he had what would be considered advanced technology for footwear. The shoes he wore were not only made of various skins, but also it seems each skin had its own purpose, one of which was to make them nearly waterproof as he walked on the snow. Inside the shoes was woven grass, worn to keep his feet warm in the same way we wear socks. As for his gear pieces, the following were found with his body:

Primitive knives were incredibly important tools.

- Copper axe with a yew handle
- Flint knapped knife with an ash handle
- Quiver containing fourteen shafts
- Yew longbow
- Antler pressure flaker used for making flint tools
- Berries
- Two birch-bark baskets
- A polypore mushroom used to eliminate worm parasites in the body
- A polypore mushroom used as tinder for starting a fire
- Various plants (possibly for making fire)
- Flint and pyrite utilized for making sparks to start a fire

Ötzi is our first historical giant considered, but he will certainly set the foundation for the others listed here (and my approach to being outdoors as well). He had his essential tools (knife and axe), first aid items (mushroom), clothes and items to make fire (which would help him maintain his core body temperature).

SIMON KENTON (APRIL 3, 1755, TO APRIL 29, 1836)

Simon Kenton died in 1836 after an incredibly eventful life as a frontier scout. He spent most of his life in what we now know as Kentucky (my home state). As a frontier scout, Kenton was often tasked to venture far and wide in search of hostiles, suitable areas for surveying, hunting for sustenance and much more. He would regularly be gone for weeks at a time and sometimes for months. These trips were made solo most often, so he would be responsible for his well-being and sustenance in a vast wilderness. We do not know exactly what Kenton carried or for that matter what his more-famous contemporary, Daniel Boone, carried either. We do know from historical records what men of this status typically carried into the wilderness:

- Belt knife (typically of the 8- to 10-inch [20- to 25-cm] carbon-steel blade length) and a deer-antler handle
- Tomahawk
- Flint and steel for making fire
- Tinder material (such as dried bark and grasses)
- Char cloth for making fire
- Pemmican or jerked meat
- Tin cup
- Flintlock rifle
- Extra flints for the rifle
- Powder and lead balls for the rifle
- Tools for the rifle
- Tobacco
- Bedroll

We also know how Kenton carried his goods. He carried the rifle supplies in what is most commonly referred to as a rifleman's pouch. He and other frontiersman of his day also carried another bag commonly referred to as a possibles bag. This was a catchall sort of bag for everything else in the preceding list. The bedroll was often carried on a separate sling or worn on the small of the back wrapped around a large belt.

See the similarities between Kenton and Ötzi? Kenton also carried his essential tools, such as knife and axe, but he also carried a weapon for taking game and self-defense. He also wore clothes that were made from animal skins and those that he could make or purchase in towns and forts. These clothes and his fire-starting kit would have kept him warm and mostly dry during inclement weather. You can also see that Kenton started carrying items for comfort, such as a bedroll. With his capability, he often made it without such comforts but when he was able he did not avoid them. A good night's sleep was as great a morale booster for him as it is for us today.

Modern accoutrements similar in styling to those worn by Simon Kenton.

With curvature in the belly, which makes for better skinning and slicing of game, either of these knives is similar to those used by Nessmuk.

GEORGE W. SEARS, AKA NESSMUK (DECEMBER 2, 1821, TO MAY 1, 1890)

Sears was a conservationist and writer who became well known under his pen name, Nessmuk. He took this pen name from a Native American who had befriended him and taught him when he was a young boy. As a writer, he covered topics such as woodcraft, campcraft and canoeing. In many respects he bridged the gap between the historical practice of self-reliance and the utilization of those methods for the simple pleasures of recreation and enjoyment.

When you add a layer of danger to any outdoor adventure, you must plan for contingencies. One of those layers is canoeing. By purposely taking yourself off dry land and getting into an unstable boat, you add a layer. Nessmuk did this often and with ease.

Nessmuk could have easily been informed about and seen what the frontiersmen in the generation before him carried. As far as timing goes, Nessmuk was fifteen years old when Simon Kenton died. Therefore, it is not far-fetched that Nessmuk learned not only from his Native American mentor but also from his family and friends who were hacking their way through the frontier.

One wonderful thing about Nessmuk is that he wrote about his travels and his gear regularly. After his death, a 1912 edition of *Field & Stream* magazine described his "ditty bag" and its contents. The magazine made it clear that everyone has different styles and tastes, and to say Nessmuk's bag's contents were *the* contents everyone should carry was inappropriate. Everyone has different needs, and their gear should reflect those needs. I believe Nessmuk's gear shows his level of expertise and proves the adage that "knowledge weighs nothing":

- Compass
- Matchbox
- Saltbox
- Emergency ration (i.e., a tin containing smoked beef and bacon, some tea and hardtack)
- Bug repellant
- Fisherman's knife (similar to a modern fillet knife)
- Classic "Nessmuk-style" knife as seen in knife in the photo on the left
- Nails and tacks
- Needle and thread
- Candle and holder
- Razor and leather-sharpening strop
- Mirror
- Shaving cream
- Coffee
- Toothbrush and tooth powder (the precursor to toothpaste)
- Hooks, line and sinkers for fishing
- Percussion black powder rifle
- Gun cartridges
- Gun grease
- Can opener
- Rifle-cleaning rod

I have always found this list to be interesting—Nessmuk took with him health and beauty supplies. This indicates that not only did he want to do important and positive work but he also wanted to have a professional appearance and be hygienic as well. He was a consummate professional. I think it is worth noting that *Field & Stream* magazine also stated that each user should also carry "one foolish thing which the owner would not be happy without." In other words, some sort of morale booster. Being outdoors was hard. Anything to boost one's morale was, and is, a great thing.

The first time I read what Nessmuk carried, I had a pretty good chuckle—I still do, actually. Not only did he carry the essentials like Ötzi and Kenton but he also carried some creature comforts, such as hygiene items and spices for food. He was a man who knew how to enjoy himself and do so in style. Nessmuk is also our first historical giant in whom you can see a heavy influence of mass-produced items that were widely available in a settled area. Although Nessmuk was incredibly accomplished, he did enjoy the resupply opportunities he received from being in a town or city.

STEVE WATTS (JULY 25, 1947, TO MARCH 21, 2016)

If you are like me, you probably know someone who was born a century too late, someone who has the characteristics, demeanor or skill set that would have fit in nicely two or three generations prior to their birth. If the dictionary had a picture of this type of person, the person in that picture would look a lot like Steve Watts. I never personally trained with Steve, but he was so influential in the fields of woodsmanship and wilderness skills that I can see his impact almost everywhere.

Steve was the director of the Aboriginal Skills Program and the Center for the Study of Southeastern Indians at the Schiele Museum of Natural History in North Carolina. He regularly demonstrated aboriginal, primitive and near-modern skills and the gear needed for them.

Although he was incredibly detailed in his writing about various methods and gear, Steve was equally evasive in interviews of what exactly he carried. I think this is because he wanted to teach people how to make the right decisions about gear rather than telling them what to carry.

With that said, Steve did often talk about generalities. In an interview in 2011, Steve was asked by interviewer Liz Childers, "What tools do you consider essential for a wilderness trip?" Steve answered, "The specifics are determined by how I 'go out'—in what style—primitive, classic camping, 18th century, etc. But, behind the specifics are your brain, your hands, edged tools and fire-making tools. They all take different forms (depending on the style) but they are all the basic requirements no matter what the style."

Liz Childers then asked, "If I looked in your wilderness survival kit right now, what would I find?" Steve answered, "Well, with me, it all depends on which kit you look in. I have Stone Age kits, eighteenth century kits, classic camping kits, cowboy kits, etc. And, with each of them I have basic and more involved forms. To delve into the details of each is a book-length effort. All of them must meet the basic needs of outdoor living—shelter (including clothing), water, fire, food and psychological well-being."

I have had discussions with Steve's students about his gear. He had a vast selection of modern equipment for outdoor adventuring. By looking at his equipment, you can see the same common threads that our other three historical giants utilized: essential tools like a knife and axe, clothing that accommodated a multitude of climate conditions, fire-starting equipment and containers for carrying it all. Even with today's huge selection of advanced and very technical gear, Steve proves that the most important considerations are where you're going, what you're doing and making sure you've always got your basics covered.

What can we learn by considering these historical giants individually and collectively? I believe we can glean three important principles.

First, you must do you. I mentioned this already, but I hope it has been emphasized by these people. They spent the better part of each day, sometimes for months at a time, in the outdoors. Take my words to make the best decision for you. I certainly have a range of experience to share. I am sharing it with the sole purpose of your utilizing it to make the best decisions for yourself.

Second, knowledge weighs nothing. Each of these people had vast experience and wisdom in the outdoors. That differs greatly from simple knowledge. I tell my students several times during each class, "I am now giving you permission to spend *more* time outside." I'm certain this book will prove to be an invaluable resource to you, and I am also certain it will require (and encourage) you to spend more time outside developing your own experiences while using the gear I cover.

Third, I do think it is valuable to dwindle the gear of these historical giants down in a general sense. So here it is for you:

- **PERSONAL SAFETY.** Each person had things that would protect him in the case of danger.
- **SHELTER, CLOTHING AND FIRE.** Each of them had clothes suitable for the environment and shelter options for the night, even if the need came about unexpectedly. Each and every one of them carried fire-making supplies.
- **TOOLS.** Did you notice that each man carried a knife? It is an absolutely necessary tool, which I'll cover in Chapter 2. Other essentials they used (and that I will also cover) are cordage, clothing and a pack to carry it all in.

We have many wonderful options available to use in our modern era. Each of them, and this book, are designed to help you get outside. It is now time to get you packed up with modern gear so you can be the next historical giant that someone writes about a century from now.

Author in late 1700s clothing and accoutrements.

CHAPTER 2
ESSENTIAL TOOLS

Mary gave him a brand-new "Barlow" knife worth twelve and a half cents; and the convulsion of delight that swept his system shook him to his foundations. True, the knife would not cut anything, but it was a "sure-enough" Barlow, and there was inconceivable grandeur in that—though where the western boys ever got the idea that such a weapon could possibly be counterfeited to its injury is an imposing mystery and will always remain so, perhaps.

—Mark Twain, *The Adventures of Tom Sawyer*

I CAN DISTINCTLY REMEMBER THE DAY WHEN, AS A YOUNG BOY OF EIGHT OR nine, my dad gave me my first knife. It was a classic Barlow pocketknife, much like the one mentioned in *The Adventures of Tom Sawyer*. I can still remember how that knife felt in my hand. It was with that Barlow I learned the basics of owning a knife: how to use it and to do so safely, how to sharpen it so that it would slice hairs and how to maintain it. I still have that knife, and the value of it to me is immeasurable. While it was a fine knife for a young boy who was learning the important attributes of knife ownership, that same Barlow doesn't quite cut it when it comes to regular, long-term use in a wilderness environment. While that Barlow will always be special to me, I have had many knives that have been put to a lot of work. I have a Case three-blade pocketknife that I used for many years to field dress and process rabbits that I trapped. I would get off the school bus each day and check my traps on the walk home. That little pocketknife has done a lot.

At Christmas one year, an uncle gave me a classic Buck 119 that I have used to field dress more deer than I can count. A few scratches and dings later, it is still working like a champ.

Since receiving those first two knives, I have been given or have bought dozens of other knives. There are many aspects of knives that we need to understand, and I am glad to share with you my hard-won experience.

KNIVES

MORE THAN GRANDAD'S POCKETKNIFE

Nothing in the outdoor world can get a friendly discussion or not-so-friendly debate going quicker than the topic of knives. Campers, survivalists, backpackers, tactical enthusiasts, farmers and many others carry some sort of knife with them every single time they go out—and for good reason. Knives are the gold standard of a multiuse item. There are several categories I will divide knives into. For the sake of simplifying our understanding here, I am considering knives as those tools that can be used to cut and only those with fixed blades. Please note that this does not mean I am going to ignore folding knives; I will cover those at the end of this section. This section will not cover large cutting tools like machetes and what I refer to as choppers (axes and the like). For those tools please see pages 40–44.

A small knife, even a good folding knife, can withstand the rigors of use that come along with camping, backpacking and small-game hunting. However, once I started hunting big game such as white-tailed deer and doing larger knifecraft tasks, it was apparent that a small folder was not going to be enough. I have used my Buck 119 for over 35 years to field dress dozens of deer. On the right of this page, you will see that same Buck 119 with labels on it to understand the various nomenclature of a knife. While it has proven to be a great knife, it is not a be-all, end-all knife. There are many other choices and considerations to keep in mind when choosing a knife.

I have a two-blade approach to carrying knives. I carry a CRKT® M21™ (approximately $70) with me everywhere I go. However, anytime I go into a wilderness, whether it is on a picnic or a backcountry adventure, I carry an L.T. Wright Genesis (approximately $170, see photo on the next page).

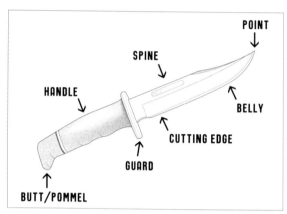

Classic Buck 119 with labels indicating the important parts of any knife. Knowing the name of each part will help you navigate this chapter and select the perfect knife on the market for your needs.

My CRKT M21 folder is a great all-around knife to use every day and to accomplish bigger tasks when needed. It has a drop point blade, which allows me to puncture easily, and it has a skeletonized handle on it that makes it easy to utilize when my hands are wet or dirty. The other reason I really appreciate this blade is because it has a double-locking mechanism on it, making it secure and not easily folded during use. I have carried this knife for over ten years. I typically sharpen it about once per month to help maintain it. It has a light coating on the blade so it does not rust, even when it stays wet for extended periods of time. However, it is not designed to take the punishment that the dense hardwoods of Kentucky can have on a knife, even when used properly. That is why I carry the L.T. Wright Genesis when going outdoors. You will note from the photo on page 38 that they are similar in shape. The full-tang Genesis is a workhorse of a knife. I have not found a woods chore requiring a small cutting tool that this knife cannot handle easily. I have used this knife for hours doing

The well-worn and used L.T. Wright Genesis that I use nearly every day when doing woods tasks.

bushcraft work and it is comfortable in my hand, it stays sharp and it has held up to abuse. It is 1095 carbon steel, so it has a natural patina to it that serves to protect it. If I allow it to stay wet for extended periods it will get some rust on it, which I very easily knock off with some steel wool after rain-soaked trips into the woods.

Despite the overwhelming variety of knives you can use in a wilderness setting, if you boil it all down, you only need an edge and something you can safely and easily hold in your hand. That is why I have said for years that if you can get a good edge on a typical household dinner knife, you have all the tool you need to get things done *in an emergency*. With regular wilderness travel and continued use, you need something different. You will need a tool that works well in hand and does so for the long-term.

Following are my preferences for a go-to knife that does a lot of tasks well in the wilderness:

- Tang style (this page): Full
- Blade material (page 28): 1095 carbon steel
- Handle material (page 32): Micarta
- Blade shape (page 32): Drop
- Edge style/grind (page 33): Scandi or sabre
- Coatings (page 34): None
- Sheath material (page 36): Kydex

In the pages that follow, I will go into the complete details on what the preceding items mean and what you need to consider when choosing the best knife for your purposes.

TANG STYLE

The tang of a knife is that portion of the blade that extends into the handle and connects to it with pins, epoxy or other fasteners. The following are descriptions of different tangs available, and there is an illustration of the different types on the next page.

- **FULL TANG.** The tang of the knife extends fully to the entire length of the knife and, most often, the width of the handle as well.

- **SKELETONIZED TANG.** This is a more modern invention. It is like a full tang. However, portions of it are removed within the outer limits of the handle portion. This serves to reduce weight and create better balance. Most often this portion is covered by the handle and the user never realizes this. Lately, makers have been exposing these with different styles and sometimes even putting small survival items, such as fire tinder and fishing line, within a removable handle for use in an emergency.

- **PARTIAL/HALF TANG.** The blade extends one-half to three-quarters the length of the handle. Most often this is surrounded by the handle material. Narrowing tangs are a type of partial tang.

- **HOLLOW TANG.** Hollow-tang knives are those made famous by the Rambo movies. Gil Hibben made an exceptional knife for that movie. It is my estimation that knives mass-produced in this manner are poor imposters of Hibben's creations. They are not of high quality. The weakest points are in front of the handle, making the spot where the blade meets the handle more susceptible to breaking.

- **RAT TANG.** Also called stick tang, this is a much narrower portion of the blade that extends to the butt of the handle and sometimes has threads on the end. It is used to help secure the handle with a threaded nut or other pinning mechanism.

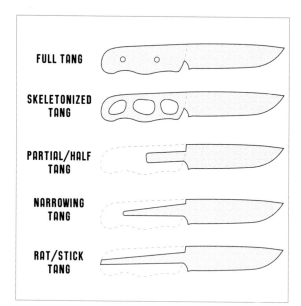

FULL TANG

SKELETONIZED TANG

PARTIAL/HALF TANG

NARROWING TANG

RAT/STICK TANG

Please note the various widths and lengths of these tangs. The wider and longer a tang is, the stronger and more durable a knife you will have. Note that because a "hollow tang" doesn't actually have a tang extending into the handle, it is not shown.

"So, what does it matter what sort of tang that I get?" you wonder. Thanks for asking that question. It matters a great deal and is mostly dependent on the area in which you will most often use your knife. In mixed hardwood forests, like the ones in my home state of Kentucky, a full tang knife is a must. Certain woods' density—such as hickory, oak and locust—seem to be hard as rock. To put pressure on a handle with woods as dense as these, you want to be holding onto as much handle as you can. The partial tang varieties are not made to handle that sort of abuse. It does not mean that the steel will break. It does mean that simple physics on the handle will dictate that it is weakened at the point where the partial tang stops.

My recommendation for tangs? It must be a full-tang knife. I have others that work well, but if I could have only one, I would go with the heartiest of the bunch. Simple physics tells me it must be a full tang. If it has proper steel in it, it will be the strongest.

BLADE MATERIAL

Understanding the blade materials you need for your purposes is important. If we consider it broadly, the most common steel used for knives can be broken down into four categories: (1) carbon, (2) alloy, (3) tool and (4) stainless.

CARBON: Carbon is steel that is determined to contain carbon up to 2.1 percent by weight. You will most often see carbon steels listed as 1095, 1075 or similar. This means, for example, that a 1095 knife has 0.95 percent carbon and a 1075 knife has 0.75 percent carbon. This is important to note because a knife with a high carbon content translates into a blade that is more resistant to wear. This also means it cannot handle lots of hard, improper use. Carbon steel knives will be affected by corrosion more than others. You must be prepared to maintain and store them properly. I store my knives outside their sheaths and always keep a light coating of food-grade oil on them, such as vegetable or coconut oil. I have completed several formal and informal studies of oils and corrosion resistance, and I have found these food-grade oils to be as useful as higher-priced knife oil. The food-grade oil has the added benefit of not being a health hazard when I use my knife to cut into my venison steak around the campfire.

➤ *(Right) I have a lot of knives, and I use them a lot. I have used each of these at length for various tasks. As with all tools, lots of use and training can make any of these knives a useful tool.*

From left to right: Bright Forest Forge Long Knife, Wander Tactical Megaladon, Mora Companion, BHK Muk, L.T. Wright Genesis and Green River Classic are all knives from my collection that have seen ample use and success in wilderness-based tasks.

TOOL: Tool steel is most often used on tactical or combat knives. It is a very hard steel and therefore holds its edge well. The downside is, if you don't possess ample sharpening skills, getting an edge on this type of steel is difficult.

STAINLESS: Stainless steel is any steel with a minimum of 11 percent chromium. It is very easy to maintain. It is highly unlikely a stainless blade will ever rust, hence the name. The benefit of the hardness is also the downside for sharpening: It is hard to get an edge on a stainless knife.

I realize the preceding information may be overwhelming, but I believe is important to understand. So, I have put it all in a table for your comparison. In the table below *Durability* is the ability to withstand abuse; *Sharpened* is how easy the steel is to sharpen; *Keeps Edge* refers to the knife's ability to stay sharp; *Strength* is the hardness of the material; *Affordability* refers to the price points for the most common knives I have used and the most common knives I see my students bring to class.

The best tool for the wilderness should be determined by your desire to properly take care of it. Carbon steel is the best choice, in my opinion. It makes a great balance between being relatively easy to sharpen, maintain and afford. It takes more to maintain, but that is a good thing. Familiarity with your knife is invaluable. The more you use, clean, oil and maintain it, the more effective you will be in utilizing it safely and properly.

ALLOY: Think of alloy steel as a carbon steel with just a hint of chromium added. Chromium adds strength to the material, which creates an extremely tough blade. Since it is still primarily a carbon blade, it too will have corrosion issues but nothing like carbon blades. Alloy steels are easy to sharpen and hold an edge well.

In this table, 1 is best and 4 is worst.

	DURABILITY	SHARPENED	KEEPS EDGE	STRENGTH	AFFORDABILITY
CARBON	4	1	4	2	2
ALLOY	3	2	2	3	3
TOOL	1	4	1	1	4
STAINLESS	2	3	3	4	1

REAL-LIFE SKILLS: ONE-STICK FIRE

Being able to make a fire is paramount to both survival and the simple enjoyment of being in a wilderness. Fire provides warmth for our bodies, assists in food preparation, boils water and provides a great morale boost to any camp. With a lighter, a knife and one stick you have the beginnings of a fire that will last all night, even when the conditions are wet. Follow these steps to make a one-stick fire.

1. Choose a dead branch or twig that is about as tall as you are. Its diameter at its base should be slightly larger than your thumb.

2. Break it into manageable segments roughly the length of your forearm.

3. You can tell a branch is dead when you break it. It should have an audible snap and break cleanly into two parts. Also ensure the branch is a softer wood (e.g., aspen, poplar, cedar, birch). You should be able to make an indentation in the wood (not the bark) with your thumbnail.

4. Use the spine of your knife to scrape off the bark. If conditions are wet or damp, discard the bark. If conditions are dry, save it to put on the fire later.

5. Carefully use the knife's spine at a 90° angle to scrape off fine shavings of wood, scraping slowly away from you to prevent the blade slipping and injuring you.

6. Use your blade to cut off thicker shavings. You can also leave these attached to the stick at the bottom to make them easier to move about. If you leave the shavings attached you have what is referred to as a feather stick.

7. Create a base on the ground from pieces of the original branch. I call it a fire raft. This will serve to keep your fire off the ground.

8. Start with the smallest portions of your stick and add them to the fire-making materials. Slowly add larger pieces until you have a great starter fire.

9. Use other dry pieces of wood that you accumulated prior to starting this process if you want to prepare a bigger fire.

10. Light the wood shavings or firestick with your lighter and place it on your fire raft.

I can take one simple stick and turn it into the material I need to get a fire started just by breaking it and using a sharp tool, such as the axe pictured here.

HANDLE MATERIAL

Safety and comfort are the name of the game when it comes to handle material. You do not want a knife to slip during use. You also want a knife that does not cause hot spots or blisters when you use it regularly. Let's look at some of the most common handle materials and discuss a few thoughts on each.

WOOD: Wood is tried and true. Wood handles work. I prefer a handle that is of a hard, dense wood so that it will take abuse over its lifetime. Hickory, oak (especially live oak), dogwood, ash and Osage orange are extremely hard. I have had great success with Osage orange and hickory on many knives I have made—my sandpaper wears out quickly due to their hardness.

ANTLER: Antler has historically been a good choice for knife handles. Frontiersmen and settlers used antler because it was readily available; these people used everything on the animals they harvested. In modern times, antler is not such a good option. Much of what is used as antler today is harvested from pen-raised animals or is faux antler, both of which are subpar materials. If you live in an area where it is legal, get a knifemaker to make a knife for you with elk or deer antler—it will be a prized possession.

RESINOUS POLYMERS: Resinous polymers present an extensive range of materials with varying results. Usually this kind of handle is an indicator of mass-produced blades, as they are more affordable to make in large quantities. Unfortunately, this also means poor-quality materials.

MICARTA: Micarta has fast become my (and many others') favorite. Micarta is compressed fabric with impregnated resin. It is incredibly comfortable and can be formed much like wood. I have used several knives made with micarta handles to hammer materials. While I do not recommend treating it that way, micarta has stood up to even that amount of abuse.

RUBBER: Many knives have either complete hard rubber or partial rubber on the handles. These make great choices for knives that you will use when your hands are wet. However, these handles cannot stand up to regular use over the long haul.

BLADE SHAPE

The blade shape you pick is entirely dictated by the tasks for which you will likely be using it. Some points are designed specifically for piercing, others are designed for stability in wood processing and bushcraft tasks. Like so many other things with knives, the blade shapes available are only limited by the knifemaker's imagination. I will cover those that will assist you in a wilderness setting.

NORMAL STRAIGHT: Simply put, normal straight points have a spine that extends entirely to the point.

DROP POINT: Drop points have fast become my favorite. They are a great all-purpose blade shape and will perform tasks well. They also boast strength and durability. The back of a drop point knife curves from the handle to the point and is unsharpened along its entirety. This means

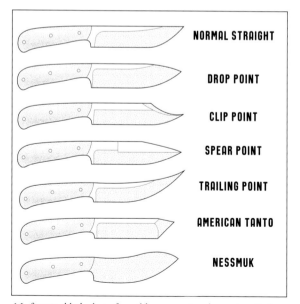

My favorite blade shape for wilderness use is a drop point. Each point has its own value and in the right hands will be a useful tool.

it stays strong for long-term use. Drop points have a large cutting edge as well. I think the drop point covers two tasks that I engage in often: animal processing and bushcraft tasks.

CLIP POINT: Although I enjoy my drop points, I have recognized that most of the people who come to my classes enjoy a clip point blade. A quick look at data on sales proves to me that clip points are one of the most popular shapes used today. The back of a clip point starts at the handle then stops about midway along the back. It then takes a drastic straight line to the point. Therefore, you have a sharp point to utilize. This makes it a great choice for piercing, such as in animal processing. The classic Buck 119 I was gifted when I was a teenager has a clip point on it. It stays with my deer-hunting gear. I have used it to field dress over 100 deer and domestic farm animals as well. While the clip point provides a good piercer for that process, the disadvantage of this shape is that it is weak at the point. This makes it a poor choice for wood processing tasks.

SPEAR POINT: Spear points are made so that the blade is symmetrical on top and bottom. They come with two variants: one has both sides sharpened, another has only one side sharpened. This allows the point to be both strong and sharp. Spear points have a fair amount of what I refer to as knife "sexiness" to them, meaning they look cool and for that reason alone they are somewhat popular. Unless you are into throwing knives as a hobby or you think you will regularly engage in self-defense, spear points should be avoided for wilderness use. They are not that useful as a wilderness tool, especially if they are sharpened on both sides. I will use the back of my knife for tasks, such as scraping sticks for tinder, nearly as much as the sharpened side. If both sides of the knife are sharpened, I do not have that option—in addition to having a knife that is more dangerous to use.

SKINNERS/TRAILING POINTS: This shape of blade is optimal for the specific task of skinning animals. The back edge will curve upward from the handle. Most will also have a large belly on them, which provides a long cut for cutting and skinning. Due to the point being up and away from the handle it makes it weaker simply due to the physics of use.

TANTO: I am reluctantly mentioning tanto blade shapes because they are not worthy for serious wilderness use. I do bring them up because they are popular for their "sexiness," as I mentioned earlier. The current style of tanto that is popular is a version known primarily in the United States. The actual historical tanto-style edge used in Japan is not like the current popular version. The style popular in the United States has a very sharp and angular point. It also has a belly that comes to a distinct angle near the point as well. These two aspects serve to make this knife weak in that area and susceptible to breakage during regular use. They do have their use in self-defense and are therefore appreciated by many in the military and law enforcement communities. Just leave them at home when you head into the woods.

NESSMUK: Nessmuk-style points are a type of skinner/trailing point. They are easily recognized by the blade's larger belly and swept-up curvature.

EDGE STYLE/GRIND

As I was growing up, my dad regularly admonished me to work smarter, not harder. Unfortunately, I did not always heed that advice—if I had a task that needed a knife, the best knife for the job was the one that happened to be closest at that time. As I grew older and more experienced, I discovered that my dad's words were wise ones. There is a wide range of grinds on knives to choose from these days, and many grinds are made with specific tasks in mind. While I feel that I can get most things done with even a sharpened dinner knife, I have come to understand how easy some tasks are when you choose the right grind.

The grind of a knife is the style of sharpened edge that it has. As I started studying grinds for tasks such as backpacking, camping and bushcraft, I found that they each have their own strengths.

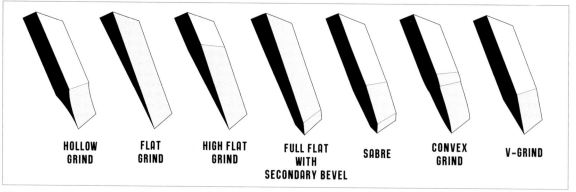

HOLLOW GRIND   FLAT GRIND   HIGH FLAT GRIND   FULL FLAT WITH SECONDARY BEVEL   SABRE   CONVEX GRIND   V-GRIND

These are the most common grinds on knives you will find for wilderness use. This chapter goes into detail on the uses of each, including sabre, which is my favorite to use.

HOLLOW: A hollow grind is a concave grind, and I've found it to be useful while processing game with my Buck 119. Although it does dull rather easily, that is not an issue when I go hunting. In that situation, I can utilize it and sharpen it on the same day.

FLAT: Flat grinds start at the top of the blade and continue all the way to the edge. They are good for light- and medium-duty bushcraft skills and camp needs. High flat grinds start about halfway down and offer more stability. A full flat with secondary bevel is shown in the illustration above as another variation of a flat grind.

Scandinavian (or Scandi) grinds are common on knives used for survival training because they work well for wood processing, which involves cutting, chopping and slicing at times. In short, they get used a lot but are also relatively easy to sharpen in the field. I have many Morakniv knives with Scandi grinds that new students borrow in my classes so they can get a feel for what knife works for them. Many of my students and I regularly come back to the Scandi grinds for such use. Scandi knives are the most popular style of high flat grind.

SABRE: Sabre grinds are my personal favorite, as they handle nearly all tasks I can throw at them, including campcraft, firecraft and bushcraft and are still relatively easy to sharpen in the field and at home.

CONVEX: Convex grinds are an excellent choice for those that are hard and abusive on knives. These knives work well as choppers and cutters. They can be sharpened but because of their heartiness hold an edge through lots of use for long periods of time.

V GRIND: V grinds are more common in hand use tools than your typical woods knife. They make good self-defense edges.

As I mentioned earlier, sabre grinds are my best recommendation to you. What they slightly lack in usability they make up for in durability. With proper use, they can do anything any other grind can do.

COATINGS

There is a range of coatings out there. Each is proprietary to the manufacturer; therefore, the details are too numerous to cover. There are a few general things about coatings you should know, however.

Coatings will cover nearly the entire knife but most importantly, not the belly of the blade. This will require you to continue to take care of the edge so it does not rust.

Some knife companies use both stainless and carbon steels under the coatings. Understand the difference (see pages 28 and 30) and what that means for you regarding maintenance.

REAL-LIFE SKILLS: TEN SIMPLE STEPS TO BUILDING YOUR OWN INEXPENSIVE KNIFE

If you are new to knife building, I suggest you first go about it with a kit. Don't go for hammer-forged just yet. I have put together many of them (such as the bottom knife in the photo on page 30). Here are the steps I use and a few hints on each:

1. Choose a blade and handle style that you like. Cover the sharpened portion of the knife with tough tape so you can work with it without the risk of cutting yourself. I prefer wood handles for beginning knife makers.

2. I like to take some sandpaper to the interior portion of the handle that will be covered by the exterior handle. In so doing, the epoxy will adhere more strongly.

3. Mark the pinning holes on your handle and drill at 90° to the handle. Choose a drill bit that matches the hole size on the handle. If you have two scales rather than one handle, drill through both scales at the same time while they are bound together. (Scales are material that come in two equal parts and are attached on either side of the handle.) This will ensure the holes match up.

4. If you use a piece of solid material for the handle, cut it into scales now.

5. Make sure the surfaces of the handle, steel and scales are free of any dust or similar debris.

6. Gather everything together and then apply epoxy to both the knife handle and the scales. Place all the pieces together, including the pins. For simplicity and ease, I usually just use nails the same size as my holes. You can purchase specific pinning material.

7. Clamp the handle material together, ensuring that it is making good contact along the knife handle. Let the epoxy dry for the recommended time. Do not shortcut this step.

8. Once the epoxy is dry, cut the excess handle material from the blade with an X-Acto–type knife and then start the process of filing and sanding the handle down to make it feel good in your hand. Be careful if you are using an electronic belt sander—it will get the pins hot and melt the glue, making the glue unstable.

9. When the handle is complete, apply liberal amounts of linseed oil to help preserve the wood. I do this by wiping it on with a cloth and letting it sit in a warm spot so that it soaks up the oil.

10. If you prefer, you may want to finish the handle with wood stain. This will also help preserve the handle.

A forced patina on left, natural on the right. Both serve as a protectant.

From left to right: a leather sheath that came from L.T. Wright Handcrafted knives, a very old leather cowhide leather made by myself that holds two knives, my kydex sheath for my L.T. Wright Genesis with optional ferro rod holder and a handcrafted leather sheath for my classic long knife from Bright Forest Forge.

Coatings on the spine will essentially round it over and not allow a sharp 90° edge. This will make it more difficult, if not impossible, to use the back of your blade as a scraper on wood, ferrocerium (ferro) rods and similar. You can alter this by using a file to remove the coating. Ensure the spine is 90°.

A big positive to having a coating is customization. Some manufacturers will offer you options on color. You can get knives ranging from flat earth camo to zombie fluorescent green. Those in the tactical community often prefer knives with black or camouflage coating. A bright coating may be a good choice for beginners. Beginners to the outdoors will often lay their knives down (never a good idea). If it is brightly colored, it is easier for them to see it for safety reasons.

A forced or natural patina on a knife (see photo above) is also a good protector. A patina is a thin layer on the surface of carbon steel knives that comes from age and use. It is a very light level of corrosion that helps protect the knife from further decay. Some knife companies use vinegar and various acids to force this process. Often, this is done to make unique designs.

SHEATH MATERIAL

Sheaths are rather simple in materials. You can't go wrong with any sheath material with some minor exceptions that I will note. A good sheath should be one that does not allow the blade to slip out, either by having a snap closure or being formed to fit the knife perfectly. If you have a kydex or leather sheath formed for your knife and no other holding mechanism, your knife should "snap" into place when put in the sheath. Anything else and you risk the possibility of your knife coming out. This can be dangerous because you can unexpectedly wind up cut or stabbed. It can also be unfortunate because you may lose your knife.

LEATHER: Leather is the most classic choice of the bunch. Leather sheaths are very versatile, and with minimal effort you can make your own. Avoid faux leather sheaths, as they are not hardy at all; choose one made from cowhide or a similar material.

KYDEX: It took me many years, but kydex has become my preferred choice for sheath material. Kydex stays rigid and is a good choice for tactical use and activities where the sheath is likely to get wet. Kydex drains easily and there is room for moisture to evaporate.

ONE-TOOL OPTION

As I have mentioned many times, I like to share with you *a* way of doing things. I am not so egocentric that I feel my method is the *only* way of doing things. I am a two-tool type of person. I prefer to carry a fixed-blade knife and a large cutting tool as well. However, there are many new, innovative knives that serve as one-tool options. One such tool is the Multi-Scenario Knife (MSK-1) from Ultimate Survival Tips. This knife, and those like it, are designed to be utilized as both a chopping tool, like a small axe and a cutting tool. This allows the user to not carry the extra weight of two tools and still complete most any task. This knife also has the following features:

Ultimate Survival Tips MSK-1 is a good choice for a multi-tool option.

1. ferro rod striker on the pommel

2. steel bow drill divot in the handle

3. integrated mini survival kit

NYLON: If they are made of nylon, these sheaths are a poor choice. If the knife has plastic or kydex inserts to hold the knife within the nylon sheath, then they work much better. Many nylon sheaths are compatible with Modular Lightweight Load-Bearing Equipment (MOLLE) and can be attached to packs and belts easily.

PLASTIC: Many plastics do not hold up well, especially in freezing conditions. I carried a very high-end knife in a plastic sheath for a while and had the sheath break in freezing temperatures. Not all plastics are like this; just be aware if it is common for you to be in in the wilderness in frigid temperatures.

Here are a few other items of consideration when picking out a sheath for your favorite blade:

- When your knife is not in use and is stored away, do not leave it in the sheath. Any moisture will be directly in contact with the knife and cause corrosion. This is most applicable with leather sheaths.

- Ensure the clasping mechanism on the sheath is hardy and can withstand abuse. If it is single-stitched or appears of poor quality you may be in trouble. Your knife will last a long time under a lot of use. Your sheath needs to be able to do the same.

- If given the opportunity, try a knife on before purchasing it. This way, you can see how it rides on you. You want it to be secure to you but not so rigid that you cannot move comfortably to perform the tasks you intend to do.

FINAL THOUGHTS

You can now understand why knives are such a debatable topic. There are many, many different aspects to them that you need to consider when purchasing. I have many knives that I use for various tasks. My recommendation of the L.T. Wright Genesis at the beginning of this section was quite hard for me to do because there are knives designed to do specific things that will perform certain tasks better. However, if you want to buy one knife and do a range of tasks with it, the L.T. Wright is an easy choice to go with.

FOLDERS, CHOPPERS AND MULTI-TOOLS

BIG AND SMALL CHOICES FOR MULTIPLE TASKS

Now that we have covered what I consider the best type of knife to carry into the wilderness, let's look at our fixed blade's smaller cousins, pocketknives and multi-tools. When you start looking at these sorts of knives, you need to keep in mind where the knife is manufactured—many manufacturers in China use subpar steels in their knives, leading many of them to break or become susceptible to breaking down through regular use. You'll also need to be aware of how many moving parts the knife has. The more parts there are to a knife, the more likely it is to break down or not work properly. Pocketknives or folding knives will need more maintenance.

In today's world, children will get in trouble for bringing a knife to school. Back when I was young, I would have gotten in trouble if I *didn't* take a pocketknife to school. Many young boys and girls who live in rural areas use knives daily.

Folding knives have come a long way since I carried my three-blade Case back in the day. I still have it and carry it from time to time for the nostalgic value it carries. For daily chores on the farm or even tasks in an urban environment, a pocketknife of this type will get most jobs done. With this type of knife, it is not too hard to open envelopes and boxes and cut the occasional string in your daily routine. For wilderness use, I like to carry a folding knife that will serve as a backup to my fixed blade. For my personal use, I carry a CRKT M21 (shown in the photo on the left page) because it closely resembles in make and function the same things I prefer in my fixed-blade knife.

A knife is the ultimate multiuse item, and I believe it is important to have the "two is one, and one is none" mind-set with such an important tool. There are literally thousands of variations for folding knives. For our purposes here, I suggest you get a tool that has a clip and a secure locking mechanism. Safety is paramount in the backcountry and you should be as safe as possible with your tools. The same goes for your multi-tool. I have a Leatherman Wave® (approximately $90) and a Gerber Suspension (approximately $26). Choose one that has locking mechanisms for the various tools. For most wilderness tasks, a multi-tool will get the job done. At a minimum, I believe you should get one that has a set of small needle-nose pliers. I have used my multi-tool pliers for tasks ranging from pulling out a splinter to cutting and splicing wires on a defective headlamp. Like most things in gear, manufacturers have gone too far when putting various blades on their multi-tools. Tools are getting so large that they are cumbersome to use and heavy to carry.

◄ *(Left) The CRKT M21 folder pictured here has seen more use than any other knife in my collection. I carry it daily and use to open boxes, process game, perform bushcraft tasks and lots more.*

The Leatherman and Gerber multi-tools shown are my backup tool options—one stays in my outdoor gear and the other stays in my truck at all times. In the left-hand photo, the Leatherman is in the front, and the Gerber is in the back.

Here are a few of the multi-tool implements that will make your life much easier in the backcountry:

- **KNIFE.** No serrations needed. A sharp knife edge is all one needs for most tasks, including cutting cordage.

- **SAW.** A multi-tool saw is not a good choice for cutting firewood, but it is a great choice for making cuts on traps and food items in the backcountry.

- **FILE.** Equipment will regularly develop burs, nicks or similar imperfections. A good file can knock those down and out so you can get through a trip more comfortably.

- **SCREWDRIVER.** A screwdriver is nearly a must-have for modern equipment. Get one that has a flat head and a Phillips head.

- **CAN AND BOTTLE OPENER.** If you are carrying consumables that will require an opener, make sure you get a multi-tool that has one. It will keep you from carrying an extra opener.

- **JOB-SPECIFIC TOOLS.** Multi-tools are becoming so popular that companies are designing them with tools for specific tasks. For example, there are tools for working on mountain bikes and AR-15 rifles, for whittling and more.

LARGE CUTTING TOOLS

For your typical backpacker, a large cutting tool like an axe is a luxury not worth carrying the extra weight. However, if you are packing your gear in a car or canoe or if you don't have to walk far with your gear, a large cutting tool will make a nice addition for some larger tasks. Simple physics tell us that an axe is going to be more effective and efficient at large cutting tasks than something like a machete. I want to examine these two tools and share with you some reasons why I think one greatly out performs the other for wilderness use.

MACHETE

There is no denying that a machete is the must-have tool for a jungle or arid environment. In those habitats you mostly find herbaceous materials that can be cut with a swift, thin blade. The density of this sort of plant life is hollow or pithy. This means that the thin and broad design of a machete can make quick work of these types of materials. It also means that a machete can be used for much longer periods of time than other large cutting tools. One summer during college I worked on a survey crew for a natural gas utility company. It was my job to cut through dense hardwood forests so the engineer could take shots with his transit to survey the proposed pipeline. This meant I was basically hacking my way

I keep this L.T. Wright Overland Machete in my truck as a backup tool for large tasks. I have used it on numerous occasions to clear trails and roads in the backcountry.

Axes come in several sizes for any task you are looking to complete. They are a must-have item for use in hardwood forests.

through small branches on trees, multi-flora rose bushes and similar vegetation. A machete worked great for this. I would utilize it nearly all day long during my twelve-hour days. By the end of that summer, my forearms looked like Popeye the Sailor Man's.

Another great use for a machete is cutting through bamboo and cane. Since these plants are composed of chambered sections with little hardwood in the center, a machete will make short work of cutting through them. For example, I have used my machete to cut more Kentucky river cane than I can shake a stick at (pun intended).

I think it is evident that unless you are going cross-country clearing brush and small limbs, machetes are not necessarily the best choice. I wanted to bring them up simply because a large segment of the outdoor community considers them a viable option for regular backcountry use. I do too, but only when you are cutting herbaceous-stem plants.

If you need to cut through larger and woody-stemmed material like you will find in a mixed hardwood forest, an axe is a much better choice.

AXE

To say I am a fan of axes is an understatement. Unfortunately, I have spent the better part of my outdoor life using subpar axes. When I started using Gränsfors Bruk axes (approximately $130 for my favorite, the small forest axe), I was surprised at how much easier it was for me to get jobs done.

I also grew up throwing tomahawks in competitions that were both formal and informal (the only prize at stake was bragging rights). I also grew up in a house in which we use firewood for warmth; there was never a shortage of wood that needed to be cut. For home use or car-camping use, a basic wood splitting maul is the best choice for firewood. However, with a head weighing in at 4 to 5 pounds (1.8 to 2.25 kg), a wood-splitting maul is not a viable option anywhere else. That is where a good, sharp axe becomes the best choice.

Axes are no different than knives. They have specific handles and heads to accomplish the various tasks they are used for. (Look at the illustration on the next page for the basic nomenclature for axes.)

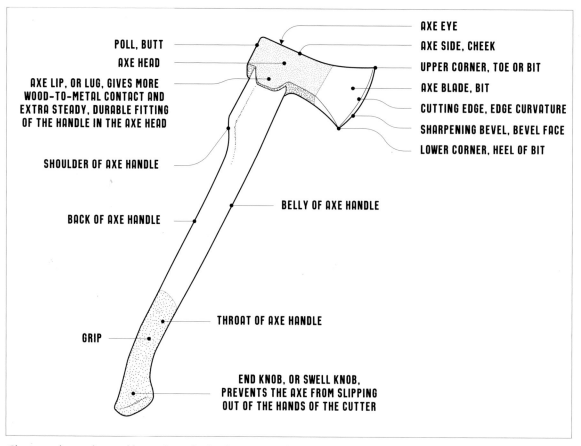

POLL, BUTT

AXE HEAD

AXE LIP, OR LUG, GIVES MORE
WOOD-TO-METAL CONTACT AND
EXTRA STEADY, DURABLE FITTING
OF THE HANDLE IN THE AXE HEAD

SHOULDER OF AXE HANDLE

BACK OF AXE HANDLE

GRIP

AXE EYE

AXE SIDE, CHEEK

UPPER CORNER, TOE OR BIT

AXE BLADE, BIT

CUTTING EDGE, EDGE CURVATURE

SHARPENING BEVEL, BEVEL FACE

LOWER CORNER, HEEL OF BIT

BELLY OF AXE HANDLE

THROAT OF AXE HANDLE

END KNOB, OR SWELL KNOB,
PREVENTS THE AXE FROM SLIPPING
OUT OF THE HANDS OF THE CUTTER

Classic wood axe styling used by woodsmen for decades. Knowing the nomenclature will assist you in this section.

I am a traditionalist when it comes to handles—and not just for the sake of aesthetics. I have used handles made of fiberglass, polymer and steel, all with rubberized grips on the handles. However, in my experience there is no better handle material than solid hardwood. Hardwood handles absorb a greater amount of the shock that gets transferred to your hands while chopping. When used properly, they also last an incredibly long time. Most handles that are made of a composite plastic or similar material will have a rubberized grip. Under regular and sustained use, this rubber does not last. Once it is gone, the handle is uncomfortable and unsafe to use due to the lack of grip. Hardwood handles eliminate these problems.

Not all hardwood handles are made the same, though; there are some aspects you should look for. The first is the type of wood. Hickory is one of the most popular choices, and for good reason. It is very hardy, does not splinter easily and has a tightly packed grain. This gives it great strength and the ability to withstand abuse. Another good choice with similar qualities is ash. Outside of those two, you will start to have issues due to the grains of the wood not being long and straight.

One of the first things you should look for on the end of the axe handle is the direction in which the grain is running. It should run the same direction as the head. If it is running perpendicular to the direction of the head, you will have a subpar experience with it. Due to the

UTILIZING AN AXE SAFELY AND EFFICIENTLY

1. **Ensure your axe is sharp.** I use a Lansky Dual Grit, Multi-Purpose Sharpener. It is easy to carry in the field and easy to use. It comes with great directions on how to use it.

2. **Ensure the head of your axe is stable and in place.** Replace the splice in it from time to time, as well as the handle when it gets worn to the point of being unsafe. Any handle becomes unsafe when you notice it is becoming harder to grip properly. This is most often recognized when the handle material is wet. If you cannot keep a good grip on the handle at any time, you should consider replacing it.

3. **Whenever you start to cut, assume you are going to miss your target or you are going to cut through it completely on one of your cuts.** Do a follow-through cut to see where the axe head goes. If it goes toward your body in any way, you need to readjust for safety. You can do this by cutting from your knees as well as ensuring there is ground or another log between you and the axe (see the next point for more details).

4. **Put something made of earth or wood between you and your target in case you miss.** When I use a very small woods hatchet, I kneel rather than stand. A small woods hatchet is used with one hand; this gives you little control over it once you bring it down on your target. If I am on my knees and I miss, or my axe goes through unexpectedly, it is then embedded in the earth. Doing this regularly is not advised, however, because regular cuts into the earth dulls a blade rather quickly.

5. **When splitting wood, always aim for the side farthest away from you.** This allows for the axe-head to hit the center of the wood if you miss your exact target. If you choose the side closest to you, the axe comes back toward you.

6. **When splitting wood, go for the cracks and avoid knots.** This allows you to work with the wood rather than against it.

7. **When cutting wood on the side, swing the axe at a strong angle.** If you go in straight to the wood at 90°, you will not cut effectively. If you go at a real small angle, then it is easy for the axe to glance off.

8. **Once you get close to the end of a piece of wood and are nearing a cut-through, take your time.** Large cuts that go through may catch you by surprise and go in an unexpected direction.

9. **Becoming proficient at cutting wood with an axe takes time, patience and lots of effort.** Recognize when you are getting tired and losing your focus. That is the time to stop and take a break.

A quality axe should have a handle in which the grain runs parallel with the axe head.

Cleaning and sharpening of all your wilderness tools is a must-have skill set.

nature of swinging and then stopping the axe in wood, perpendicular grain will start to split and splinter more easily. That is a dangerous situation for the user.

The axe head is the part that does that work for you if you use it properly. Your axe head should make a good "bite" into the wood. This means it cuts and does not glance off easily. An axe should be sharp in the same way that a knife should be sharp. For some reason I have found that many of my students understand the need for a sharp knife, but feel they can get away with having a dull axe. Just like a knife, the most dangerous axe is a dull one. Keep your axes sharp. You can do this by getting an axe head that is a composite of different steel hardness. Low carbon should be throughout the head itself. If you then ensure that you have a higher carbon steel on the cutting edge, you will find it is easier to sharpen. This allows the axe to have some flex to it, and at the same time the edge is hearty enough to hold both the sharpened edge and endure the abuse you will be giving it by cutting. If you are new to cutting wood with an axe, refer to the sidebar on the previous page for some pointers that will help you stay safe and make your work easier.

FIELD AND HOME CARE OF KNIVES AND AXES

It's important to remember that if you are using your tools and they are not made from stainless steel they will develop rust on them. As a matter of fact, it is my opinion that if you are not getting a light coating of rust on them, you are most likely not using them enough. Even if you take your tools to the wilderness with oil on them, you will quickly wear that off with use. Expect a slight bit of rust.

Unless you are using your tools several hours a day, you will most likely have no need to sharpen your knives or axes on a stone or something similar. A good leather strop will go a long way in keeping your tools sharp in the field. To avoid carrying a leather strop in the field just for this purpose, you can use a belt or leather boot to get the desired effect. When my knives are used to field dress animals, I will use leaves and grass to clean excess waste from the knife and wash it with water in a puddle or creek—or even in dew from the grass—to clean it off. Once you are home, you should clean all of your blades with soap and hot water. When you do get light rust on them, you can take it off with steel wool very easily. Take time to always sharpen your blades before storing them. I prefer to store my knives out of their sheaths, because the sheaths will sometimes hold moisture. Make sure to store them in a safe place. If you have small children or those untrained with knives in your home, put all knives and axes under lock and key.

CORDAGE

TIE IT UP, TIE IT DOWN, MAKE IT STRONG

Tying up a tarp, hanging a bear bag, binding an injured limb and even keeping your shoes on means that cordage is a much-needed piece of wilderness gear. There is a lot of cordage out there. Some of it you should never go into a wilderness without; others you should never take into a wilderness with the intention of seriously using it. In the following section, I am going to detail the various aspects of rope that you should understand so you can find what is best for you and your intended task.

CLIMBING ROPE

Climbing rope is referred to as kernmantle rope (from the German words *kern*, which means "core," and *mantel*, which means "jacket"), because this rope has an outer sleeve that provides abrasion resistance for the strands inside. Those strands provide the actual strength. Climbing ropes come in two varieties:

- **DYNAMIC:** Dynamic climbing rope is flexible rope designed specifically to take falls from those engaged in rock climbing or similar activities.

- **STATIC:** Static climbing rope is not nearly as flexible and has very little give to it. It's most often used for rappelling and by SAR teams.

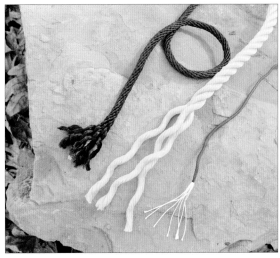

Braided (left), twisted (middle) and kermantle (right) ropes each have strengths and weakness in various tasks.

Each type of rope will have a tab at the end of it designating when it was made and its strength and fall rating. Climbing and rappelling are dangerous activities in which your life depends on those pieces. Black Diamond ropes are my preferred choice for climbing and rappelling. Please get good training and a dedicated source for rope education and information before engaging in these activities. Climbing and rappelling are both skills that help you meet your fears head-on, but safety is all-important.

In this chart, 1 is best and 5 is worst. See opposite page for more details on the ranking.

	FLEXIBLE	KNOTTABLE	WEIGHT	RESISTS WATER	STRENGTH
CLIMBING ROPE, DYNAMIC	3	2	5	5	2
CLIMBING ROPE, STATIC	5	5	4	4	1
PARACHUTE CORD	1	1	2	2	3
TWISTED	2	4	1	1	5
BRAIDED	4	3	3	3	4

TOP KNOTS FOR WILDERNESS USE

1. **BOWLINE:** Fantastic knot for rescue

2. **FIGURE EIGHT:** Safe and useful way to create a connection point on a rope

3. **PRUSIK:** Slips when you want it to slip, tightens when you want it to tighten

4. **TWO HALF-HITCHES:** Workhorse method of attaching cordage to anything

5. **FISHERMAN'S:** The go-to way to tie and untie two lengths of cordage

6. **ALPINE BUTTERFLY:** Used to form a fixed loop in the middle of a rope

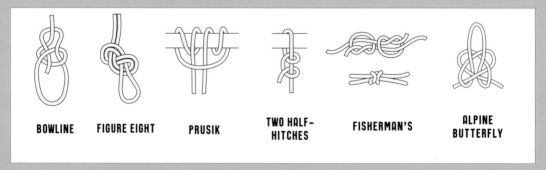

BOWLINE　　FIGURE EIGHT　　PRUSIK　　TWO HALF-HITCHES　　FISHERMAN'S　　ALPINE BUTTERFLY

These are favorite knots that get regular use in wilderness tasks. My personal favorite is two half-hitches.

PARACHUTE CORD

Often referred to as paracord, this cordage, in my estimation, is the number-one choice for wilderness gear. Paracord is the same cordage specifically designed and utilized on parachutes for the Unites States military. Paracord is made to brutal military specifications (mil-spec) and is also a kernmantle style of rope. It has an outer sheath and seven strands of braided rope inside. Mil-spec paracord goes through rigorous testing to ensure that it can withstand a minimum of 550 pounds (247.5 kg) of pressure. Hence, another name is 550 cord. Because each strand is in itself very strong and has many uses, you should carry some with you. If you are carrying 100 feet (30 m) of paracord with you, you are carrying 800 feet (240 m) of useful cordage (i.e., 7 strands and 1 outer sheath). The most affordable mil-spec paracord I have been able to find is made by Rothco.

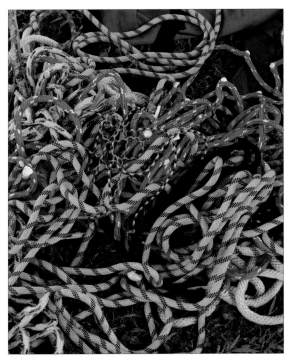

Various ropes have their own specific uses. For general wilderness use in hiking, camping and similar activities, paracord is my go-to choice.

TWISTED ROPE

Twisted rope is sometimes called laid rope and you will see it in nearly every hardware and discount store. This rope kinks easily, is hard to tie into knots and it is not very strong. Its redeeming qualities are that it sinks and it is not impermeable by water. If you have those two specific needs, then get some twist rope; if not, then please don't.

BRAIDED ROPE

Braided ropes are made by weaving various fibrous strands together. Braided ropes are either hollow-braided or double-braided. I prefer double-braided ropes due to their increase in strength: They do not kink as easily as twisted ropes, and they tie and untie more easily than twisted.

To the left is a table that will help break down the issues I view as most important when it comes to cordage in the wilderness. I ranked each of these in order of best (1) to worst (5), considering the available choices. *Flexible* refers to how easy it is to use, store and carry. *Knottable* refers to how easy it is to tie and untie knots and maintain the cordage. *Weight* refers to the lightest (1) to heaviest (5) options. *Resists Water* refers to how well the cordage withstands water and other contaminants. *Strength* refers to tensile strength.

It is my opinion you should never head into the wilderness without the essential tools discussed in this chapter. Each of those items can make many other tasks much easier to accomplish. Next up are items you can take with you to keep yourself out of danger or *get* out of it if you find yourself in the middle of it.

CHAPTER 3
MAINTAINING YOUR PERSONAL SAFETY

I have never been lost, but I will admit to being confused for several weeks.

—Daniel Boone

SOME OF THE GREATEST JOYS I'VE EVER HAD IN OUTDOOR EXPERIENCES CAME from wandering, much like Daniel Boone did, in the beautiful hills of Kentucky. Whether hunting animals, searching for edible and medicinal plants or simply looking around for the fun of it, I do enjoy making my way through the woods.

Also like Boone, I have never been seriously lost, but I certainly have been out a few times and not really known where I was. One of my most memorable was when I was practicing land navigation with a new GPS unit I had purchased. My wife and daughter had taken the vehicle and the dog and gone around the road to pick up my son and me at a different location. It was my intent to navigate off the trail and through a wilderness area, teach my son some things about map reading and GPS and then rally with the rest of the family at the other location. Before heading out to enjoy the day, I showed my wife my expected route on the map and my contingency plan should something go wrong. The contingency plan was to basically go back the way we came and meet them on the road later. (I always tell my family my plans, when I expect to be out and for how long and my alternate plans. This saves a lot of time and effort should I need assistance getting out.)

My son, who was only about ten years old, and I ran into a little problem after getting started. There had been either a tornado or a severe windstorm in the recent past that had destroyed a large swatch of the area I had intended to traverse. Due to the topography of the area (high cliffs on either side of a ridge), we were definitely not going to be able to travel my planned route. We took our time making our way back to the road, throwing rocks into a wildlife pond or two, looking under logs for bugs and grubs to study and just enjoying the day.

We easily found the road we had started at utilizing the map and GPS and hiked on the road to the alternate location. It was a long trek on blacktop and our feet were tired, but we were safe and had enjoyed a wonderful day walking through the wilderness.

DIRECTION FINDING

GEAR TO GUIDE YOU

One of the most unique experiences I have had utilizing land-navigation gear occurred a few years ago while I was setting up a land-navigation course with Tracy Trimble, who teaches land navigation at Nature Reliance School. After we set up the practice course, I went back through it to verify that we had set and marked all the points properly. It was snowing hard and my hands were extremely cold as I had set up the points without gloves. As I started to go through the course, I put my gloves back on to keep my hands warm. When I pulled out my compass and set myself up to take my first azimuth, I was surprised to see the needle jumping back and forth like you might see in a cartoon. After thinking that I was standing on some sort of spot leading to the third dimension, I realized the culprits were the tiny little magnets holding my gloves' finger coverings back. Lesson learned for future reference: Get hook-and-loop fasteners next time.

While I am sure there are some people who may want to walk into a wilderness and never return, most of us want to be able to go out and return home. That is why we need to be able to navigate safely and efficiently. There are several tools that help us achieve this. As an SAR supporter and outdoor enthusiast, I have seen an incredible amount of people who own land-navigation tools but do not know how to use them. While I am a fan of technology, I also like to share gear that does not require any power to utilize it effectively. Land-navigation tools are no different. I want to cover the use of maps and compasses, then we'll dive into GPS as well.

TOPOGRAPHY MAPS

If I were given a choice to go into a wilderness area with either a map or compass but not both, I would choose a map. Maps are incredibly useful tools and you can navigate rather easily with a good one.

Topographic (topo) maps are the way to go as they offer you the ability to see lots of detail in an area. United States Geological Survey (USGS) maps are the gold standard of topo maps. These are easy to find at https://store.usgs.gov and relatively inexpensive at approximately $9.

Large-scale trail maps are another option as well. These maps do not have the detail of topographic maps but will most often give you a better overview of the trail system you are using as well as interesting local features. If you plan on staying on a trail, then this type of map will work just fine for you. Please note that that some of the more sensitive areas do not allow you off established trails. These large-scale trail maps will be great for keeping you on the trail.

One of the biggest benefits of modern technology is the ability to print maps from online sources. Some of these options are fee-based, others are completely free. Here are some great choices:

- **SARTOPO.COM.** This is the go-to choice for Nature Reliance School instructors and students. It is free, but you can purchase a membership that allows you to save your maps for later use. This site also prints out a quick response (QR) code that will take you directly to the map that has been printed and its details. This makes it incredibly easy to share maps with others in your family, team or unit.

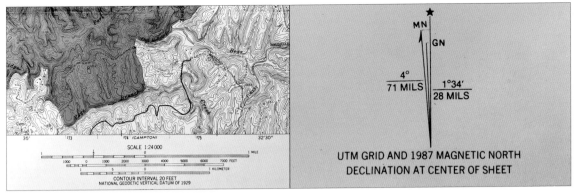

SCALE 1:24 000

CONTOUR INTERVAL 20 FEET
NATIONAL GEODETIC VERTICAL DATUM OF 1929

UTM GRID AND 1987 MAGNETIC NORTH
DECLINATION AT CENTER OF SHEET

The scale (left) and declination (right) portions of a map are important information for any land navigator.

- **MAPPINGSUPPORT.COM.** This site integrates easily with Google Maps and allows for easy overhead use of satellite imagery.
- **MYTOPO.COM.** This is a great site if you know you are going to travel primarily in one location. You can get a customized map (they will waterproof and laminate for you as well) for a fee of approximately $20.

At the time of this writing, the use of your cell phone as a handheld GPS unit is still not warranted in my opinion. Although Gaia GPS does have a great app for handhelds, you need to check it in the area you intend on traveling to ensure you will have the ability to download maps or have service. With all that said, let's dig into the most common map features as seen on topo maps.

Being able to read and understand maps is the key to properly using them. When understanding topo maps, we need to consider two key things: color and specific features like scale, grid system and north arrows.

Each color on a topographic map means a particular thing:

- **RED:** Primary and secondary roads
- **GREEN:** Vegetation areas (i.e., forest)
- **BLUE:** Water-related features
- **BLACK:** Man-made features (e.g., buildings, cell phone towers)
- **BROWN:** Elevation numbers and contour lines
- **WHITE:** Areas where vegetation is sparse (e.g., arid areas, cityscapes, rocky or bouldery landscape)

There are many other things to note about topographic maps. Following are the top three features you must understand, particularly when communicating with others.

SCALE

USGS maps are made on a 1:24,000 scale. This means that 1 unit on the map corresponds directly to 24,000 units on the actual Earth. If you use the scale to find and measure 1 inch (2.5 cm) on the map, the distance you just measured is 24,000 inches (60,000 cm), 2,000 feet (610 m) or 0.38 miles (0.6 km) on Earth.

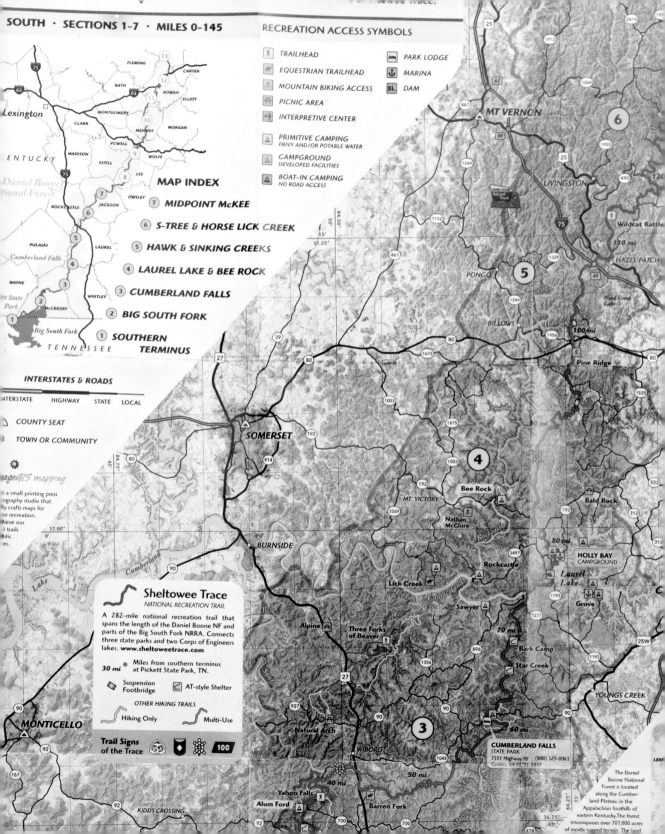

SOUTH · SECTIONS 1-7 · MILES 0-145

RECREATION ACCESS SYMBOLS

- TRAILHEAD
- EQUESTRIAN TRAILHEAD
- MOUNTAIN BIKING ACCESS
- PICNIC AREA
- INTERPRETIVE CENTER
- PRIMITIVE CAMPING — PRIVY AND/OR POTABLE WATER
- CAMPGROUND — DEVELOPED FACILITIES
- BOAT-IN CAMPING — NO ROAD ACCESS
- PARK LODGE
- MARINA
- DAM

MAP INDEX

7 MIDPOINT McKEE
6 S-TREE & HORSE LICK CREEK
5 HAWK & SINKING CREEKS
4 LAUREL LAKE & BEE ROCK
3 CUMBERLAND FALLS
2 BIG SOUTH FORK
1 SOUTHERN TERMINUS

INTERSTATES & ROADS

INTERSTATE   HIGHWAY   STATE   LOCAL

COUNTY SEAT

TOWN OR COMMUNITY

...ageGIS mapping
...e a small printing press
...ography studio that
...ly crafts maps for
...or recreation.
...lieve our
...s trails
...blic
...res.

Sheltowee Trace
NATIONAL RECREATION TRAIL

A 282-mile national recreation trail that spans the length of the Daniel Boone NF and parts of the Big South Fork NRRA. Connects three state parks and two Corps of Engineers lakes. www.sheltoweetrace.com

30 mi ● Miles from southern terminus at Pickett State Park, TN.

◇ Suspension Footbridge   ⊏ AT-style Shelter

OTHER HIKING TRAILS
Hiking Only   Multi-Use

Trail Signs of the Trace   100

CUMBERLAND FALLS
STATE PARK
7351 Highway 90   (800) 325-0063
Corbin, KY

The Daniel Boone National Forest is located along the Cumberland Plateau in the Appalachian foothills of eastern Kentucky. The forest encompasses over 707,000 acres of mostly rugged terrain. The land...

GRID SYSTEMS

1. **LATITUDE AND LONGITUDE.** The lat/long system is the oldest known method for map grids available. It's still heavily used by pilots of ships and aircraft.

2. **UNIVERSAL TRANSVERSE MERCATOR.** UTM is a metric-based system commonly used by SAR personnel.

3. **UNITED STATES NATIONAL GRID SYSTEM.** USNG is a metric-based system that more modern first responders, including the Federal Emergency Management Agency and SAR teams, are starting to use.

4. **MILITARY GRID REFERENCE SYSTEM.** MGRS is the system used by the U.S. military.

CRAIG'S TIPS FOR USING A MAP

1. Always keep maps where they are easily accessible while hiking or otherwise moving through a wilderness. You should reference them often. Recognize various points that you will encounter (a creek crossing, for example) and note it on the map when you come to it.

2. It helps to orient your map north to keep from confusing yourself. This means when you are looking at your map, have the top of the map facing the actual direction of north.

3. Use some sort of waterproof case with maps. Rain, dew and sweat will ruin a map quickly. You can get cases made for this purpose or use a sealable plastic bag for a more budget-minded choice. An even better choice that is very inexpensive is to cover your maps with clear packing tape. This makes the map easy to fold up. You can also use permanent or dry erase markers on it as well.

Rain, fog and sweat are problems for paper maps; using a map covering can fix this problem.

GRID SYSTEM

Think of a grid system as a language with which to communicate. If I speak only English and you speak only Japanese, we are going to have a difficult time understanding each other. If I use a map that has a Universal Transverse Mercator (UTM) grid system, and you have one that uses only a latitude and longitude (lat/long) system, we cannot communicate points effectively. This communication also works solo when you have a map that indicates one grid system and your GPS is

◄ *(Left) Understanding the various features on maps can open another level of wilderness travel and adventure.*

detailing another. Make sure everyone you communicate with and all your gear is set on the same grid system. At Nature Reliance School, we train all of our students—which include public sector outdoorsman; federal, state and local law enforcement officers; and emergency medical service and SAR personnel—to utilize the United States National Grid System (USNG). It is a metric based system that mirrors what the U.S. military uses. Once you get used to utilizing a metric-based system, you will see why most people who use it regularly do so. It is much easier to determine distances, share your position with others, and find other key map points of consideration. See the sidebar about grid systems (above) for more details on these and others.

NORTH ARROWS

You can typically find north arrows in the bottom-center of topo maps. You will see several arrows indicating north. True north refers to the longitude lines of a map, which end and begin at Earth's poles; magnetic north refers to the north pole and is where an accurate compass will point (due to Earth's state of magnetic flux, this value is constantly changing slightly); grid north is north as it relates to the various grid systems available.

You may run into some issues while utilizing topo maps. They are worth noting here.

UPDATES

USGS quadrangle maps and those that are based on them are not updated often. This means in some areas trails are sometimes rerouted and will not be displayed accurately. There is a bird-watcher's proverb that I keep in mind with such things: "When the bird and the bird book disagree, always believe the bird." The same is true when using topography maps if you are on a trail and regularly checking your route along the way—you may see a deviation in the trail itself from the map you are using. Often the entity responsible for trail maintenance will post signage in those areas, but not always. It is rare for a trail to be completely abandoned. You will most likely make your way back to the trail you were on after the reroute.

TERRAIN ASSOCIATION

The technical data is represented easily enough on the map and in this book. Applying that to the real world is difficult for some. What I recommend to you is the same thing I do in my land-navigation classes. You must get out in a known area with your topo maps and look at ridgelines, waterways, ravines and saddles and see how things in front of you appear on the map.

SCALE

When you print a map from a website, make sure your printer settings do not adjust your map's scale in such a way that it is no longer accurate. If you choose options

Recreation trail maps often have some topography details, good trail identification and even local points of interest details

such as "shrink to fit to page," then the scale will not be accurate unless the program is designed to adjust the map scale when doing so.

USER UNFRIENDLINESS

With all the details, scales, symbols and more, topo maps are not pick-up-and-go–style resources. You will need to invest some time in how to use them. If your wilderness travel doesn't require such details, a trail map will most suit your needs.

LARGE-SCALE TRAIL MAPS

National Geographic has some of the best trail maps available (approximately $12). They include topography, trails, points of interest and lots more. These maps will show trails and areas of interest specific to your needs. While they don't offer nearly the detail that you can expect from a topo map, they make up for it with more easily understood information for the casual outdoorsperson.

For the occasional user, large-scale trail maps are the best choice for the following reasons:

- You are a day hiker or adventurer with little-to-no experience and you expect to stay on a trail and not deviate.

- Symbols on trail maps are more user-friendly. Signage on a trail will often coincide with the map that represents it.

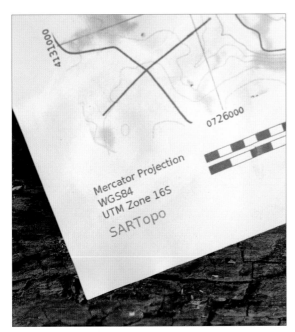

Printing your own map from a site such as SARtopo.com allows you to customize the map specifically to your needs.

Shown here is my favorite baseplate compass, the Suunto MC-2. With proper training, this tool, accompanied with good maps, has allowed me to go on and off trail to many wonderful locations.

- Trail maps are updated more frequently. Some maps are updated annually.

- Trail maps come pre-folded and are easy to carry.

- Trail maps are sometimes printed on water-resistant paper. This makes them more durable against rain, sweat and humidity.

Go to any sporting goods store, tourist area or visitor center and you will find some form of trail maps. Some will be free in visitor centers, others will be offered for a fee. I sincerely believe that if you plan on staying on the trail, these maps will assist any beginner very well. Once you start to go off-trail (when it's legal to do so) and pursue more technical wilderness travel, you will need to have some topo map skills. You can assist yourself even further by having a combination of trail and topo maps.

As your skills as a wilderness traveler increase, you will need to be more involved in your own maps. I believe the best method is to find an online supplier (SARtopo.com

is my favorite) and create a map specific for your use. This customization will allow you to do a number of things that will offer you a wider range of wilderness sites and even keep you safer while doing exploring. You can highlight trails or areas of interest for your trip, get coordinates for places you want to see and even track yourself with a GPS then download those points to your mapping software when you get home.

COMPASSES

Compasses are one of those gear items that various brands take to the extreme in order to separate themselves from their competitors. The bells and whistles are more confusing than helpful, and you should rely on something that is simple. I can easily divide compasses into two different types to discuss them. You cannot go wrong by using either of them. I have one of each that I use regularly and I will make it clear why I do so in the following paragraphs.

BASEPLATE COMPASS

For nearly all the things I do outdoors, I use a Suunto MC-2 compass. This type of compass is an excellent choice for the typical hunter, hiker, backpacker or outdoorsperson. It has a clear plastic base containing scales that correspond to most common scales used on topo maps. The bezel surrounding the face of the compass indicates the degrees of angle and are most often in increments of 2° with each tick mark. When choosing a compass make sure that the liquid inside the bezel has some oil rather than just water. Water expands and contracts easily and will allow bubbles to form. If you have bubbles in your compass, it cannot be accurate and should not be used.

Baseplate compasses are incredibly affordable. My Suunto MC-2 cost around $50. I prefer it because it has a sighting mirror that makes it more effective. If you do not need that sort of function, a good alternative is a Suunto A-10 (approximately $15). It does not have the sighting mirror but will do nearly everything that you will need to do with it.

The arrow in the bezel is your north arrow. Usually the north arrow is the red arrow and south will be either black or white. Different manufacturers have their own colors, so ensure you know which arrow points north. The direction-of-travel arrow is most often at the front of the compass and should be used to show which direction you are facing (see the sidebar on page 59). Although a simple baseplate compass will get most navigating tasks done, I do prefer those that also include a sighting mirror. The sighting mirror gives me a bit more accuracy when utilizing it. If you feel that you may utilize a compass at night, I recommend you get a compass that has luminous arrow accents on the north arrow, direction-of-travel arrow and bezel as well.

Baseplate compasses can have some issues, which are outlined in the following list, along with some easy solutions.

- **BEZEL FLUID EXPANSION/CONTRACTION.** Keep the compass close to your body during cold weather and don't leave it in your car or an unheated area of your home.

- **ROUGH HANDLING.** These are not mil-spec compasses—they will get scratched up easily and can break under a fair amount of pressure. I have dropped mine several times and have had no issue with a simple drop. However, do take care since you don't want to drop your pack and have the compass inside hit a hard surface, like a rock. This warning may seem unimportant, but you don't want to fall on a trail, drop your compass, accidentally step on it and find that you have broken it. If that were to happen in the backcountry and you were off-trail, you would have to rely on more advanced map skills, such as terrain association.

- **SIGHTING MIRROR BREAKS OR COMES UNGLUED.** If you use a baseplate with a sighting mirror, it is not uncommon for it to come out. (Another use for that superglue in your first aid kit.) Also, with rough use it could easily break.

LENSATIC COMPASS

I also have a Cammenga Tritium 3H lensatic compass, (approximately $100). Lensatic compasses are the type most often associated with the U.S. military. The Cammenga brand is the standard that all other compasses are measured against.

Lensatic compasses, when used properly, have more precision than the baseplate compasses detailed earlier. The thumb loop is used to secure it to your hand during use. The siting wire will assist you in taking accurate readings (see the sidebar on page 59). The lens bracket is slightly magnified, which assists in seeing both the sighting wire and the degrees. You will also notice that

▶ (Right) This is the incredibly tough mil-spec lensatic compass made by Cammenga. It is my favorite compass to use for nighttime land navigation.

The proper way to hold compasses. From left to right: a basic baseplate, a baseplate with a sighting mirror and a lensatic on the bottom. Refer to the sidebar How to Hold a Compass on the following page for tips.

HOW TO HOLD A COMPASS

1. Ensure that rings, necklaces or other magnetic metals do not interfere with the use of your compass. To determine if metals are interfering with your compass, place these items near the compass. They will "pull" the needle slightly off.

2. Ensure the direction-of-travel arrow is facing away from your body.

3. Hold the compass so the base is flat and allows the needle to move freely. I do this by twisting my compass and ensuring the north arrow stays pointed in the correct direction.

4. Center-hold is done by using a baseplate compass without a sighting device. Hold it near the center of your chest so you can look down on the readings.

5. Cheek-hold is done by placing the compass near your dominant eye and using the sighting device on the compass (i.e., wire on lensatic, "gunsight" on others).

the compass can be used to measure both degrees (which are in red) or mils (which are in black). Mil-spec lensatic compasses are the style that is most often replicated by cheap gear manufacturers. Avoid these knockoffs at all costs. The Cammenga Tritium Compass 3H is heavy and bulky for something its size. This is one of those items that is worth the extra money invested in it. The knockoff versions are hardly ever accurate and are made of lightweight plastic. I have seen dozens of them in my classes and the knockoff versions are rarely accurate.

While typical mil-spec compasses do have some gradients for measuring distance and scale, they are not as easy to use as those on a baseplate. They are also more useful with a large-scale map and longer distances. Therefore, if you are on a trip that is going to take you over a long distance, such as a through-hike (in which you hike the trail end-to-end within one hiking season), a lensatic compass will serve you well. Lensatic compasses are also nearly bombproof. Due to the rigid standards and needs of the military, they can handle lots of abuse. If you are in law enforcement or related tactical fields in which you will be hitting the deck a fair amount of the time, I highly recommend you get a Cammenga lensatic; it will handle any abuse you can throw at it. For all other contexts, I recommend a simple baseplate compass.

COMPASS FIELD AND HOME CARE

Compasses will be negatively affected if they are stored near metal with a strong magnetic pull. This can serve to "spring" the compass; that is, the needle gets pulled slightly off magnetic north and stays that way. You can also develop bubbles in your compasses if you store them in temperatures below freezing. It is not that they will freeze—it is that the temperature changes from cold to warm will cause the liquid to expand and contract, which causes bubbles to form. I store my compasses inside where the temperature remains moderate.

WILDERNESS FIRST AID

FROM BOO-BOOS TO SEVERE TRAUMA

I bet you did not expect me to start a first aid section with a story about blackberries, but that is exactly what I am going to do. I love them, my wife loves them and we enjoy getting out and picking them. When you find a patch of them, you sort of just let the blackberries guide you to where you are going. On one such trip, my wife had walked up and down some hills, on uneven terrain, picking a couple of buckets full of the juicy delights. As she was coming out of some high grass, she could not see her foot placement and twisted her ankle severely. I always have a first aid kit nearby, so it was rather easy to get her wrapped and splinted up. Without a good first aid kit she would have certainly lived; however, by securing her ankle, we ensured that her ankle was not injured further so she could get to the vehicle and back home, where we could take care of it more properly.

First aid equipment is a set of items that often get overlooked, mainly because people think that nothing is ever going to happen to them. I look at it very differently. I have trained many first responders—such as law enforcement officers, EMTs and SAR personnel—in wilderness safety and survival. I have heard countless stories of first aid issues happening in the backcountry. None of the people affected ever purposely put themselves in situations where they knew they were going to get injured. I repeat: none of them.

A fundamental first aid kit will include items for small open wounds and illness.

Gear is a game changer and a lifesaver when it comes to wilderness first aid. I am a proponent of taking first aid gear with you every day no matter where you are, so much so that I think it is foolhardy to go into a wilderness setting without any. Unexpected events happen to even the best and most experienced wilderness traveler.

I like to divide first aid supplies into two groups: (1) wilderness kits and (2) trauma kits. Individual first aid kits (IFAKs) should be customized to you as an individual and often will change based on the geographical location in which they will be used. The first two lists that follow are things that are fundamental to all wilderness first aid situations. In the third list I will include some other items to consider for customization.

WILDERNESS KIT

- Two 4 x 4-inch (10 x 10-cm) gauze pads
- Roll of surgical tape
- Irrigation syringe
- Two pairs of gloves
- One triangle bandage with safety pins
- Ten adhesive strips (6 large, 4 small)
- Two 3M™ Steri-Strip™ skin closures
- One roll vet wrap elastic bandage
- Two povidone-iodine pads
- Two alcohol prep pads
- Two packages ibuprofen
- Two packages antihistamine
- Two packages aspirin
- Triple antibiotic ointment
- Two packages rehydration salts
- One instant cold pack
- One moleskin (for blisters)
- Duct tape
- Booklet that covers first aid and other important issues for reference (this is a great tool to have when you need to think clearly under stress)

TRAUMA INDIVIDUAL FIRST AID KIT (IFAK)

As the name indicates, a trauma IFAK is for incredibly serious medical issues. Each of the items in the follow list require the user to have sound medical training to avoid misusing them. While these items are most often used by EMTs, paramedics and similar medical professionals, with training from a good instructor, most everyone can recognize when the need to use them arises. I often get scoffed at for recommending these items because "they are overkill and you need good training to use them properly." That is correct. I believe everyone who ventures into the wilderness should have such training. As I mentioned earlier, the folks I have trained have completed too many body recoveries and severely injured carry-outs for me to ignore it. The reasons not to carry a trauma IFAK are obvious: Weight and space are important. I can assure you that the following items, when assembled, weigh less than 1 pound (450 g) and can easily fit in your back pocket or on your belt.

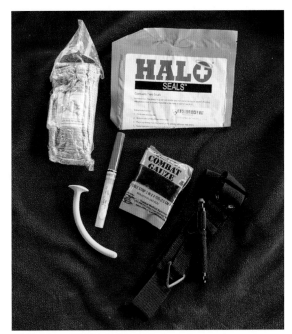

Trauma kits include items that require more than basic first aid training but are absolute lifesavers when needed.

FIX THE MOST-LIKELY INJURY IN A WILDERNESS: MAKE IT FAT AND SASSY

Wilderness Medical Associates is one of the nation's top providers of emergency medical training in the wilderness. They also have an extensive collection of data on wilderness injuries, sicknesses and other problems. I want to help you be prepared for what they have determined is the most-likely injury you might experience in the outdoors, a twisted or broken leg below the knee. Follow these six steps to make a hurt leg "fat and sassy":

1. Loosen the strings on the person's footwear so their leg injury has room to swell.

2. Wrap soft gear—such as a shirt, jacket or sleeping pad—around the injured leg. This is the "fat" part—it will serve to protect the affected area and allow it to swell.

3. Use something rigid to support the injured leg, as it will be held in place in step 4. This is the "sassy" part. Employ stout limbs from the wilderness or aluminum stays from your pack, such as tent poles. Your goal here is to ensure the injured area cannot be moved. The supports on the leg should protrude below the foot. They will protect it as much as possible if the person stands up. You do not want them to put pressure on the injured leg directly.

4. Wrap material above and below the injury to keep all the "fat and sassy" material in place. This additional material could be other articles of clothing, paracord, duct tape, vet wrap or rolled gauze.

5. If possible, leave the person at your current location, go get help and bring it back to them. Give the patient resources to protect them from the environment while they're waiting. You should also mark the location on the map before you leave and note the coordinates to share with SAR support.

6. If self-rescue is a must, have the patient place their same-side arm across your shoulders for support and make your way out. Encourage them to not put pressure on the injured leg. If you are alone, the splinting portions of this work is vital. Any mechanical injury will cause you to move erratically. This can cause your injuries to be more severe if you determine you need to self-rescue. If during preplanning you shared your location and time of return with someone, you should shelter-in-place if at all possible. It is safer to let the SAR personnel extract you. They will give you first aid onsite and pack you so you are less likely to be injured further during transport.

TRAUMA IFAK

- Tourniquet
- Israeli bandage pressure dressing
- Nasopharyngeal airway (aka NPA or nose trumpet)
- Hemostatic gauze
- Two chest seals
- Chest decompression needle

There are also some medical conditions that not everyone deals with (e.g., allergies and unstable blood sugar) but the people who do have these issues must have an answer for them in their IFAK. You should know the members in your group to know if they have any conditions and how to treat them. Following are a few examples of individualized items someone might need to carry in their IFAK.

CUSTOMIZED ITEMS FOR IFAKS

- **EPINEPHRINE PEN (AKA EPIPEN®).** These can be obtained with a doctor's prescription and are for people that have allergic reactions to various things such stings, bites and even nuts. This will serve to reduce the swelling in the throat so the patient can breathe more easily.

- **GLUCOSE TABLETS.** These tablets will help those with hypoglycemia or diabetes by raising their blood sugar after it has fallen to an unhealthy level. You can also use any form of sugar. Some individuals, particularly type 1 diabetics, respond differently to various forms of sugar, so make sure you know what works well for them.
- **PRESCRIPTION MEDICATIONS.** Make sure you take your prescription medicines with you during outdoor travels. I have had students cut their class time with me short due to leaving their blood pressure, heart, migraine or other medicine at home. Although being outside is great for your health and may assist you in getting off some of these medicines, you should not expect that to happen instantaneously. Plan accordingly.

FIELD AND HOME CARE FOR FIRST AID ITEMS

Since we hope to never need first aid items, it is easy to just keep them in your pack or throw them in quickly when you are ready to leave. When I unpack after a trip, I always recheck my first aid kit and replace items I have used. This way, I always have items available when I need them. For years before I developed the habit of rechecking, I would keep a notebook with me and write notes along my trips so I would not forget gear items I needed to replace before the next trip. This also included the first aid kit items.

HOW TO USE A TOURNIQUET

For many years, using a tourniquet was frowned on because it was assumed that it would lead to extensive nerve damage and the loss of a limb due to lack of blood flow. Battlefield use of tourniquets has shown that only 0.4 percent of patients had loss of limbs and most of those were due to reasons other than tourniquet use. Only 1.5 percent of patients experienced permanent nerve damage. There is no substitute for good training from a qualified medic, so get some training on your own. I queried three EMTs, one of whom was a former Special Forces medic with extensive battlefield experience. Here are the seven steps they suggest when utilizing a tourniquet.

1. Ensure the area where the patient is located is safe for you to enter. Whatever caused their problem could cause the same for you. As an example, you might see a friend writhing in pain and holding their leg, but they cannot tell you what happened. If you were to rush in, you might cut yourself on the same rock they did.

2. Put on medical gloves if you have them available.

3. Verify that the wound needs a tourniquet. You will recognize a significant amount blood pooling and blood may be spurting in rhythm with the heart.

4. Put firm and direct pressure on the wound. For the leg, this is done on the inside of the thigh, close to the groin. For the arm, it is on the underside of the arm near the armpit. The patient will not like it, but one of the best ways to do apply pressure is to kneel on that area. Your goal is to not make the patient happy but to save their life.

5. Place the tourniquet on the affected limb and place it as high as you can. Get as much slack out of the tourniquet as you can. I prefer the SOF® Tactical Tourniquet Wide. It allows you to easily pull the slack out of the tourniquet through a simple buckling device.

6. Use the windlass handle to create more pressure until the blood flow is reduced. This will most likely cause pain to the patient again.

7. Lock the handle into place and note the time so you can share it with medical personnel.

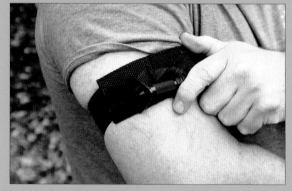

Many people suggest they will use boot strings, belts, pack straps and other equipment under these circumstances. This is foolhardy at best and should not be considered the way to stop extensive blood loss. You should get training, get a tourniquet and practice with it under stress.

With proper training, tourniquets can slow bleeding in a person with a large arterial bleed.

DEFENSE AGAINST PREDATORS

DON'T PET THE BEARS

One of the barriers that keep people from traveling into a wilderness area is an unfounded fear of wildlife. I do not feel that we should be afraid of any animal in the outdoors. I do, however, have a healthy respect for all animals, especially those that may prey on me and my family and friends while we're outdoors. A little knowledge on wildlife will go a long way when it comes to your safety. I want to consider the tactics and gear pieces you can use to be safe around them all. Let's break them down into two categories: (1) prey, those animals that are food for predators; and (2) predators, animals that hunt or seek out other animals—including humans—as food.

There are very few animals that will actively seek out humans as prey. There is evidence to suggest that the mountain lion is the only animal in North America that has actively hunted humans. Other predatory animals, such as grizzly bears, may seek out humans to get their food, but most often it is because they are opportunistic and not necessarily seeking out humans as the food source. With that said, there are tactics and gear we need to know for each of these categories.

For prey animals like deer, elk, large raptors and more, the simplest tactic is to not get between them and their young or their food. If you are a barrier to their getting to either one, it could cause problems. Often, simply making sure they are aware of your presence will cause them to leave an area before you get close to them.

Predators are different. They often have either claws or teeth that allow them to kill other animals for food. Surprise them and they will attack in self-defense. If you get between them and their food or young, they will attack in defense of them. Here are certain animals in a typical wilderness that get the most attention as well as advice on how you should handle yourself around them and the gear you'll need to stay safe.

GRIZZLY AND BROWN BEARS

Wear a bell on your gear to announce you are coming. This will often cause a bear to leave. Carry bear spray with you if you are going to be in an area that has bears and keep it within arm's reach. The active ingredient to look for is capsaicin. The Environmental Protection Agency requires that percentage of capsaicin and related capsaicinoids in the bear spray range between 1 percent and 2 percent. Capsaicin affects the eyes, nose and throat of the bear so you will need to spray the animal in the face. Keep your food in a bear-proof container (Garcia and Counter Assault are two great brands) and sleep in a spot separate from where you cook and store food.

BLACK BEARS

Black bears are less dangerous than grizzly bears because they are herbivores, whereas grizzlies are omnivores. However, they can attack if you catch them by surprise or threaten them or their young. Much like their brown bear cousins, black bears are attracted to smells. During a class in Pennsylvania one year, I came back from lunch to find a black bear digging underneath my hammock. I had attracted it by spitting out my toothpaste on the ground. Keep anything with odors closed and be cognizant of your waste as well.

MOUNTAIN LIONS

These big cats do not like for people to fight back. If you are attacked, then fight back with all you have and you may avoid further damage. You can do this by throwing rocks or sticks or any other instrument that could cause blunt trauma. Some other strategies that also help are traveling in groups and not wandering around in the dark. One simple thing you can do is add fake eyes or a mask on the back of your head or hat. It seems silly, but many people with experience with mountain lions say it is beneficial because mountain lions always attack from behind. The thought is that they may not be able to determine whether you are looking at them with the fake eyes.

Fake eyes are one small possibility of defense against a mountain lion.

VENOMOUS SNAKES

Avoidance is the key with snakes, and let's be clear on one thing for certain: There is only one gear piece that will help you with a snakebite. That gear piece is a set of vehicle keys. They will help you get to a hospital to get proper care. Snakebite kits are completely ineffective tools on snake venom and one of the largest marketing schemes ever placed on an uneducated public. Snake venom is one of four types: (1) proteolytic, (2) hemotoxic, (3) neurotoxic or (4) cytotoxic. Each of the venom types attaches to the respective areas of the human body and no extraction device will pull it out. A tourniquet is also a poor choice to use on a snakebite as it will help hold the toxin in a localized area of the body and will cause rapid tissue decline.

One other thing that will help protect you from wildlife is a dog. Dogs make great hiking companions and have much better senses and situational awareness than humans. If you are traveling with a pet you know well enough to read their body language, they can alert you about other animals before wildlife can cause an issue.

SIGNALING

NO CAMOUFLAGE NEEDED

Signaling is rather simple, really. Signaling items can be gear pieces that you carry specifically for that purpose or the colors you choose for other equipment. If you are a hunter and wear camouflage, you especially need to carry some sort of signaling equipment.

We cover this on a regular basis in our tracking courses at Nature Reliance School. The concepts taught there are exceptional for making sure people see the things in a wilderness we want them to. The two concepts we teach are baseline vs. disturbance:

- **BASELINE:** The way an environment looks under regular conditions.

- **DISTURBANCE:** Any change or adjustment to an environment that is different than baseline.

There may be a need for you to be recognized by others. Whether it be an SAR party or your friend who came to the hunt, hike or picnic later than you did. The way to do this is to appeal to the other person's senses of sight and hearing.

SIGHT

You can appeal to a person's sense of sight by movement and colors. If you put the two together, you are more likely to be seen. Keep in mind that moving with these signaling devices is far better than using them while staying still. However, you may not always be able to move, which is where color comes in. To keep things incredibly simple, when you choose a pack, jacket, hat or similar item, choose one that's brightly colored. The human eye is more sensitive to some colors than others. Do you remember "Roy G. Biv" from school? It is the acronym that helped us remember the color spectrum: red, orange, yellow, green, blue, indigo, violet. Your eye is more sensitive to colors in the yellow-green portion of the spectrum. A yellow, particularly fluorescent yellow-green, is going to be more easily seen. That is why most highway laborers utilize this color for safety. You are most likely thinking that you do not want to go into a wilderness looking like a neon sign. I don't either. It is worth your trouble to carry a neon yellow-green or orange signal panel in your pocket. I am a fan of bandanas simply because they can be used for signaling and so many other uses.

Flashing light is nothing more than light that is moving. If rescuers are looking for you from the air or across a mountainside, flashing light will get their attention rather quickly.

Carrying smoke and signal flares is not likely for the average backpacker. Even I recognize that this is overkill. They could be a good choice when you travel by vehicle (like a car-camping, canoeing or all-terrain vehicle trip). I keep these in my vehicle for serious emergency use. Comet makes great signaling devices for maritime use that are equally useful in a wilderness.

Although it is worthy of discussion here, please consult pages 70–72 for details on the uses of lights for both safety and everyday needs.

REAL-LIFE SKILLS: MAKING SIGNALS

1. **SIGNAL MIRROR.** While looking through the aiming hole, shine the mirror on your outstretched hand. This ensures you are getting plenty of sunlight to it. As you look through the aiming hole you will see a bright dot on the reflective material in it. You can then move the dot toward the distant object you want to signal. Please note that you can signal in this manner across a ridgeline, open field or similar location. It is not to just for aircraft. Most searches do not utilize aircraft, so this should be one of several ways to signal for help.

2. **WHISTLES.** The international distress signal with a whistle is six blasts. However, most people do not recognize it. The more widely known three blasts will accomplish the same end goal. Your goal should be to get the attention of those looking for you. Three sharp blasts on the whistle on a regular basis can accomplish this. Although knowing Morse code is a benefit, it is not necessary; however, if you want to signal SOS specifically, give three short blasts, three long blasts and three short ones again.

3. **FIRE.** You can use fire to signal in many ways. Forming three fires in a triangle is a distress signal to aircraft. Building a fire that produces a lot of smoke can also be seen by aircraft and smelled by searchers on the ground. Remember the concept of baseline vs. disturbance, though. Putting green material on a fire will create white smoke, which shows up well against a green area. If you are in a snow-covered area, white smoke will not be easily seen. Utilize an oil-based product on the fire to create black smoke. This could include plastic, cooking oil or similar substances.

Using a signal mirror (left) or a signal panel (right) are good ways to bring attention to your position. See page 67 for details on panels.

USING A WHISTLE TO FIND MY CHILDREN

One year for Christmas my wife gave me an MSR Whisperlite™ International stove (see Chapter 7 for more details). I was excited to try it out. We packed up the kids and headed out into the snow-covered Daniel Boone National Forest to have a fun day playing and enjoying some hot chocolate made on the new stove. I failed to check the weather before leaving—and that was a big mistake. The wind was strong, so we set up the stove in a small ravine to keep the flame from blowing out.

As we were setting up the stove my kids, who were approximately five to seven years old at the time, wanted to go play in a small field about 30 yards (27 m) away from us. We could still watch them play from that distance, but before they left we went over what to do if they got lost—which included blowing their whistle. I also told them that if they heard me blowing mine that they should stop what they are doing and wait for me to come to them. At the time, I thought it was simply a good opportunity to reaffirm a lesson they had previously been taught. Shortly after they left, it started to snow a bit harder, and then it began snowing in a way I had never seen before. I literally could not see my hand in front of my face, the snow

was coming down so hard. I immediately set off to track my kids in the snow. The tracks were already covered up. I then got to the edge of the field and blew my whistle. I heard nothing in response and my heart sank. I blew it again three times, as I had instructed my kids to do. I was relieved when I heard another whistle off to my left and started walking that way. My daughter and I continued blowing our whistles in this call-and-response fashion, and I found her and my son huddled under a hemlock tree out of the snow. We packed up the gear and headed out to drink the hot chocolate elsewhere.

HEARING

Do you remember our discussion regarding the need to signal to keep bears away? A bell is a constant sound that helps, but its range is short. A great choice to keep attached to you is a whistle. I carry a Fox 40 brand whistle with me each time I go outside, as do all well-trained SAR personnel. The average human voice and typical whistle can only reach around 90 decibels on a good day.

A whistle made for outdoors can reach more than 120 decibels. This means the sound is louder, which allows the sound to go farther. I keep my whistle attached to my pack. I personally believe every child going into a wilderness should be required to wear a whistle on a breakaway lanyard. See the sidebar for a misadventure of my own that will help you to understand why I feel this way.

LIGHTING

LIGHT UP THE DARKNESS

Sometimes there is simply not enough light in the day to enjoy time in the wilderness. Thankfully, you can employ artificial light. Whether you want a great headlamp to run an ultramarathon or to play card games at camp, gear pieces that illuminate are becoming brighter with each season and at the same time becoming more affordable and lightweight. That is a nice combination. The key to illumination is understanding how this equipment works and comparing features and specifications. There are a few factors to consider when deciding on what to purchase.

LUMENS

Lumens is the technical term for the intensity of light. During product testing, this is determined with a new light utilizing fresh batteries. The lumens of a light will slowly decline as you use it. Lumens will range from 20 lumens, which is enough to do small tasks directly in front of your line of sight, up to 3,000 lumens, which will nearly replace the sun. This is only one small part of the effectiveness of any given light. The type of beam also plays a big role. The beam allows you to have a spotlight or floodlight. Spotlights focus the beam farther away and covers a small area more intensely. Floodlights widen the range of the light but make it less intense. Both are incredibly useful for various tasks. If you want to use your light to see what is going "bump" in the night, use the spotlight. If you want to brighten up a whole campsite area to find more materials for your fire, then flood it out. I prefer a light that adjusts easily between the two. That way with one unit I can cover both tasks well.

Handheld lights are a standard, reliable source of illumination in any situation.

POWER

Most small handheld lights will be powered by either AA or AAA batteries. I like to have multiple pieces of equipment that all run on the same batteries, so I have to carry only one type of backup batteries. It also means that I can pull batteries out of one device and use them in another device in a worst-case scenario. For example, I may pull batteries out of my GPS unit to use in a headlamp because it is not likely I will be using both at the same time. There is one exception to this: handheld flashlights. I prefer to carry a tactical flashlight on me always. High-performance flashlights such as these run on CR123 batteries. These allow the light's brightness to be incredibly intense at high power and very long-lasting on low power. I carry a PowerTac E5 light (approximately $70) that has three output settings, one of which is termed "moonlight." This is a very low output setting that can do all my necessary camp chores. This low output, coupled with high-efficiency batteries, equals a light source that will last several more hours than I have ever had need of. With this type of light, I can also use it on its highest setting in contexts such as self-defense. If left on this setting, though, the light will only last two to three hours.

USE

Technology has come a long way with illumination and some innovations are very beneficial. I prefer to use lights that have more than just an on-and-off switch. If available, I prefer a light that has levels of brightness and, whenever possible, a setting that blinks for safety (I would only use that feature in a lost-person situation). As noted in the section about signaling (pages 67–69), that is extremely valuable.

The following paragraphs detail several kinds of lights and the uses they're best suited for. Keep these details handy as you purchase lighting equipment so that you can make the best decision.

HANDHELD LIGHTS

There's nothing like the tried-and-true standard flashlight. Flashlights come in shapes and sizes to meet both your needs and your wants. Most come in plastic housing. Plastic does not last as long and is more susceptible to breaking, especially during cold weather. Anodized aluminum housing is my choice for handheld flashlights. It is incredibly durable, has better grip when you're wearing gloves and typically contains a clip, allowing it to remain secure as you move. And the clip makes it easy to fasten the light to your pants, shirt or pack or hang it from a tent or hammock. Just ensure the flashlight you get has O-rings to maintain its viability in wet conditions. As I mentioned previously, my top choice for a handheld flashlight is the PowerTac E5.

HEADLAMPS

In the South, when something is very useful, you might hear us remark, "That is as handy as a shirt pocket." Headlamps are even better than that. A headlamp stays out of the way, doesn't weigh but a few ounces and is easy to use. The elastic will eventually wear out on a headlamp, so expect that to happen. Some manufacturers have replacement bands, so look for those when you're purchasing your headlamp. I utilized a Petzl TACTIKKA® (approximately $40) for a couple of years until the casing broke in cold weather. I have a number of military and SAR students who use them regularly. I have now adjusted to utilizing a Streamlight Sidewinder® light (approximately $70). It is a light that falls into the tactical category, so I detail it in a later paragraph.

CAP LIGHTS

Cap lights are like headlamps, except they clip on to the bill of a ball cap. That is a nice innovation but I do not always wear a ball cap when I am in the wilderness. If you feel the same way, purchase a headlamp instead. After all, you always take your head with you when you go outdoors.

TACTICAL LIGHTS

The U.S. military is good at coming up with innovations that we can utilize in the public sector. There are any number of lights called tactical because they came from this type of design. What it means is that these lights have MOLLE clips, infrared illumination, adjustable head angles and much more. I have had a number of headlamps, each of which have become unusable due to my using them a lot. I have been using a Streamlight Sidewinder light the last seven years with no issues (see photo on page 73). The Sidewinder offers more options than some other tactical lights. For example, the light can be unclipped from the head strap and worn on my pack strap or belt or easily clipped inside my hammock. It is designed to be a multiuse tool. It is definitely more expensive than your typical headlamp (approximately $70); however, in my estimation it is well worth the investment.

RECHARGEABLE LIGHTS

It may be overkill, but I also have an inexpensive rechargeable light made by Coleman®. It is my fail-safe method meeting my nighttime-illumination and emergency-preparedness needs. These lights are invaluable for keeping in your pack or similar outdoor gear. They weigh very little and never need the batteries replaced. Just give them a few cranks and you have light for a while. When they get dim again, crank them back up.

LANTERNS

I grew up around an old Coleman white-gas lantern that my dad still uses today (the new ones cost approximately $78). We have used that lantern for nearly 50 years now. Think about that for a moment. That is a long time. Coleman still makes very good lanterns—some work on white gas (referred to as drip gas, naphtha or Coleman fuel, depending on regional vernacular), some crank, some use solar cells or batteries. I find no fault in any of them. For camping trips with the family or similar excursions where you will be traveling by vehicle, they are great to have.

Battery, solar or gas-powered lanterns are a great choice for car campers.

FIELD AND HOME CARE FOR LIGHTS

Batteries are the big culprits when it comes to lights. I keep an extra lamp and batteries in a small reserve kit that goes in my pack each time I use it. Some flashlights have enough room in the housing to store an extra lamp as well, which I recommend when it's possible. I also learned how to check the amperage on my batteries with a volt meter. This way, I don't have to guess on the batteries' value before trips. If they are close to being fully charged, I will leave them in the light as I begin a new trip. If they are less than half-charged, I will replace them before leaving so I start with fresh batteries. On trips where there is significant rain, I will always break down all my electronics when I get home to dry them out if moisture makes its way into the sensitive circuitry.

➤ *(Right) The Sidewinder is an incredibly useful light that works great as a headlamp, as a handheld device or when clipped to a pack.*

CHAPTER 4
SHELTER

It always rains on tents. Rainstorms will travel thousands of miles, against prevailing winds for the opportunity to rain on a tent.

—Dave Barry

MANY YEARS AGO, I REGULARLY SPENT A GREAT DEAL OF MY FREE TIME backpacking. It was during that time that I had one of the most memorable experiences in the outdoors. My good friend Brian and I were hiking a section of the Sheltowee Trace National Recreation Trail in Kentucky. We were on the first leg and had been dropped off with only one way home: We had to hike the roughly 40 miles (64 km) to where we had left my vehicle.

As we started off, it started to rain. The clouds did not think that was enough so they decided basically to pour water on us in their best waterfall imitation. At the time, we had some of the best gear that two poor college kids could afford. Hiking was no problem; we and our belongings stayed relatively dry, thanks to some great rain covers. Then nightfall crept up on us. We stopped for the night and set up our two-man tent, put our sleeping bags down and climbed in to eat a snack before going to sleep.

Sometime in the middle of the night, I woke up to running water. As I lay there, tired and sore, I thought it sounded soothing and very close. Then I realized that was because the water I was hearing was running down the middle of our tent between our two sleeping bags. Yeah, it was that bad.

This soggy situation was the product of our own poor choice of campsites, as well as a poor tent choice. Adding to the learn-from-my-mistakes moment, we had sleeping bags that were now soaking wet. (I hope it is obvious that they do not insulate in that state.) We had at least one more night out in the wilderness with them. I try to find the positive in all situations and don't like saying that the next night was miserable, but it was miserable. I can reflect on such trips now with warm fuzzies. Back then, though, warm and fuzzy was nowhere to be found. I have never had an experience like that since, due to a lot of study about sheltering. Strap your boots on, and let's look at how to stay warm and dry sleeping in the wilderness.

CLOTHING

GETTING COOL THINGS WARM AND WARM THINGS COOL

The purpose of your wilderness shelter system is maintaining your core body temperature for comfort at best and survival at worst. In this chapter, I am going to discuss how to stay comfortable by primarily focusing your attention on maintaining your needed temperature in cold weather. I regularly tell my survival students that the best *and only* heaters we carry with us are our own bodies. I believe you need to consider that deeply. Many outdoor enthusiasts think that a jacket or sleeping bag is the secret to staying warm in cold weather. This is only partially true. We *must* have all the other things in place to allow our bodies to heat properly. They do an exceptional job if we can set them up for success. Understanding how your body loses its heat will help you know what option is best for shelter. Your body loses heat in five ways:

1. **RESPIRATION.** You experience normal heat loss by breathing. You can only stop this by not breathing, so let's not put that into practice.

2. **RADIATION.** Since heat rises (even in human bodies), you most often lose heat through your head, neck and face through radiation. Keep in mind that you can lose heat through any exposed portion of your body. This can be fixed with quality clothing and a sleeping bag. I will also show you the "Caudill Family Secret" to regulating your body temp while you sleep at night.

3. **CONVECTION.** Convection is heat being removed from an area due to wind. This can be corrected with proper insulating layers and shelter placement, as well as shelter choice.

A proper clothing investment allows you to get out when the weather is less than perfect.

4. **PERSPIRATION.** Any water loss from your body, or addition of water to your body from outside influences like rain, will assist in pulling heat from you. You already know this because humid air feels warmer than dry air. Your body works the same way. Heat from your body goes into the moisture—be it sweat, rain, snow or a river drenching—and cools the body down. The best way to correct this issue is to choose your clothes wisely. At its root, perspiring is a form of conduction. You can counteract this by employing by proper base layers and good rain gear.

5. **CONDUCTION.** Think of your body as a temperature scale. If it contacts something that is cooler, then heat will flow from your body to the cooler item. The ground is a perfect example of this. It will pull heat from your body. You can correct this issue by good site placement and setup and a good sleeping pad.

As I mentioned previously, your body is a heater. If you understand it is the most important aspect of staying warm, then you we can move forward with putting together a clothing system that will work with your body. Too many times people look at clothing as some sort of miracle apparatus. Especially in cold weather, many think the more they put on the warmer they will be—nothing could be further from the truth.

One of the many benefits of growing up in a farming family was that no matter what the weather was like, I had go out and get work done. Cattle must be fed no matter what the conditions are. Farming helped me develop a system of dressing that works. It works whether you are involved in high-intensity activities (e.g., throwing hay bales or climbing up the side of a mountain) or low-intensity activities (e.g., climbing into a tent to go to sleep or sitting motionless while hunting). No matter what you are doing outside, I am here to help.

I consider clothing in tiers. While each tier will be discussed in-depth in the following pages, let's look at them briefly here.

Tier 1 is your base layer. This is the layer that will be in contact with your skin. Out of each layer I will be covering, this one is of primary importance. If you get the base layer wrong, it will not matter what else you wear. Base-layering properly is critical to heat management.

Tier 2 is the layer you will put on to go about your regular activities in moderate temperatures.

Tier 3 is needed when temperatures start to get uncomfortable for you. After years of being outside with an incredibly wide range of people, I have noticed that everyone's definition of *uncomfortable* is different: I sometimes have people in class who are going through our studies together with a T-shirt on while someone right next to them is bundled up for cold weather and still chilled. As I stated in the introduction, you will need to take my recommendations and do you. Find what works best for you in your environment.

Tier 4 is the clothing you will wear when your Tier 3 is simply not keeping you comfortable. These clothes will assist your body to function when wind, extreme temperatures or a combination of the two are bringing you dangerously close to hypothermia (see the next page).

I will get into each tier system shortly, but to understand them better we also need to have a good grasp on the fabric choices that are out there first.

COTTON

The saying "cotton kills" is so cliché for those of us who spend a lot of time in the outdoors, but it is incredibly true. Cotton holds moisture in its fibers and is not conducive to helping that moisture evaporate. What is problematic is many companies still make clothes that look "woodsy" but are 100 percent cotton. For years cotton was the go-to source for comfortable clothing, and it still is. Comfort while wearing it around the house does not translate into usefulness in a wilderness. Cotton still holds moisture in hot weather, which serves to cool you down; otherwise, avoid it.

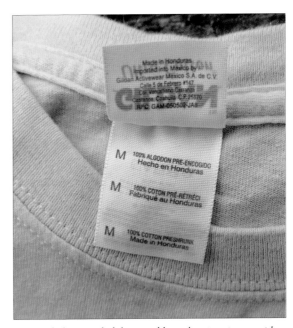

Cotton clothes are a liability in cold weather situations; avoid them when possible.

SIGNS OF HYPOTHERMIA

Hypothermia is the dangerous condition in which you lose too much of your core body temperature. When this occurs, your body takes over and attempts to do some things to keep you safe. If you recognize the following symptoms, especially early, you can take corrective action and avoid hypothermia. You will notice the mild symptoms in yourself, so fix them. If you recognize these happening to other people, you must take corrective action.

SYMPTOMS OF MILD HYPOTHERMIA (START TAKING CORRECTIVE ACTION)

- Mild shivering
- Lack of fine-motor function and coordination
- Difficulty speaking clearly
- Increased heart rate and breathing
- Hunger or nausea
- Feeling of cold or numbness in hands and feet

SYMPTOMS OF MODERATE TO SEVERE HYPOTHERMIA (TAKE CORRECTIVE ACTION IMMEDIATELY OR DEATH MAY RESULT)

- Worsened shivering (or cessation of shivering)
- Deterioration of fine-motor function and coordination
- Drowsiness
- Significant confusion
- Slurred speech (similar to intoxication)
- Weak pulse

CORRECTIVE ACTIONS

- If the person is wearing anything that is damp or wet, get it off them—even if it means undressing them in cold weather. Do to this in a tent or other shelter when possible.
- Get the person out of the wind, if applicable.
- Have the person rub their core or do it for them. You can also get the person engaged in light exercise, such as jumping jacks.
- Once the person begins to warm up, put them in a sleeping bag, bivy sack or reflective blanket to maintain their body heat.
- Lie next to them when possible so they can benefit from your body heat, as they may not be generating much of their own. Your body is functioning properly and will create heat they can utilize.
- Warm some liquids, even if it is just water, for them to drink. This will assist in warming up their core.
- Keep the person off the ground.
- When possible, build a fire for warmth.

Under Armour makes comfortable cold weather caps that wick moisture well.

POLYESTER

Polyester is a great choice for outdoor clothing due to its usability and affordability. I have several pieces of both expensive and inexpensive clothing made from polyester, ranging from Under Armour to our Nature Reliance School shirts that we get screen printed. It has been my experience thus far that polyester clothing greatly depends on the weave and fit as much as the fabric itself. The Under Armour weave is excellent to hold shape and resist abrasion. Inexpensive clothes made with the same material but different weave do not hold their shape as well.

One disadvantage of polyester is that it holds odor. Odor is a manifestation of bacteria growing on the fabric. You can get some antibacterial sprays to use on trips, but that is not a realistic option on backpacking treks or similar adventures. You can also wash the clothing along the way. This will help somewhat, but will never get rid of all the odor.

I have also found that, due to its tightly woven pattern, polyester makes some people "feel" colder when it's against their skin. It is much better than cotton in transferring moisture, but it does hold it on the surface. That is another reason that the polyester blends are problematic. For example, if you have a polyester-cotton blend shirt, you will still have similar issues as if you were wearing cotton. Those cotton fibers will still absorb water and make you feel colder. However, for hot weather polyester-cotton blends can work to your

SPECIAL FORCES CORE-BODY RUBDOWN

One of the simplest, yet greatest, lessons I have ever learned was from a Special Forces soldier who was attending one of our survival classes. This technique is rooted in your biological makeup. When you start getting cold your body prioritizes blood flow to your organs to maintain your viability as a human and all-around good person. It does this by restricting blood flow to your arms and legs. This is first felt in your cold fingers and toes. By rubbing your torso with your hands, you warm up your torso and your organs. When this happens, your body releases the restriction and regular blood flow occurs in the fingers and toes and they warm back up. So yes, you can rub your belly and warm up your toes!

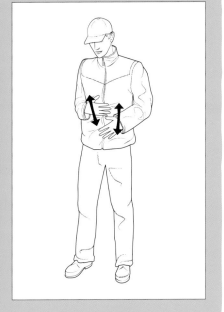

	COMFORT	DURABILITY	MOISTURE REMOVAL	WEIGHT	COST
COTTON	2	1	5	5	2
POLYESTER	4	3	2	2	1
NYLON	5	4	3	3	3
SILK	1	5	4	1	4
MERINO WOOL	3	2	1	4	5

advantage. They hold some moisture, which helps to cool you off, but not so much that it feels like you are wearing a wet towel.

NYLON

Nylon is like polyester in that it is a man-made fabric. It does absorb water into its fibers more readily than polyester but not nearly as bad as cotton does. I have found nylon clothing to be much more resistant to wear and tear than polyester fabrics. This is good for people like me, who spend most of their time off-trail, doing wildlife habitat–improvement work, studying nature, tracking or bushwhacking. Nylon is also more tightly woven than other fabrics, offering more wind resistance than polyester and cotton.

SILK

Silk does not move moisture away from your skin as well as nylon and polyester. There are silk blends that are now treated to do so, but with regular use the treatment is worn and washed away in a short time. Silk's redeeming factor is its weight and comfort. Silk is very soft and adds little to no bulk in your pack or on your body. The softness and comfortable weave also make it prone to abrasion—not the type of stuff for a person who is rough on gear like me.

WOOL

You should get some wool clothes sooner rather than later if you do not already have it. For many years wool had a reputation of being itchy and uncomfortable to wear. I spent many days in a deer stand as a young boy with itchy wool sweaters. A polyester wicking undershirt makes wool more comfortable and the best option for keeping you warm, in my opinion. The modern wool options are much better than what I had as a young man. Modern wool, particularly merino wool, is breathable, wicks moisture and is incredibly strong. In the 1990s, the Smartwool company developed merino wool (which comes from merino sheep) for clothing products. They only use wool of a small diameter, making for a much tighter weave pattern a very comfortable piece of clothing that is not itchy. I use merino wool products for my socks, Tier 1 layer, hats and gloves. I highly recommend it. Look for merino wool fabric, regardless of brand or manufacturer. There are several companies that now offer it.

I should also add that the most comfortable socks I have ever owned for cold weather were made from llama wool. Llama wool is incredibly soft and has the same warmth and wicking properties of other wool. That is the largest benefit to utilizing wool in any portion of your tier system of clothing. It does not hold any moisture on the outer portion of the fibers, though this is not something you can actually see with your eyes or feel with your hands. Studies show that under

➤ *(Right) Wool is a great choice for jackets and caps as it continues to insulate even when wet.*

a microscope, the outer fibers do not hold the water molecules. You can think of it to being similar to the fabric being "sticky." Water molecules do not "stick" to wool fabric as easily as others. This serves to keep moisture away from your skin.

That is a lot of information on fabrics. I've broken it down for you in a table (previous page) that compares materials from most favorable (1) to least favorable (5).

Despite merino wool getting a 5 on cost, I want to emphasize it is well worth it. As more manufacturers are making it, the price is coming down even further. I have as much merino wool clothing as I can afford. For those pieces that I cannot afford, I get a polyester-nylon blend. Now, let's dig in to putting these fabrics into a system that will keep us operating at peak efficiency.

TIER 1

Tier 1 clothing can make or break your next adventure. It is all about heat and moisture management. You should also consider the core of your body its primary heat source. Your arms and legs will not need as much coverage and insulation as your core does. That is why your shirt and underwear should be of primary concern. This tier of your clothing system should do the following:

- **WICK MOISTURE.** This serves to move the moisture away from your skin and onto the fabric itself.
- **ASSIST EVAPORATION.** If the fabric holds the moisture (like cotton), then it does not evaporate readily.
- **ALLOW FOR AIRFLOW.** Without airflow, you will feel clammy and your garments will stick to you. Airflow increases the ability for evaporation to occur in your Tier 2 clothing. You will have garments to stop wind flow if you need to. The layer that goes directly against your skin should be tight enough to make contact but not so tight that it restricts blood flow at all. Please keep in mind what I stated earlier: Your body is the only heater you carry around with you. By wearing tight-fitting clothing, you will restrict blood flow. This blood flow is your body's main heating system.

Darn Tough socks have a lifetime guarantee and are also very comfortable.

Many years ago, I queried many military personnel I was training. Keep in mind that many of these gentlemen spent weeks at a time without a hot shower. I asked them what their go-to method was for underwear in hot conditions. The group was nearly split between those who wore wicking underwear beneath their pants and those who went "commando," meaning they did not wear any at all. I have tried it both ways as well. There are many classes I teach in extremely hot and humid conditions, and I am simply not able to change clothes. On those sorts of trips, I go commando to increase airflow where it is needed. I also follow a certain hygiene protocol that I detail in Chapter 9.

My go-to choice for undergarment shirts is polyester-nylon blends. I get a number of these each year from events that I attend. I save some money buying inexpensive ones so I can use my pennies on my other gear.

This Tier 1 group should also include good socks. I always wear socks—ankle-high versions most of the year and taller boot or hiking socks the during the cold season. My first choice for socks is merino wool. I am huge fan of Darn Tough socks simply because of their lifetime guarantee. Socks play a vital role because they cover the body part that is farthest from your heart—blood flow is key to warm feet. I wear merino wool socks all year long doing wilderness activities. I wear thin ones in the hot months, thicker ones as it gets cooler and then thin liners and oversocks during cold weather. You might think wool is made for cold weather only. Technology has come a long way in recent years, however, and merino wood is the go-to choice for adventuring socks—including hot-weather adventures.

Many, but not all, serious backpackers also find great benefit in wearing liner socks. Liner socks are incredibly thin socks worn under your regular socks. They serve to keep any rubbing inside your footwear on the sock layers and not directly to the skin of your foot.

I prefer to change out my underwear and socks each day for a clean pair. If I am traveling light and living out of a backpack, this means I carry only two pairs of each. I wash and dry one pair each day in that situation. Many times this washing and drying is nothing more than a rinse in whatever water source is available and allowing them to air-dry.

TIER 2

Tier 2 is the layer that includes pants or shorts and another top depending on the weather.

Your choice of pants will greatly depend on the activity you intend on doing in them. For most everything that I enjoy, I need a pair of pants tough enough to handle being in contact with thick vegetation and the ground when I'm on one knee. They also need to have some "give" to them so I can move about freely. I find that most of the pants offered as hiking and backpacking pants are simply not tough enough for the activities I regularly engage in. If you spend more time enjoying hiking and similar pursuits, you will find (as I did when I hiked more often) that you will want some lightweight pants, preferably those that convert to shorts by zipping off the legs. I had one particular pair of Mountain Hardwear pants like this, which I wore for years on backpacking trips. What I am seeing my students wear now from Mountain Hardwear, Outdoor Research®, Columbia, Arc'teryx and similar brands have taken this style of pants to an even higher level of moisture

5.11 offers pants that have ample movement, are water resistant and have extra pockets.

wicking, comfort and resistance to wear and tear. You should plan on playing close to $200 or more on pants of this caliber.

However, I am the type that spends enough time kneeling while studying nature, carving something or otherwise going through heavy brush to warrant a tougher pair of pants. My favorite pants are 5.11 Tactical® pants (approximately $50). Although the word *tactical* is in the name, these pants are not just for those with that type of interest. They work exceptionally well as outdoor pants. They have everything that I feel you need in a pair of pants for the outdoors adventure: They are made from a stretch nylon fabric that has plenty of stretch around the waist and hip area. This makes them great to do the up-and-down tasks that I do when bushcrafting, camping and studying nature. They also have a water-resistant coating. I have had many pants through the years with such coatings. These are the first that have lasted for a considerable amount of time. I have one pair that still sheds water well after three years of weekly use. In addition to those advantages, they have several pockets. While it is cumbersome to put heavy objects in cargo pockets I still believe there are certain things you should keep on your person, such as a trauma IFAK. The basic trauma IFAK (page 61) is so light that it does not impede my work in any way.

What I require from shorts is no different than pants. It is rare that I wear shorts in the wilderness because the things I do require me to be off-trail most of the time. However, I can wear shorts during downtime that are able carry the same tools as my pants; for example, 5.11 makes cargo shorts that have the same exact pocket and materials as their pants.

Keep in mind that I am very hard on my pants every day. I am also in regular contact with large amounts of students who do not engage in the same activities I do. They, and you, may be satisfied with pants from Patagonia, Mountain Hardwear, REI and other outdoor manufacturers. Just take the time to read the preceding sections on fabrics to find the type of pants you need for the areas in which you live.

TIER 3

As I mentioned earlier, your Tier 3 gear is going to vary widely and is dependent on two contributing factors:

1. Your area and its climate conditions
2. Your internal heater and how efficiently it works

There are three pieces of gear that I think are mandatory for everyone to have: (1) a vest, (2) rain gear and (3) a windbreaker. The need for each of these pieces is based on objective science rather than the subjective feelings of the individual. Regardless of how hotblooded or coldblooded you are, these garments will help ensure your survival and comfort.

VEST

I sincerely hope you also find time to follow my school on YouTube and Patreon. If you watch any of our several hundred videos, you will most likely notice that I am wearing a down vest from Cabela's (approximately $130) in nearly every one filmed during cold weather. For many years working in cold weather on the farm I thought vests were some sort of trendy clothing choice for affluent, stylistically inclined folks. Many years ago,

I started testing gear more earnestly and studying the physiological effects of the natural elements. I discovered that vests are scientifically sound pieces of equipment. When you start to cool down, your body systems will restrict blood flow to your limbs; therefore, your hands and feet are the first to feel uncomfortably chilled in cold weather. Your body does so to ensure there is adequate blood flow to your organs. Your body is smart. It knows that without your organs functioning properly, you'll die. If your arms get cold (or even get frostbite), you will still live. So, your body prioritizes blood flow to the organs to keep you operating efficiently. A good vest helps this process along. It aids your core in maintaining its warmth. There are many different fabrics and styles when choosing a vest, and they each have their own pros and cons. I have two vests that are great options when it comes to outdoor wear.

There are a few types of material you'll need to consider when purchasing a vest:

- **FLEECE.** You will note from the photos throughout this chapter that I have a dark green fleece vest from REI (approximately $80). I have had that vest for over twenty years now. It is an indispensable part of my layering system. Fleece, particularly PolarFleece, is lightweight, warm and insulates when it is wet. Because it is easily cleaned in the washer, that vest has seen a lot of use and abuse. I wear it in the spring and fall on hunting trips, hiking trips and picnic trips with my family. I also wear it under my Tier 4 gear in colder weather. I like fleece that is deep-pile rather than smooth. In a layering system, deep-pile fleece allows for heat convection to work more properly and keeps me warmer. My vest has a softer fleece added to the neck to make it more comfortable and offer extra defense against the chill.

◄ *(Left) Wearing a vest on its own or under a jacket helps maintain core body temperature warmth.*

My two favorite vests that have seen years of use: REI fleece on the left, Cabela's down on the right.

- **DOWN.** Another more recent innovation in vests and jackets is what is lovingly referred to as "puffy" garments. These are mostly down-filled pieces of outerwear that have channels in them to offer more heat retention and increase the efficiency of down. When made properly, they have extra down in areas that need more warmth and less where it is not needed. However, they are not very abrasion resistant. That is why my down vest is the Cabela's Fleece-Lined Woodsman. It is made of a durable, lightly oiled canvas fabric. It is incredibly hearty material and withstands most of the abuse that I throw at it. If you are planning on light hiking, camping or even backpacking, a puffy vest is the way to go. If you plan on getting down and dirty like I do on hunting trips or while bushcrafting, you will need something a lot tougher. The only problem about down is that it does not insulate when it is wet. So, if you plan on utilizing one on a canoe trip or in the rain, you should have a backup option to ensure you stay

dry for your safety. Keep in mind that all vests are not the same. Many will have the look of a puffy or down-filled vest but will instead have a cheap fill that does not insulate.

- **WOOL.** I must say that I would like to own a wool vest. The only reason I don't already is because of the first two that I already own. I do own a wool anorak pullover that works exceptionally well. Wool insulates well when it is wet, is comfortable to get work done in and layers well.

RAIN GEAR

I have mentioned multiple times that I enjoy hiking and doing nature study in the rain, particularly on warm summer days. My wife thinks I am crazy at times because often I will get my gear ready to go when I see rain forecasted. For me, it is enjoyable—but being out in the rain also helps you to embrace uncomfortable situations. The mental fortitude gained from it can be directly applied to many aspects of life. I think there are a couple variations of rain gear that should be used for different situations: ponchos and rain suits

A poncho is basically a tarp with a hood on it. The benefit of having one is that you can easily put it on yourself and your backpack and everything underneath will stay relatively dry. Ponchos make getting a fire started in the

Ponchos accomplish many tasks, including being able to hike with you and your pack covered.

Frogg toggs® are lightweight wind and rain barriers that I use often.

rain easier as well, because you can use them to cover your area and materials to keep them as dry as possible while you are starting the fire. Any number of tasks can easily be completed in a poncho, as its shape and size allow for a great range of movement.

My go-to choice for a poncho is from Wilderness Innovation (approximately $130). They provide an ultralight version sewn in such a way that it can be used as a poncho, shelter or impromptu hammock. They are incredibly tough, and I have abused mine on more trips than I can count. It still looks nearly brand-new. These ponchos are so tough because they are made with a hardy and thick nylon. They are pricey but worth it. If that does not meet your budget, I recommend you find a good military surplus retailer and get one there. Military ponchos are extremely tough and versatile. They are definitely made with one person in mind. If you were to use them to build a freestanding shelter, they would not provide much protection. They are primarily meant to be worn or fastened with others to make a larger shelter.

I have tried several different types of rain suits and have finally settled on two different ones. The first is a GORE-TEX® mil-spec suit (approximately $250) from the U.S. military. It is a tad bulky but is incredibly tough. Mil-spec clothing can be incredibly hard to come by, but you can purchase less-expensive copycat versions

from companies such as Propper® or TRU-SPEC®. This will allow you to get non-camouflaged versions if that interests you.

I am also a big fan of frog toggs® rain gear (approximately $50). Avoid the ultralight versions, as I have owned two sets and they ripped within minutes of going through a wilderness in them. The thicker layers of this brand are a great combination of packability, durability and minimal weight. Keep in mind that virtually every rain gear setup needs to have the latest technology in it, such as GORE-TEX. If you get the old-style rubberized suits, you will keep the rain off you for certain but without breathability, you will sweat and your clothes will get soaked anyway. Invest in GORE-TEX or similar fabrics for rainproof gear that breathes as well. GORE-TEX is so widely known that I mention it here, but you can also find comparable fabrics, such as eVent, Sympatex, Omni-Tech, NeoShell®, OutDry®, DryVent™, H2No® and MemBrain™. These are all proprietary versions across other brands that work just as well or better.

WINDBREAKER

I like to keep things simple. Certain things need redundancy and others don't. As I mentioned earlier, I am a fan of frog toggs® rain gear, one reason being that I also wear it as a windbreaker (aka windcheater). As wind travels across and around you, it removes the heat from both you and the clothing you are wearing that has trapped your body heat. By wearing a windbreaker, you can significantly reduce this heat loss. Since frog toggs is so affordable, I have three jackets in my supplies reserved for students. When I have a student show up with inadequate clothing and I notice them getting cold, the windbreaker will often take care of their needs. There are also dedicated windcheaters that I have seen people wear in class (FirstSpear™ and Hill People Gear come to mind) that I am certain will also get the job done very well. My mother-in-law is not the most outdoorsy person in the world, but she regularly admonishes us to "have a lightweight jacket" wherever we go. Be more like my mother-in-law and have a windbreaker handy.

A wool anorak is comfortable enough to work, play or hike in.

LAYERING JACKETS

Beyond vests, rain gear and windbreakers, I believe you should also find the jacket of your choice. If there were a Jackets Anonymous group available, I would have to go through their twelve-step program. I have lots of jackets—a whole lot of them. Just ask my wife. I have convinced myself that I am field-testing them for companies that request my feedback (which I am doing), but I have a tough time giving them up.

You will often find me wearing my wool anorak. There are many organizations that make them and similar ones, but I received mine from Asbell Wool. They are a small shop and they do great work and have many options. I don't think this type of jacket would be appropriate for backpackers (I will list those products shortly). I do, however, think it is perfect for those who camp, bushcraft, nature study, go on short day hikes, hunt and a lot more. It is 100 percent wool and fits snugly so it is not cumbersome but not too tight. My favorite part is that it has a kangaroo hand warmer pocket in the front. You can keep some essentials there or just keep the wind off your hands. It also has a nice zippered pocket on the front that does a good job of holding a cell phone or a hand warmer.

Just like shoes, there are many options out there and I want to help you determine what will work for you and your needs. Following are some other options that are great choices in and of themselves. I have some of each of these choices (I told you I had a problem).

Fleece Jackets

You just cannot go wrong with a comfy fleece jacket. They are easy-on, easy-off. Fleece wears well and takes a fair amount of abuse. My only criticism is that fleece melts easily if you get it too close to the fire (don't ask me how I know). My favorite fleece jacket also has Polartec® Windbloc® married to it. This means that it blocks most, but not all, wind. That is a nice feature to have. I recommend choosing a jacket that has a hood on it. That way you can easily ventilate (see sidebar on page 90) some of the heat off you when you need to and cover up when you don't. *Never* dry Polartec® Windbloc® materials in the dryer. Don't ask me how I know this either.

Puffy Jackets

Are puffy jackets a trendsetting type of outdoor gear? Yes, they are—but for good reason. Puffy jackets are jackets that have the latest high-tech insulating material possible and the craftsmanship sets it up for success. My favorite to use is PrimaLoft®. PrimaLoft insulates very nicely, compacts down incredibly well and still offers some insulating qualities when it is slightly wet. For these reasons, I would choose PrimaLoft® (see photo on page 84) over down for a puffy jacket. I choose different materials for safety. Since down is susceptible to moisture, I prefer to have my outermost jacket made of something different. This way, moisture on the outside does not immediately decrease the ability of my clothes to insulate. Be aware that the shells of puffy jackets are notoriously weak and not resistant to harsh conditions. At the very least, choose a shell that has ripstop nylon so you don't rip the front of your jacket open on a greenbrier bush.

Three-in-One Jacket Systems

This certainly seems like a great idea. You get one system that contains an outer jacket that is windproof and water proof, an inner jacket that is either fleece or puffy and you can also wear the two together for colder temps. However, I have yet to see someone who has one that doesn't feel constricted wearing it all together (including me). If you do get one, choose one that lets you zip off the sleeves. I had a three-in-one years ago, and I just cut the sleeves off the fleece inner jacket so it would be more comfortable. With my new vest and outer jacket my core was still warm, and I could do more tasks easily.

ROUGH AND TOUGH

I have included this category for those that work daily in a wilderness setting. Whether you are like me and are an environmental educator, wildlife biologist or forester, you will need something that is tougher than those jackets previously mentioned. Carhartt is your friend. I and many of the Nature Reliance School "family" were models a few years ago for Carhartt's fall line of clothing. Carhartt used to make clothes primarily for farmers and ranchers, but not anymore. They now have an incredible line of clothes with many of the same qualities I have discussed and are incredibly tough. I did a test on a Carhartt jacket that a local company sent me a few years ago. I dragged it behind an all-terrain vehicle for several miles through Kentucky wilderness, sunk it in a pond and left it for a month, then left it laying in an open field in direct sunlight for another month. It came out of the ordeal like a champ. That jacket is still tough to this day. It looks a bit used, but it functions like new.

ZIP UP VS. PULLOVER

To zip or pull over—that is the question. There is a time for both, and I do so throughout the cold season. Where I am from, we have four distinct seasons, but the winters are not incredibly cold. Zippers on your outer garments are the fastest and easiest way (along with removing your hat) to cool down when you feel you are overheating. Overheating leads to sweating,

which leads to cooling down and staying there. That is not a good combo. However, when it is cold enough I know that no matter what is going on I can ventilate by only exposing my neck and head, I wear a pullover. If I am bushcrafting, I wear my wool pullover from Asbell that I mentioned earlier. If I am engaged in more tactical-related activities or those that are more athletic endeavors—such as rucking, tracking or orienteering—I will wear a polypropylene pullover from Polartec that was designed for the United States Marine Corps.

LONG UNDERWEAR

Another portion of my Tier 3 system is long underwear pieces. This includes tops and bottoms. My first choice is made by Polartec and is waffle knit. Waffle knit works similar to puffy vests and jackets. Waffle-pattern insulating layers made of fleece and similar materials work more efficiently than counterparts that are not waffled. The channels in these patterns of clothing trap warm air and allow it to circulate. The benefit of having these garments is that they don't hold as much moisture and they are much warmer. Even during deer hunts in temperatures of 20°F (–7°C), I will regularly go into the woods with a long-sleeved wicking T-shirt, a waffle-pattern insulating shirt and my down vest. I rarely get cold with that sort of setup, even after sitting or slowly stalking most of the day.

Waffle-pattern insulating layers are excellent choices for a Tier 3 level base layer.

ENSURING WARMTH AND MOISTURE MANAGEMENT DURING SLEEP

- Wash and dry yourself for proper hygiene before climbing into your sleeping bag. If it is considerably cold, you may have to do this by exposing only one body part at a time.

- Dry yourself off well with your bandana or towel.

- Put on a wicking fleece or a wool hat.

- Employ the "Caudill Family Secret" for ventilating excess heat. I get a sleeping bag that zips both ways. In favorable temps, I keep only a small portion unzipped so I can stick my bare leg out. This allows extra heat that may cause me to sweat inside the bag to escape. As soon as I get that first hint of chill in my bag, I pull my leg back in.

- Make sure you go to bed hydrated. When you are hydrated, your blood flows properly and therefore you stay warmer. Drinking hot tea helps warm your core organs, which saves your body some energy in doing so. For proper hydration it is best to drink pure water without coffee or tea, however. It is absorbed by the body much faster.

- On trips where I have plenty of extra space and it is easy to carry, I have a separate bottle just to urinate in at night. If you hydrate properly, you will need to urinate during the night. There are also many female urination devices.

- I like to be slightly chilled when I first get in my bag. If I am already warm, I am nearly guaranteed to overheat and start sweating. Sweating in cold weather, even in a sleeping bag, is not good for you. To cool down before getting into your sleeping bag, simply strip down in the cold and then slide in. If it is excessively cold (well below freezing) I will take my clothes off in the bag itself. I will also leave them in there so they are warm to put on in the morning.

- Each morning, hang your sleeping bag and any other sleep gear up to dry whenever the weather is suitable to do so.

- Keep a set of clothes for the sole purpose of being used as sleepwear. They can also be backup emergency gear when needed. Keep in mind that sleepwear should be very lightweight layers. Anything more and your body will have to heat those up before it can heat up the sleeping bag. This causes a lot of extra work for your body. The light layers (Polartec makes some great ones) are there mainly to pull moisture from your body. I also most definitely wear a merino wool or fleece pullover at night. For years I have worn an Under Armour wicking cap with COOLMAX® in it. I like it so much that I have sewn the inner lining in several times after it's come loose. As I write this, I have been using a handmade merino wool cap made by Rotten Friends Nature Crafts that they sent me. I believe it is going to be my new favorite moving forward. It is soft, wicks moisture and I can pull it down over my eyes and ears in cold weather. Recently, I used it on three different overnights in near-freezing temps, and it worked extremely well.

You are obviously not going to carry all layers in the tier system each time you go out. Here are some simple steps to follow during the preplanning process so you know your needs are taken care of.

- Check the weather, but keep in mind that weather is an incredibly hard thing to forecast past three or four days. You need to consider contingencies for an abrupt change. As an example, if the forecast shows a 30 percent chance or better of rain, I will have rain gear available.

- Know the weather patterns of the area you'll be traveling. Opposite sides of a mountain can have drastic weather changes; camping near a creek or river may give you temperatures up to ten degrees cooler than forecasted; if there is no tree canopy to provide shade, direct sunlight will drain your energy. You should have clothing plans to cover these issues if they arise.

- A lightweight frog toggs® jacket is a great layering piece. It weighs very little, compacts well, will keep rain off your core and it serves as a wind barrier. It is one piece that has served me well many times when weather patterns have unexpectedly changed.

- Especially on day hikes, always consider what would help you stay alive if you unexpectedly had to stay the night outside. Whatever that is, you need to take it with you. One good choice is the Wilderness Innovation poncho I discussed on page 87. It does so many things well.

TIER 4 GEAR

Tier 4 gear is the clothing that you not only want but also need to stay alive in outdoor activities. My Tier 4 system includes more robust versions of the things in my Tier 3 system, with the bonus of hats and gloves. As an example, the puffy jackets and vests here are traded for a puffy coat. My Tier 4 is various combinations of what appear in my Tier 3 system.

Some essential accessories are hats and gloves. It has been said that we lose 60 percent to 70 percent of our body heat through our head. This is only partially true. If our head is exposed we do lose that much heat through it. However, we would lose that much heat from any exposed portion of our body. If we had a nice wool hat on and nothing covering our arms, we would lose body heat through our arms.

For example, if I am out and need to chop wood or engage in some other activity that requires a lot of exercise, I will often be dressed exactly as I just described. I will have

a hat on and go down to my base layer T-shirt and a vest. This helps to maintain my core body temperature properly. Excess heat travels out my arms, which are doing most of the work, and I do not overheat. If I recognize that even then I am overheating, I will decrease my activity level.

The beauty of this setup is the ability to ventilate heat and moisture away from me. You must pay strict attention to how you feel when you are doing activities outside and act sooner rather than later. Most often I do this by unzipping or unbuttoning my jacket and removing my headgear if I am wearing any. When I expose my upper chest, neck and head a lot of heat and captured moisture will be released. At the first hint of being chilled again, I will zip back up to keep my heat. You cannot ignore what your body is telling you. If you listen and have the right gear, you can have the most marvelous time in the outdoors even in inhospitable conditions. Now I want to more specifically consider how headgear and gloves can help you accomplish this.

Everyone needs a good ball cap to provide protection and keep the sun out of your eyes.

Headgear is an essential piece of my Tier 3 and Tier 4 gear. Your choice of headgear should be specific to your climate. Here are few thoughts about my first choice of headgear, a baseball cap:

- It shields your eyes and most of your face from the sun, so you can see where you are stepping and moving more clearly. It seems small but this may be the one simple thing that keeps you from tripping and twisting an ankle or breaking a wrist in the woods.

- Most of us dislike bugs crawling on us. I use liberal amount of deet or permethrin on the outside of my ball cap during the spring, summer and early fall when mosquitoes and other pests are problematic. If you have ever attended one of my classes or seen me on YouTube or TV, I will likely have that hat on. It looks like it needs an oil change. Most of that is simply spray residue.

- It is easy to use as a temperature regulator. If I get too hot, I take it off and release some heat.

- It is customizable. I am not a slave to fashion, as you can probably tell. But I do like to wear hats with a hook-and-loop attachment point so I can show support for my school and others I have trained or trained with.

- When I wear hooded jackets, the brim of my hat helps keep the hood from falling over my eyes. This is especially helpful in the rain or heavy snow.

- Ball caps can be insulating. I have a GORE-TEX hat lined with a wicking liner that I wear during rainy and cold days so I can keep my head warm and dry.

One thing a baseball cap does not do is keep the sun off my ears. I wear a boonie-style hat for occasions in which I will be in direct sunlight for long periods of time. There is a large volume of data that suggests wearing bug sprays and sunscreens on your skin is detrimental to your health. In my line of work, where I am outside every single day, that is impossible to do. I screen myself from the sun and perform pest control with clothing whenever and wherever I can to avoid putting those chemicals on my skin directly. For example, on a summertime fishing trip in Alaska, I ended up wearing a bug net over my head and neck to keep the mosquitoes off me. Had I not had that simple bug net, my trip would not have been tolerable. Sometimes a simple piece of equipment can go a long way.

COLD-WEATHER HEADGEAR

During cold weather, a nice warm hat can not only keep you warm but it can also increase your morale. My go-to hat in cold weather is an Under Armour beanie. The hat that I wear is lined with Under Armour's HeatGear® (approximately $30) lining, which serves to wick away moisture and keep my head dry. The earliest versions of this hat, which I have since worn out, were lined with another nice liner called COOLMAX, which serves the same purpose. Under Armour's beanies are made of their proprietary polyester blend and weave. I do spend the extra money on these hats; other hats I have had do not hold their shape as well.

I also have a range of basic fleece and wool hats for the same reasons I mentioned in the Tier 2 section (page 83).

Buffs come in various patterns and colors to meet the preferences of the wearer.

There are some other items that I have used off and on through the years with great success that deserve mentioning. Most of these are used to gain specific benefits.

- **SCARVES.** Scarves are easy to use to keep your neck and chest warm. They are also easy to pull off as temperature control. I find that they tend to get in the way if I am doing anything active. If I am in a campsite with my family or otherwise not doing a lot of activity, I enjoy having a scarf along for the ride. They don't take up much space in or on the pack.

- **BUFFS.** I was a student in a man-tracking class with some highly qualified law enforcement officers. I had avoided buffs up to that time because I thought they were simply a trending novelty piece of gear. These fine officers convinced me otherwise and I am pleased they did. My buff has served as a facemask, neck covering, head covering and more. Buffs are a very simple yet versatile piece of equipment. Like everything else you will use in cool or cold weather, choose a fabric that will wick moisture from your skin rather than hold it there.

- **NECK GAITERS.** These are the buff's thicker, warmer cousins. Neck gaiters are typically used in severely cold climates. As with buffs, you will often wear these over your mouth. By doing so you will breathe through them and condensation from your mouth will eventually collect and soak them. I simply rotate the wet portion to the back so it can dry out when that occurs.

- **RUFFS.** In very severe climates, having a ruff around the edge of your hooded jacket can be of great importance. A ruff will provide extra warmth around your face and neck and will also keep wind and snow from blowing in your face at full force.

- **HEADBANDS AND EAR WARMERS.** Another good lightweight choice is to wear something to keep your ears protected from the elements and wear no hat at all. My family has several of these that we wear during outdoor exercise and hikes.

GLOVES AND MITTENS

I want to remind you that if you keep your core warm, your hands will be warmer too. That said, gloves and mittens are indispensable pieces of equipment for staying warm. I am never going to be a hand model, that is for certain. My hands are rough from working on the farm for so many years as well as from hard work in the wilderness teaching courses and doing wildlife habitat–improvement projects. There are some jobs and environmental conditions that I will get out my hand covers for. Think ahead of the activities you'll be doing and choose the appropriate hand protection:

- **MITTENS.** Mittens are my go-to option for cold weather. I wear a pair of Cabela's mitten and glove combo (approximately $10). Do you remember the heat-conduction principle from page 90? The same is true for your fingers as well. If you wear insulated gloves, each of your fingers must heat up the individual finger sections in the gloves for them to stay warm. Your individual fingers do

Mittens that can expose your fingers keep your hands warm and able to do fine motor skills when needed.

- **WORK GLOVES.** Mechanix Wear gloves are the best of the best for work gloves, in my opinion. They are thin but very tough gloves. This means my hands do not get overheated, they are protected and they still have a fair amount of sensitivity to do small tasks.

- **INSULATED GLOVES.** I have had the best success while wearing Thinsulate™ insulated gloves. Thinsulate does a good job of keeping my hands warm. I find that thick insulated gloves make tasks requiring fine-motor skills difficult. However, thick gloves are great if you're trekking, sitting in an animal blind and so on.

PUTTING YOUR LAYERING SYSTEM TOGETHER

The following paragraphs walk you through an example of a layering system for cold weather and how I would use it to regulate my body heat.

Below the waist I wear merino wool socks. If I am going to be doing a lot of walking, I will have a liner pair of merino socks as well as a regular pair.

My next layer will include wicking underwear and a sleeveless wicking T-shirt. This allows the areas of my body where I need moisture management to work effectively. I choose a sleeveless T-shirt so I do not get too much material around my arm pits and shoulders, which causes discomfort when I'm working.

Next is a long underwear bottom and top made of light fleece waffle knit. The top is a zip-up mock turtleneck that I zip up around my neck when I feel chilled and unzip when I feel myself getting warmed up to the point of sweating.

I then layer on my pants. My pants have an elastic waistband in addition to the belt I always wear. One of the keys to regulating body temperature is to have good blood flow. If I wear a belt too tightly, it restricts blood flow below my waist. An elastic waist band helps to hold my pants up and at the same time will flex and not be too tight and restrict that important blood flow.

not put off much heat. If your fingers are next to one another, they will warm one another by heat conduction. Therefore, mittens are a good choice to keep your hands warm. My method is to have a pair of thin liner gloves under my mittens. My favorite mittens are the ones whose finger pad folds back and attaches to the back of the mitten. This exposes your fingers easily when you need to perform work that requires fine-motor skill. Liner gloves will help keep the elements off your fingers while you do work and at the same give you ample amounts of sensitivity. When used in concert with insulated gloves, liner gloves also provide your hands with a moisture-wicking barrier. I never wear these solo. I most often pair them with mittens to do the types of things that I do. If the weather is not incredibly cold, I don't wear liner gloves under the mittens.

The next layer includes my vest of choice. As I stated previously, I will wear the deep-pile polar fleece if I am moving around a lot. If I am at a base camp and not moving around a lot, I will wear my down vest.

In addition, I then wear climate-dependent clothing. For example, I will put on a rain jacket if it is warm enough to just rain, an insulated coat if I just need to shed snow or cold, or a windcheater (rain jacket for me) to keep the wind off me. Each of these will have a hood on them as well.

My students were quite aware that I was writing this book so they regularly sent me ideas for it. One student sent me a blog piece on how it seems that outdoor adventurers are more focused on fashion than utility while in the outdoors. First and foremost, I have shared with you the clothing choices you can employ to stay safe. I have also shared a number of brands that, although they are fashionable, also keep you safe. It is my sincerest desire that you spend more time outdoors and do so for the fun of it, not just because it's stylish.

FOOTWEAR

To say that my dad and I did things in a minimalist fashion when I was young is an understatement. At certain times I felt like my dad was offering some experiences to give me joy in the outdoors and others to build my character. One character-building trip was at the Red River Gorge in east-central Kentucky. My dad, uncle, cousin and I had gone to the area to camp, fish and stay the night. We were doing it carrying our gear in Native American–style pack baskets. This trip had three memorable experiences rolled into one.

The first is that we hiked through this beautiful area and I distinctly remember taking a shortcut along a path to get to our location near the river. This shortcut involved walking along a rock shelf that was about 16 inches (40 cm) wide and had a very large drop-off to the bottom. (I can remember my dad telling me to not look down. That is never a good sign, is it?)

Hiking boots, sandals and off-trail shoes are all options for wilderness footwear. If you take care of your feet, they will carry you longer and more safely.

Second, for bedding my dad had brought a piece of plastic and what he called a sheet blanket. He still has it to this day in his camping gear. This sheet blanket is 100 percent cotton and I am confident it was designed to specifically give the impression that it will keep you warm when it won't. We set up our sleeping area on an incline and I kept sliding off the incline to the foot of the hill and rolling off in the night. My dad kept waking me up and bringing me back to the bed.

My third memory is where footwear comes in. I was hiking in a pair of Chuck Taylor knockoffs, the kind with the wide white sole and canvas upper. Mine were royal blue and I was most pleased with them. I had spent most of the trip "accidentally" getting my feet wet in the river and other surrounding waterways. At night, as we sat around the fire, I took my shoes off and placed them next to the fire on a rock to dry them off.

My dad suggested that I move them back so they would not get too hot. Me being the all-knowing preteen that I was at the time, I felt I knew better how to dry my shoes, so I shifted them around a bit but left them nearly in the same place. My dad again suggested I move them back and I suggested they were okay. My dad then allowed me to learn a very valuable lesson that night. Since it was cold, either my dad or my uncle kept a small fire going through the night to warm us. When I woke up the next morning, refreshed from the exercise of sliding off the plastic all night, I found that the soles of my shoes were on the rock—but not much else was. There were no canvas uppers, and only one somewhat usable shoestring. I had the joy of hiking out barefoot that day and each step was a reminder of a very valuable lesson. Read the sidebar for my tips on how to dry boots and socks around a campfire.

Let's look at footwear for outdoor adventuring. It is a major source of problems for people in the outdoors. I am going to help you fix that.

HOW TO DRY YOUR BOOTS AND SOCKS AROUND THE FIRE WITHOUT BURNING THEM

As I told you, I am a victim of poor observation skills when it comes to getting footwear dry. Please heed my instructions so you can avoid a similar pitfall and make memories with dry feet.

- **The most uncomfortable portions are going to be the insoles.** Remove them first and set them in the sun if it is out. If not, you can put them on a rock from the fire. This rock should be uncomfortable to hold due to its warmth, but not so hot that it immediately burns your skin. If you set insoles next to the fire, they will melt easily.

- **Stuff your boots with any dry material from your environment.** Leaves and grasses work well. Stuff the boots full and tight. Those dry materials will soak up a lot of moisture. Once they are full of moisture, remove them and do it several times until the material no longer soaks up water. If you don't have natural materials to use, you can do this with a bandana or other nonessential garment. If you have none of these, skip this step all together.

- **Heat up rocks that you find from dry ground (never from a waterway) and place them in your boots.** Just monitor them closely to ensure they do not burn or sear the inside of your boots.

- **You can place your boots and insoles next to the fire but sit right next to them.** If you are getting too hot, they are getting too hot. Monitor them regularly. Don't just sit back and relax. Drying footwear, including socks, by the fire is an active-participation event, not a passive one.

Footwear is likely to be the most personal choice that I cover in this book. Take a cursory glance at any retail or online provider of outdoor shoes and you will see hundreds and hundreds of styles. They come in every shape, size and color available. I will share with you my favorites and then give you the tools to make good decisions when purchasing.

When it comes to boots, Merrell wins in my book. I must say that I started wearing Merrells long before they became cool. I bought my first pair of Merrell hiking boots circa 1989, only eight years after they became a company. I have been wearing them ever since, and I currently wear a pair of Merrell tactical boots (approximately $155). There have also been times in which I have been disappointed with a certain style that I purchased and turned my back on them. I had one pair that I absolutely wore out in about four months. I also remember a pair that I wore nearly daily for 7 to 8 years. I have worn Danner, Tactical Research, KEEN and many other brands along the way. While they all served the purpose, I never could find in those other brands the perfect combination of fit and durability. Keep in mind that others will have their favorite brand and you should too. Companies have manufacturing processes, foot beds and materials that stay similar throughout their line of footwear. Therefore, when you find a brand that works for you, it is probably best to stick with it. That is why I keep going back to Merrell.

My 8-inch (20-cm) Merrell Tactical boots have proven to be comfortable on day hikes, in and around water, as well as when carrying heavy packs.

Let's consider some other types of footwear so you can determine what will work best for you no matter what brand you choose. I am a vocal proponent of going to your favorite small outdoor store to get your footwear. These stores will almost always have a person who is dedicated to footwear and they will do all they can to find the right pair for you.

CROCS ARE A SUPERIOR CHOICE FOR OUTDOOR WEAR

Ask any of the students of Nature Reliance School what my biggest quirk is and many of them may tell you that I am a huge fan of Crocs footwear. I lovingly refer to them as "Croccasins" because we all know that sounds cooler. Here is why I like them so much:

- **THEY ARE COMFORTABLE.** The wearer's feet are comfortably and nimbly massaged with tiny bumps on the foot bed of the shoe.

- **THEY ARE EASY-ON, EASY-OFF.** Slide your foot in and then slide it out. No tying, no bending over, no stress.

- **THEY CAN BE WORN WITH THE TOP DOWN OR UP.** The retention strap is easily put in the up position to create a true slip-on. You can keep the strap down for strong retention when going over rough terrain in search of adventure.

- **THEY COME IN CAMOUFLAGE.** Enough said.

- **THEY ARE QUIET.** When stalking the woods in search of the wild asparagus, you can do so nimbly and quietly. There is enough protection to keep your feet from injury, but not so much that you cannot feel the sticks under your feet before they break and give your position away to your prey.

- **THEY FLOAT.** Dive into the lake for a midday swim or wade through your favorite creek reeling in some smallmouth bass. Lose a shoe, no problem. They float up to the top and come back to you.

- **THEY COME IN TWO-WHEEL-DRIVE AND FOUR-WHEEL-DRIVE VERSIONS.** This is my cute way of saying some have basic outsoles, and others have deep lugs for better traction in soft terrain.

- **THEY ARE QUICK TO DRY.** In the rain or early morning dew, you can wear them without socks and your feet will dry quickly.

- **THEY OFFER VARIABLE TEMP RATINGS.** By wearing them with socks (especially white merino wool ones) you can effectively decrease the temperature and your feet will be comfortable and look really cool doing it.

My go-to camp shoes are Crocs. They are comfortable and dry quickly in wet conditions.

Sandals are great choices for warm weather as they allow your feet to quickly and easily dry after getting wet.

The first thing you need to determine is the purpose for which you will most likely be using the footwear. You should choose one of five main styles of footwear that is best for you:

1. **TRAIL SHOES.** Trail shoes are usually low-cut or mid-cut varieties designed with light hiking, day hiking, or short excursions in mind. Often these will look like beefed-up versions of running shoes. Usually, they will be exactly that. They are lightweight, rarely have waterproofing and can be comfortable on the trail or on campus.

2. **ROUGH-TRAIL SHOES.** This name most accurately describes what I wear from Merrell. I am currently wearing the Merrell Moab 2 Tactical (I have both a regular shoe and an 8-inch [20-cm] boot). They are great shoes and are incredibly comfortable. Rough-trail shoes like these have more rigidity and flexibility and provide me exactly what I need. Keep in mind that at this stage in my life I am no longer a long-distance backpacker. Putting 20 miles (32 km) under my feet in a day is not a concern of mine. For that type of activity, you will want the next step up in rigidity. However, I am the type that at any time I may just walk off into the woods. Therefore, for my daily routine I wear a rough-trail shoe. When I want to put a pack on and hike for enjoyment or ruck for exercise, I wear my taller boots. I like having a little more security and support for my ankles.

3. **BACKCOUNTRY AND OFF-TRAIL SHOES.** Most footwear of this type is made with more durable specifications, such as full-leather uppers and even more rigidity in the sole. These shoes are designed for more hard-core backpackers that know they are going to be crossing rough ground with a heavy load. If that is not you, I do not recommend this type. You will be wearing and paying for more shoe than you need.

4. **MOUNTAINEERING BOOTS.** I mention these here simply because they are out there and some people will go with the biggest and baddest shoe they can possibly get. These boots are for those climbing tall mountain peaks that require great amounts of technical proficiency. They are also designed to accept ice crampons more securely. Since they are most often worn in snow, they will be the most waterproof options available, but for regular use in a typical wilderness this will cause your feet to sweat excessively.

5. **SANDALS.** Chaco sandals have become one of the most popular brands of footwear in the outdoors. They are different than most in that they offer a binder for your big toes, which keeps the sandals more stable for hiking duty. Chaco sandals are the favorite of everyone in my immediate family and many of my friends. I wore KEEN sandals for many years and really enjoyed them as they offered a bumper for your toes so they were protected. My choice now are Crocs and my reasons why are detailed in the sidebar on page 98.

The next question you should ask as you choose footwear is: How does it fit? If you have no other criteria than this one, you are doing well. When it comes down to it, this is the most important aspect of footwear. My advice is to get a boot that will support your heel and does not let your heel move around as you walk. The toe box should not constrict your toes in any way. I have heard many people suggest that you should get tight-fitting boots, wear them in water so they "stretch" and let them dry on your feet in that stretched position. *Do not* do that. If you purchase footwear that has stretch to it, you are buying the wrong pair.

In many outdoor stores you will notice a small ramp near the shoe area. You should walk on this ramp to see how the footwear feels on your feet going up and down the ramp. Your toes should not bunch up and hit the front of the boot when you are going downhill and your heel should be secure and not rub as you go up. Either of these two problems can be corrected with better choices in footwear. It is another reason I suggest going to a small-business outdoor shop. You simply cannot get the feedback you need online or from a big-box store. See the sidebar to the right for getting proper sizing assistance at the store.

Hardiness is next on my list for things to consider. My feet do a good job of sweating. Therefore, a solid leather upper is a no-go for me. I say that begrudgingly because for hardiness, leather is your best choice. My choice is to find a pair that has genuine cowhide leather and a mesh upper combo. This gives me the durability that I need and allows airflow to occur as well. Keep in mind that a full-leather upper is going to be more durable in rough terrain, especially rocky outcroppings. I would avoid leather that is not genuine cowhide or those that have a "suede" look and feel to them. That type of leather is genuine, but it tends to be more abrasive and catches on more debris than does other leather choices. I also pay attention to the stitching throughout the shoe.

An aggressive outsole is important for any off-trail travel.

Raised stitching puts the stitched material on the outside and in direct contact with surrounding debris. This makes them more susceptible to abrasion and a breakdown of the fibers. I look for stitching embedded or within channels so it is more protected. This allows the footwear to last longer. The stitching should also be double- or triple-stitched around the toe box because it receives most of the stress from flexing. I also prefer a shoe that has a toe bump on the front for protection. One piece of advice you can get from online sales is to see the reviews on how well a product holds up. The most likely culprit for a shoe's breakdown in the wilderness is the sole coming unglued. That is another reason I look for solid stitching; I also keep superglue and duct tape in my supplies for emergencies.

Support comes in many different aspects of outdoor shoes. Internal support is provided by either shanks or plates. This is the material that is below the foot bed insert and the outsole. When they are included they are there to protect the foot from hard material on the ground. You can imagine if you removed the outsole and strapped it to your feet it would not be very rigid. The shanks and plates provide this protection for you.

ENSURING A GOOD FIT IN THE STORE

There is a considerable amount of information to process here because footwear is important to your overall enjoyment of being outdoors. Take the information I have given you here to discuss with a footwear specialist and follow these steps at the store and beyond to get a good fit.

- Go to a store that can take measurements of your foot. This will include not only its length and width but also your arch. Arches vary greatly across brands and the specialist will know what brands will work with your arch.

- If your physician has prescribed orthotics for you to wear, make sure you take them to the store with you.

- Take the socks you would normally wear on a hike and wear them while trying on shoes. If you forget them, buy another pair at the store. You need another pair of socks anyway.

- Don't just sit down in the chair and wiggle your toes around when you try them on. Get up and walk around and use the ramp I mentioned earlier, when it is available.

- Check with the store to learn their return policy on shoes. Once you make a purchase, wear your boots indoors so they do not get scuffed up and damaged. This allows you to walk around the house and get a better feel for how they will fit after wearing them for a while. Make sure you know the return policy because some stores will not take shoes back with signs of wear and tear.

- At the store and during any trial phase, you should be paying attention to whether your toes feel cramped, whether your heel is moving about too much and whether you feel any hot spots. If you experience hot spots, they will eventually become blisters under long-term use.

- Before wearing new shoes on your first serious trip, break them in and get used to how you maneuver in them. I will spend a minimum of 5 miles (8 km) in a pair of boots to help break them in. Cumbersome footwear is a big contributor for a sprained ankle, which is the number one backcountry injury. REI has a great return policy in which you can return boots even after several trips. Check that out for certain and always verify with the retailer what their policy is. Many do not allow this. If you want to support local businesses like I do, it may be that you wear your boots around the house so you don't get them scuffed up and dirty.

Outsole grip is another important consideration. Vibram® is the most popular outsole in my neck of the woods. I know this because I spend a large amount of my time tracking other people. That little Vibram logo on the bottom of these boots is literally placed on the ground all over the world. (Brilliant marketing, huh?) I do believe it is widely popular for good reason. I think Vibram has done an excellent job of providing the right mix of grip and firmness. If an outsole has more grip by being more pliable, then it wears down too easily. If the outsole is so firm that it withstands all abuse, it does more sliding than gripping and doesn't allow the wearer to get good traction. When looking at a new pair of boots, I push my thumbnail into the sole. If I cannot push in the sole with my thumbnail, it is too firm. If I can move a whole lug around with just my thumb, it is too soft. I try to find that sweet spot that will offer me good grip and long durability as well. I find this to be true for basic hiking and backpacking. My mountaineering friends suggest a more durable sole for their work. Often crampons are used on such boots.

Weight will be our last consideration here and it is very important. Modern manufacturing and materials have allowed hardy outdoor adventure shoes to be incredibly lightweight. Unless you are looking at very tough mountaineering boots, you will be roughly in the same area of weight for the various offerings. If you go for the inexpensive knockoff brands in big-box and department stores, you will not get the quality of craftsmanship and weight will increase. Merrell, Asolo, Salomon, KEEN, LOWA and Vasque are all big-name brands with quality craftsmanship.

FIELD AND HOME CARE FOR FOOTWEAR

Outdoor footwear can be expensive, so you should take the time to clean and maintain them so they last longer. After each use I recommend you use a brush to remove any excess debris such as mud and dirt. You can use dishwashing soap and warm water to scrub into the fibers of the boot to get them clean. Do not use detergents because they often have cleaning additives that can break down your leather and your waterproof membranes. Rinse them with water thoroughly after utilizing the soap. Remove the insoles and wash them in the same manner. Keep insoles and boots separate to dry in normal temperatures. Do not dry them by a heat source, such as a heater or a fire. Heaters will prematurely age the leather and can cause glues in the shoe to dry out to quickly. I used to use oils on my leather boots, but stopped because I found that it prematurely breaks down the stitching. When speaking with professionals in the footwear industry, they confirmed that conditioning leather is not necessary. A thorough cleaning after heavy use will keep your leather boots in good working order for years.

SLEEPING SYSTEMS

SAFE COCOONS ARE NOT JUST FOR BUTTERFLIES

At its root, a sleeping bag is a piece of equipment designed to act as a pliable convection oven. They capture your body heat (remember, you are a walking heater) and then utilize it to help maintain your core temperature. When you are purchasing or utilizing a sleeping system, there are several different items you should consider:

- **COMFORT:** Do you get rest while sleeping in it?
- **EFFICIENCY:** Does it help maintain your core body temperature?
- **DURABILITY:** Are the materials of high quality and built to last?
- **FRIENDLINESS:** Do users find it easy to pack and use?
- **AFFORDABILITY:** Does it meet your budget?

Most manufacturers of high-quality sleeping bags will have a line of bags that have a range of three quality levels. These bags will start with good, then better and best. Each tier of quality is directly correlated to price as well. Yes, you do get what you pay for within any brand. That does not mean you must pay the highest price to get the best bag to meet your individual needs. For example, my bag of choice is a bag I purchased out of a discount bin at a big-box store. It is a TETON Sports +20°F bag. I have utilized this sleeping bag several hundred times. The cold hard truth (pun intended) is that most of us do not sleep in a tightly wrapped cocoon in our own homes. Since that is how our body is used to sleeping, we need to find the system that works best for our purpose and needs.

Modern sleeping bags are incredibly effective at maintaining your core body temperature through the night.

My daughter using one of my favorite sleeping bags made by TETON Sports.

The insulating material in any given bag is further divided into two categories:

1. **DOWN.** This is usually duck down but may be goose down in more expensive models.

2. **SYNTHETIC FILL.** This is called different things by different manufacturers. Despite the clever marketing, they each perform nearly the same.

If all you want to consider is warmth, then down is the way to go. The loft and warmth it provides are leagues above any synthetic down available. The major fault of down is that it does not continue to insulate when it gets wet. Do you remember our good, better, best classification for bags that I mentioned earlier? The cutting-edge companies of today are creating hydrophobic down. This process coats the individual down feathers so that they take three times as long to get soaked and dry three times faster. To get down of this quality, you are looking at the best version a manufacturer can offer and will therefore pay more for it.

Synthetic down comes in a large range of materials that do their best to mimic the same qualities as actual down. They are manufactured of materials such nylon, polyester and taffeta. After spending much time in various makes and models and seeing hundreds of students in classes use nearly everything that is available out there, I cannot note any major discernable differences in the various materials. It is true, however, that within any given brand of sleeping bag, the most expensive in their line is typically going to have more robust warming material in it. There are two things that will help your sleeping work well for you. One is the shelter you are in; the second is the pad you sleep on. Please refer to the sections on tents and hammocks (page 108) and pads (page 104) to ensure that you have the most effective means of setting up your sleeping bag for success.

We can also break down sleeping bags into some more defined classifications.

MUMMY BAGS

Mummy is the style most often used by backpackers. Mummy bags are tapered toward the feet to lessen bulk and be more heat efficient.

QUILTED BAGS

Quilted bags are the most common, car-camping style of bag. They look like big rectangles and are sometimes made with cotton materials (which are not good for heat retention), but they have room to move around in.

MULTIUSE BAGS

There are many varying styles and unique features of multiuse bags. These bags often have legs, arms or both so you can wear them and continue to get work done. Many in the tactical community have multiuse bags.

WOOL OR FLEECE BAGS

Wool or fleece bags are most often used as liner bags but can double as your only bag in warmer weather. These bags are thin and are great at wicking moisture away from the body. Coupled with a regular bag, they can help to take the temperature rating down another 15 to 20 degrees. (Wool or fleece bags come in a range of prices, but $20 is a good average.)

BIVY SACKS

While bivy sacks are not actually sleeping bags, they are invaluable for staying dry and warm. Many manufacturers make these bags in their own proprietary fabric. A bivy sack is one item that you should pay more for. The absolute best I have ever owned was made by the U.S. military. You can purchase them from military surplus sellers for approximately $70. I use mine on a very regular basis and have for many years. This bivy sack is part of a larger Military Sleep System, which includes warm- and cold-weather bags that can be nested together for extremely cold weather. This is the end-all, beat-all system, but—and this is a big but—it weighs 11+ pounds (5+ kg)! If you are young and have the legs of a mule, then you will love that system.

▶ *(Right) My TETON sleeping bag, Klymit pad and Hennessy hammock are my go-to sources for a sleep system in most of my outdoor adventures.*

The military sleep system is bulky and heavy, but is the hardiest and warmest sleeping system I have ever used.

Outdoor Research, Snugpak®, Black Diamond, Eberlestock and Mountain Hardwear all make great bivy sacks as well. I have one made by Snugpak that works well and is lightweight, but it is not as hardy as the U.S. military one. I've seen a variety of bivy sacks in my classes at Nature Reliance School, and I've learned that you trade toughness for weight. The lightweight sacks do not hold up to regular use in the outdoors. This can easily be resolved by taking care when choosing your sleeping area and pad placement.

Below is a table to help you determine what will work well for you. As with all the other tables, this one is based on two things: my own extensive experience and, just as important, my observations of both new and experienced students who come to Nature Reliance School classes. Keep in mind that 1 is the best and 4 is the worst in this table.

I recommend that if you need to be budget-minded, you should get a premium sleeping pad and a less pricey sleeping bag. The reason is because I have been doing exactly that for ten years now. My favorite sleeping bag of all time has been an inexpensive TETON Sports bag that I bought on sale many years ago (it's no longer made, but the TETON Sports Trailhead +20°F is a close equivalent). It is a 20°F (−7°C) bag that has PolarLite™ synthetic insulation in it. I have slept out in this bag in temperatures lower than 0°F (−18°C). When facing that kind of cold, I use a fleece liner bag and my mil-spec GORE-TEX bivy (approximately $60). This keeps me dry and warm even in heavy rain. The reason I love this bag so much is that it offers slightly more leg room than a traditional mummy bag and is simply comfortable. I highly recommend when you are considering a sleeping bag that you go to the store and actually get in it at the store. You may feel a bit silly doing so, but lie there for several minutes, move around, do some tasks while in it that you would normally do (e.g., take a shirt off). This will give you a much better impression than just reading reviews online. You never know if the person reviewing it has the same body shape or is at the same level of fitness as you.

In this table, 1 is best and 4 is worst.

	COMFORT	EFFICIENCY	DURABILITY	FRIENDLINESS	AFFORDABILITY
MUMMY BAG	4	1	3	4	3
QUILTED	3	2	2	3	2
MULTIUSE	2	3	1	1	4
WOOL OR FLEECE	1	4	4	2	1

STORAGE FOR SLEEPING PADS, BAGS, TENTS AND HAMMOCKS

You can have the greatest equipment in the world, but if you do not properly take care of it in the field and at home it will not work the way it was designed. Here are some helpful hints for you:

- After each use of a sleeping bag (even in the field), turn your bag inside out and hang it up before packing it up. This will allow body moisture from the previous night to dissipate.

- A stuff stack is not called a fold sack for good reason. Regularly folding any equipment will result in a breakdown of the fibers at the fold. Just stuff your equipment in its bag to put it away in the field. There are some sleeping pads that are designed specifically to be folded and are rectangular rather than cylindrical. You can feel free to fold those.

- When you get to your base of operations, set your equipment up to ensure it is completely dry before storing it. This is also a good time to brush off any excess sediment, leaves or other wilderness debris.

- When storing your gear do not leave any insulated equipment (e.g., your sleeping bag and pad) in its stuff sack. This will break down the loft and destroy its insulating capability. Find a place to hang or otherwise lay out this equipment so that it gets plenty of room for the loft to expand during storage. I have a shelf in my garage just for this purpose. If you do not have this sort of room, hang it on a hanger in a closet or develop a strap system in the closet.

- Make sure that each year you spray all tarps, tents and hammocks with a waterproof coating. You should do this whether you use them each year or not. Even in storage the coating will begin to break down. If you use your equipment once per month or more, do this twice per year or whenever you notice any sort of leakage.

TENTS AND HAMMOCKS

YOUR HOME AWAY FROM HOME

One of the most harrowing experiences I have had in the outdoors was on a canoe trip through the beautiful Red River Gorge here in Kentucky. The Red, as we call it, is a small unassuming river for most of its 97 miles (156 km). In the heart of the gorge, however, there are some really nice class III rapids. The issue with the Red is that it is rarely navigable unless you are hitting it after a rain event. Watching the weather forecast coming up, my friend and I saw an opportunity to paddle the Red during some very heavy rains. During the night a storm blew in on us that was throwing trees around quite substantially. We were sleeping in my Kelty Domolite two-person tent. It rained for nearly ten hours. Our canoe was tethered on land when we went to bed, but it was riding on several feet of water when we woke up. The greatest thing about this trip was that even though it rained that hard, we never got the least bit wet. All of our equipment in the tent was dry. We did not get much sleep due to the lightning continually booming through the gorge, but we definitely stayed dry. I have had several Kelty products, and they have all performed like my tent on that night: like a champ.

There are not many choices that are as important as getting the right shelter. Choose the right shelter and you will have a more comfortable stay, which increases your morale for any adventure. There are a number of choices available to you, and I have a large number of different types and models. Here are the highlights to consider:

- **TENTS.** Solo bivy tents to much larger ones for car camping and even glamping.
- **HAMMOCKS.** Hammocks have been my preferred method for the last several years. I spend over 100 nights per year in a hammock.

TENTS

Beyond that eventful night on the Red River, I have also been to Alaska and slept in a hammock in Memphis, Tennessee, during the summer. Both places have more mosquitoes than stars in the sky. We need protection from the elements and from pests. There are several items that are critical to your understanding of tents.

DURABILITY

There is a unique relationship when it comes to backpacking gear: the relationship between cost and durability. Since shelters are most likely the largest item you will carry into a wilderness, this relationship really comes into play. I have found that a tent is another item worth spending the extra money on. What this means is that when you spend more money, you will most likely get a lighter tent that is more durable than its less expensive cousins. I am hard on gear—I use my shelters often and sometimes I simply do not have the time or

MSR makes great tents in a wide range of styles and types for virtually any outdoor adventure.

Please note that some areas have very strict regulations on where you can place a tent. This serves to help both high-traffic areas as well as sensitive flora and fauna. Find a spot that you think looks like a good spot. When you stop it's best to always take time to look up, down, left and right:

- Look up to verify there are no overhangs or nearby trees likely to fall on your shelter. Take into consideration trees and how far they can reach when they fall.

- Look down to see what is happening on the ground. You should remove any large debris that might cause problems to your tent or body in the middle of the night. This includes briars and other small vegetation. I do what I can to avoid killing live plants whenever possible. You should also ensure that you are on level ground. Otherwise, you run the risk of a rough night's sleep due to sliding down as well as rainwater running into your tent.

- Looking left and right is just a reminder to be aware of where the sun comes up and where the prevailing winds are blowing from. You want to have good protection from those winds in cold weather, and you may want them in hot weather. In cold weather, waking up and having the sun on you is a wonderful thing. When you can, set up your shelter to enjoy the sunrise for both warmth and a morale boost.

- When you leave, look down so you can return the area back to its normal state as much as possible.

energy to make the area in which I am sleeping look like a baby bed when I lie down on it. I need gear that will handle a stick every now and then because I don't see them all. The floor of the tent should, at the very least, be ripstop nylon and would benefit greatly from being polyurethane. My MSR FreeLite™ (approximately $275) tent has MSR's Durashield technology in the polyurethane. This makes it a great choice for using in areas where there will be debris and regular rain.

DEFENSE AGAINST THE ELEMENTS

You need a shelter that will protect you from the elements. I like one that has a tougher material on the bottom than the sides. This means there is stitch line somewhere near the bottom. Ensure that the stitch line is a few inches above the ground line. The stitch line is the place water is most likely to get in.

You should also get protection from pesky bugs. Both my hammock (Hennessy Explorer Asym), and my tent (MSR FreeLite) have a polyester micromesh. This keeps

bugs out and me in. The mesh on my hammock is incredibly strong 30D no-see-um netting. There have been times when I have tossed and turned at night and woke up on the mesh rather than the actual hammock ripstop. It has held up well with no stretching or pulling apart at the seams. A great choice for summertime camping is a mesh top and rainfly covering. If it is excessively hot and not going to rain, I leave the rainfly off and let the dew come through on me. This serves to cool me off, while at the same time keeps the bugs away. That is a great combination.

FEATURES

Tents are great for friends who like things compartmentalized. Many models will offer you pockets and inner mini-hammocks for storing gear within easy reach. (Remember my friend's story about bear spray in Chapter 1?) You should also look for vents that will allow condensation to exit.

SEASON RATING

Tents designated as four-season are engineered to handle heavy amounts of snow. Unless you are into mountaineering and have Mount Everest on your bucket list, you will not need a tent designated as such. Three-season (spring, summer, fall) tents will take care of the rest of us and will even handle small amounts of snow.

CAPACITY

Have you ever noticed those well-dressed backpackers in the magazines, the ones that look like they will blow away with a good stiff wind? Capacity designations are made for those fine people. For the rest of us, you need to seriously consider this. There are one-person tents for those that like hitting the woods solo. Then you have two-person tents. My recommendation for two campers is to get a tent marked for two or three people. This will allow two people who don't blow away in the wind to have space for themselves and a little gear. Three- or four-person tents are almost always too crowded and tend to be uncomfortable for that many adults. For backpacking and such, I recommend getting two tents and spreading the load out among four people. This system lightens the load for everyone and the tents can handle the people and gear. If you are car camping with the family, go all the way. Get the largest tent your budget can stand so you have plenty of space. Your trunk is your backpack.

STRUCTURE

Freestanding tents are wonderful inventions. They come with a pole system that is easy to assemble. I do not use stakes unless it is incredibly windy outside. My gear inside will hold the tent down. Those tents that are not freestanding will require the use of stakes and tie-out points. It is worth it to save time and frustration during setup to get a freestanding tent.

For general use, a freestanding tent is the best choice for most campers and hikers.

RAINFLIES

You will see tents designated as double-walled. This means that the main portion of the tent is mesh and the waterproof covering is a rainfly. This greatly reduces the amount of condensation inside the tent itself. Single-wall tents are made so that the walls and the rainfly are the same thing. This is not conducive to areas where there is significant rain. It does, however, eliminate weight when hiking in arid areas. Single-walled tents are typically used by mountaineers. I recommend double-walled mainly due to the condensation issue. You do not want moisture staying in the tent with you.

➤ *(Right) Double-walled tents and bivies used with a rainfly allow those inside to move about without concern of pulling in water from the outside.*

REAL-LIFE SKILLS: SETTING UP A TENT TO AVOID GETTING WET WHEN IT RAINS

I have watched dozens of students make the following mistakes in our classes and get wet. This little sidebar is worth the price of the book you have in your hand:

- **ALWAYS INSPECT YOUR GEAR BEFORE YOUR TRIP.** Coat your shelter with waterproof sealant if you have not used it in a long while or if the sealant is cracking. This will look like white flakes over the tent. I coat my tents each year.

- **IDENTIFY WHERE THE PREVAILING WINDS ARE WHEN SETTING UP AND WHEN WINDS START BLOWING IN A STORM.** Ensure your door is not facing the prevailing winds. If it is, change its location while you have time. It is not better to hope for the best in this situation. It is better to prepare for the worst.

- **AVOID SETTING UP AT THE BOTTOM OF SLOPE.** Water naturally travels downhill. If this cannot be avoided, then dig a small "mote" around your tent to direct that water away from you.

- **USE A FOOTPRINT.** These are small tarps that fit the bottom of your tent perfectly. You can use any tarp; just ensure that it does not stick out from the bottom of your tent. When you have a tarp that sticks out from the bottom, it serves as a guttering system for water to travel under your tent. I have seen suggestions to have it 1 inch (3 cm) in from the edge, flush and much more. My experience is that as long as it does not protrude out from under the main body of the tent, you are okay. The more any portion of the floor touches the earth, the more opportunity there is for moisture to seep in. Waterbeds are not a good choice in the wilderness. Although a footprint is the easiest to use for such endeavors, it does not serve any other purpose very well. Therefore, I take a regular Equinox or Wilderness Innovation tarp to use instead. This way, I have another item with me that is multiuse.

- **ONCE YOU'RE INSIDE THE TENT, DO NOT TOUCH THE SIDES OF ANY PORTION THAT CONTACTS THE OUTSIDE WITH YOUR BODY OR GEAR.** A conduit will be created by manipulating the fibers by touching them or other equipment making contact with them. An outer barrier is made by the tightly woven fibers of the material; when the material is pushed, the fibers are pulled apart (although this cannot be seen with the naked eye), which allows moisture to pass through. This is another good reason to choose a double-walled tent. You can avoid this issue altogether by doing so.

- **ANOTHER BIG ISSUE IS SETTING UP YOUR TENT IN THE RAIN.** One way I take care of this is that I leave my rainfly attached. If it is raining when I set it up, I can pull it out and it is already covered by the rainfly. This does not work for an extended time, but does make for quick work in the rain. I also suggest you get all your tent poles out first. Put them together and have them ready to go. If your tent requires it to be staked out, then have them out and ready to go as well.

Shock cord is found in most poles and you should always carry extra in case any have problems afield.

Hammocks are gaining in popularity. Many people find them as comfortable as their own bed at home.

POLE MATERIALS

I prefer poles with shock cord and I always keep extra shock cord and duct tape in a pocket of the tent. There is nothing worse than a great tent with a broken pole. They can very easily be fixed in the field with shock cord and duct tape.

COST

I mention cost here for emphasis. I recommend you spend as much as your budget can allow, and maybe even a little more, on a tent. Spend the extra money on your shelter and not on the extra cookies. You don't need them anyway.

Since I teach so many students at Nature Reliance School, I see quite a range of tents. The two that stand out to me are MSR and REI. I see those a lot and both do really well. As I mentioned earlier, I had an inexpensive Kelty tent that lasted for over twenty years for me. It actually would still be working fine, but someone borrowed it and never brought it back. MSR tents are a bit pricier, but worth it. REI makes great tents and they are middle of the road in pricing. Kelty tends to be the least expensive of those I have mentioned here. That is why I have shared with you the materials and design features you should be looking for. That Kelty tent saw a lot of abuse and incredibly terrible weather over twenty years, but it was still working fine.

HAMMOCKS

As I mentioned earlier, I have become a big fan of hammocks. My hammock of choice is a Hennessy Explorer Asym (approximately $250). While they are certainly not for everyone, they are for me. I have slept in hammocks during most of my trips outside for the past several years. I have learned a lot and want to share it with you. If you are new to hammocks, please know they don't actually make you feel like a sausage encased between two palm trees on the beach. They have come a very long way in recent years.

Look for hammocks classified as asymmetrical. This is different from the classic style of hammock most of us are used to, which curves the user's body into the shape of a banana. In an asymmetrical hammock, your body does not lie along the center line. You lie at a diagonal on it. This offers you the benefit of a much flatter sleeping surface. I am a side sleeper and simply cannot get comfortable in a traditional hammock. Trust me, I have tried. When I first saw people trying them out, I went out and got an inexpensive model. It did not work for me and many others like me. I was gifted the Hennessy and absolutely fell in love with it.

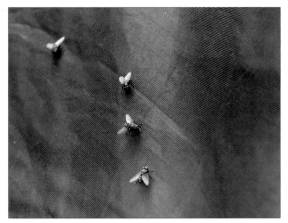

An integrated bug net is a hammock necessity in my opinion.

Straps make hammock setup and takedown fast and efficient.

I am also a big fan of an integrated bug net rather than one that separates. I have had multiple students that did not want to bring or use their bug net because they wanted the "experience" of sleeping close to the elements, after disregarding my attempts to persuade them otherwise. Many of them did not get any sleep or woke up looking like a strawberry due to bug bites.

Get some good straps. Many hammocks come with them. I have found that Kammok™ straps (approximately $30) work exceptionally well for my needs. Let me give you a big, helpful hint on the straps: do not leave them behind when packing up. It is easy to pack up the hammock to keep it off the ground and forget that the straps are hanging in the tree. Develop a process when packing up that reminds you to not leave them. The process I go through now (after leaving some straps on trees for fellow hammockers) is the reverse of what I do when finding a good place to shelter. I look up, down, left and right. I look up to verify that I have not left any gear hanging on branches, I look down as a reminder to put leaves or forest debris back so as to not leave much trace of my being there, and I look left and right to ensure I have

my straps. When I pack and unpack all my hammock gear, my hammock never touches the ground. I set its container, sometimes just my pack, at the midpoint between the trees I intend on using as anchors. My straps are on top, so I put them up first. I then clip into the strap on one side and pull the hammock out from the pack and clip to the other. This is a simple but handy method to ensure your hammock does not get covered in forest debris or moisture during setup.

Double hammocks are for lovebirds. In theory, this sounds like a good thing—you and your hiking partner in one hammock. In reality, this proves to be a good recipe for little sleep. Sleep is paramount in wilderness travel. You need to do what it takes to get good rest.

Quality of materials is important. One of the reasons I recommend good straps is because during one excessively long trip during which I stayed in a hammock for two straight weeks, one of the straps broke in the middle of the night. That is no fun at all. Ensure that your hammock or strapping system is not single-stitched. Look for good double or triple stitching along the seams.

PADS AND COTS

SLEEP LIKE A BABY

Pads are the missing link to having a good night's sleep in a wilderness setting. This is because people that are buying equipment for the first time will purchase a shelter, bag and pad at the same time to get started. The conventional wisdom is that if you save some money on one of those items, it is usually the pad. I am just the opposite. After many sleepless nights, I now have the best pads I can afford. I even have a Klymit Hammock V pad just for my hammock, and I use the Big Agnes Q-Core sleeping pad on the ground. My life (and sleep) has been enriched ever since I invested in good pads.

Recently many manufacturers have included an R-value on their pads. R-value is a material's ability to resist heat flow. The higher the R-value, the greater its insulating power. While I feel this is intended to be an objective measure of a pad's usefulness, I believe it does not have a direct correlation to comfort level while sleeping in a wilderness. As I have stated earlier, your comfort level depends on several factors: the campsite location, tent, bag, clothing and more. What an R-value rating on pads does do for us, though, is give us a quick look at pads so that we can sort through them at a store or online when purchasing them.

Pads are an incredibly important piece of the puzzle as it pertains to restful sleep.

Notice my Klymit Hammock V pad has "wings" at the shoulder and knee areas—this asymmetrical shape makes it incredibly comfortable.

Another method that you will see sellers using to try to give an objective look at pads is temperature rating. Again, while this is a good way of sorting pads prior to purchase, just keep in mind it does not directly correlate to their ability to keep you warm in various temperatures. That requires an understanding of the same factors listed in the preceding paragraph.

I have broken pads down into several classifications as they pertain to me and my use of them. Let's consider each one.

PRICE

Pads are one of those things you need to spend a few more pennies on. You will get what you pay for when you spend more money on a pad.

PACKED SIZE

For car camping, size does not really matter. For all other wilderness adventures, it matters greatly. You don't want to have a pad that is going to protrude from your pack and get snagged on vegetation. I get my air-filled pads packed up smaller than foam ones due to the design. Most foam pads take up too much space inside the pack and are therefore not efficient to carry. However, they work well when strapped to the outside. This is another good reason for a poncho or rain cover during inclement weather: I put my sleeping pad down, use my pack as a pillow, keep my clothes on for some warmth and use the poncho as a moisture barrier against dew and rain. I have used pads in the rain when I was not using a tent (due to tactical needs). This is another reason that a bivy sack is a good choice to have: Even if your pad is soaked, the bivy sack can keep you from getting your sleeping bag wet. I have also rolled my pads up in my bivy sack before so they do not get wet while I am carrying them.

WEIGHT

When it comes to pads, the differences in weight are negligible. What you can do is get a mummy-shaped pad or one that is three-quarter length that will save you a few ounces.

COMFORT

Comfort is vitally important. If you are comfortable, you will sleep better. When you sleep better, you have more energy and your morale is higher. Spend the time and money finding the best pad for you. The table on page 118 will help you sort out all the options.

I think each of those preceding factors must be considered when you are choosing a pad. Obviously, we could get a battery-powered air mattress that may even equal our comfortable bed at home, but something like that will be so big and heavy that it is not realistic to take it on a hike.

We can further break down this discussion into four main types of pads: (1) open-cell foam pads, (2) foam pads, (3) air pads and (4) down pads.

OPEN-CELL FOAM PADS

Open-cell foam pads are often referred to as self-inflating pads, because when you open the valve to the pad the foam begins to expand. It then creates a vacuum that pulls air into the pad. This will not completely fill the pad but will get it nearly inflated. You can then add your own breath to completely fill it to your liking. Keep in mind our ideas for storage for pads (see the sidebar on page 107). If open-cell foam is stored tightly and packed away, the cells will develop "memory." This means when you open them, they will stay in that packed shape, not open so readily and not pull in air as well.

Thermarest open-celled foam pads are great for the ground or on a cot as pictured.

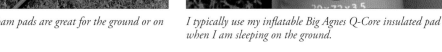

I typically use my inflatable Big Agnes Q-Core insulated pad when I am sleeping on the ground.

FOAM PADS

Foam pads are the most economical and easiest to maintain because they are nothing more than foam with no air. They come in a rolled or foldable form. You can literally have them laid out and ready to use in seconds. Most people, including me, do not find them nearly as comfortable as the other options available, however.

AIR PADS

Also known as inflatable pads, air pads have become my preferred choice. The main issue with air pads is that you must manually fill them in the field, which is time-consuming and sometimes tiresome after a long day of rucking, hiking or hunting. With that problem in mind, many companies provide either small stand-alone or integrated pumps with their pads. These allow you to use your arms or feet to pump the pad up. The first obvious benefit to this system is that you don't have to make yourself dizzy blowing a pad up with your own breath. The second benefit is that it eliminates putting bacteria into the pad itself. Once inside and then closed off, bacteria can grow and eventually form mold. Many of the more expensive pads now have an antimicrobial lining in them to thwart bacteria and mold growth.

Another thing to consider about air pads is the direction the baffles run on them. You will notice that open air pads have baffles that help distribute air proportionally while you're sleeping on them. They will run either vertically along the length of the entire pad, horizontally or in a quilted pattern (much like a zigzag pattern). I have had students remark in class that baffles that run vertically end up rolling up on their sides, which makes using the pad mildly irritating yet not uncomfortable or painful. I don't hear this complaint about pads whose baffles run horizontally or in a quilted pattern. That has been my experience as well. I now have two pads that I use: one is an insulated and quilted-pattern Big Agnes Q-Core air pad (approximately $150) that I use on the ground, sometimes with no tent or tarp under it; the other is a Klymit Hammock V air pad (approximately $105) designed specifically for hammock use. I have been using them regularly now for quite some time and I have no issues sleeping in the wilderness with them. As a matter of fact, my comfort level and restfulness in my hammock is better than my bed at home. It has made me consider how to hook up my hammock in my bedroom.

CRAIG'S SECRET TO RESTFUL SLEEP IN THE WILDERNESS

The key to restful sleep in the outdoors is to assist your spine in staying in alignment. Before setting up your sleep system, dig yourself an indentation for your lower body (i.e., buttocks and hips) and shoulder to rest in.

Everyone's body shape is different, so the depth of the hole is going to be different. I recommend you take a look in the mirror and see how far your bum protrudes out from your spine. Dig yourself an indentation even if you are using a pad. It does not matter if you are a back or side sleeper. This will serve to relieve pressure on your spine and therefore offer you a more-restful sleep.

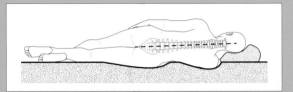

Align your spine for restful sleep by digging a small indentation at your pelvic region.

PAD USE	RECOMMENDED PAD TYPE	COMMENTS
Backpacking	Air pad or self-inflating foam	Comfortable yet packs small
Through-Hiking	Closed-cell foam	Very light, takes up little space
Winter Use	Down	More insulation is needed, so down is a great choice
Car Camping or Glamping	Self-inflating or battery-powered	Very comfortable

DOWN PADS

One of the more recent developments in pads is the use of down. Down is a superior insulator in many ways, as we have already discussed. Exped is a great choice for down pads. You should also note that down does not work well with moisture, so most companies will provide a separate or integrated pump to fill the pad up with air. This keeps the pad from getting too much moisture in it when you blow air into it.

COTS

Cots are great choices for car camping. Although it may mostly be a mind-set issue, many people like the familiarity of sleeping on a bed and a cot offers a nice bridge from being in your bed at home to being outdoors. My favorite cot is the ALPS Mountaineering cot (see the photo on page 119). This cot is comfortable without a pad on it, but I typically use one of my pads on it as well for extra comfort. Choose a cot that suits the needs of you and your team or family. Just keep in mind that they are not for backpackers, as they are heavy and bulky.

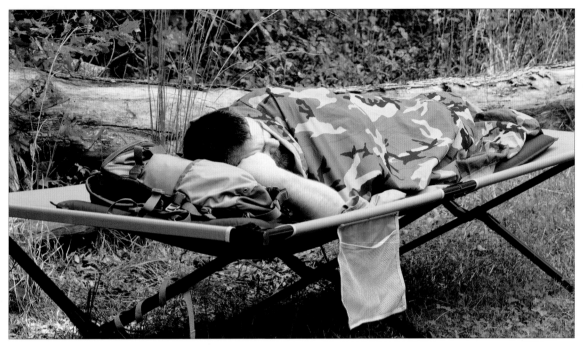

I use a cot often when I am car-camping as it gets me off the ground and is very comfortable.

FIELD AND HOME CARE FOR SHELTER ITEMS

Fire is my biggest concern in the field for the items we've discussed in this chapter. I once had a sleeping pad that I was drying on top of a tarp get blown into the fire and melt before I could get it out. That is not a good feeling when you know you have another night of sleep on the cold ground. I therefore make sure that I weight items down that could blow away. I take a needle with me to sew any of my shelter pieces that may need it. If I had this need, I could easily use the inner strands of paracord (see page 47) to accomplish this task. Duct

tape is another great resource to tape up anything that may need fixing quickly. I have taped tent poles, boot soles, injuries and axe handles in the backcountry. I have it listed earlier in this book as a first aid item, but you can always rob a little from your first aid kit to use for such needs.

I also waterproof all my rain-repellant items each year at a minimum and every six months when I am using them a lot. If I notice some water seepage on any item during a rain-soaked trip, I will waterproof it when I get home.

CHAPTER 5
FIRE

You get guys around a campfire, and they start telling their stories. That's the fellowship that they want to be in.

—John Eldredge

THERE ARE MOMENTS IN RELATIONSHIPS THAT SOLIDIFY YOU AS A COUPLE

Many of those moments may seem downright stressful at the time but with the gift of time they prove to be a part of the foundation of that relationship or a way to find humor. One such trip for my wife and me proved to do both of those things. Many of you may remember early in your relationship with your spouse how your partner engaged in activities outside their norm for the benefit of the relationship. My wife was no different. She did not grow up with as much time in the outdoors as I had growing up. When I say that, I mean basically none. Maybe a day hike or two. It was with much appreciation that I took her on her first backcountry backpacking and camping experience very early in our marriage.

As I write this, 25 years later, I can still remember heading out with a backpack full of gear for her and me. It was cold enough to have layers on and it was lightly snowing. Such a sweet, sweet moment, right? Not so much.

The hike in was actually very short. A mile or two at best. We did find a nice campsite with plenty of wood lying around for a fire that we determined would last through the evening. I took to putting up the tent and throwing in the sleeping bags and I asked her to start gathering firewood. I built a nice little camp kitchen, which included a nice bushcraft hanger setup to cook some goodies in a pot. After some fine camp dining, we sat around the fire a bit and then dove into our sleeping bags for the cold night. After less than one hour, it was very clear that the sleeping gear I had brought was not going to be enough to keep us warm. We made the decision to get up and warm ourselves by the fire. We had built a nice fire for cooking so it was not hard to get it going again. What we had not planned on, though, was gathering enough wood to keep a fire going all through the night. Which is exactly what was getting ready to happen.

I took my flashlight with me and started gathering wood and took it to her, as she began the task of breaking it up into more manageable sections. The fire was going well and we had pulled our sleep gear out around the fire. I was dozing off as I am sure she, experiencing her first overnight trip, wasn't. It was not too much later that she woke me up, saying she saw something out in the woods that concerned her. It looked like a set of eyes, she said. Me, being the true outdoorsman of the two of us, laughed it off and started to fall asleep again. Until I heard something out in the woods. She had been right all along. (Funny how that works sometimes.) Whatever it was circled our camp for quite a while. I could regularly see its eyes when the flashlight hit them. It was never close enough for me to get a good look. It continued to circle the camp through the night, but never close enough to bring us any harm. To this day, we still do not know what it was. Also to this day, I am confident that the fire we had built did two extraordinary things for us that night: It kept us warm enough to stay alive and it was enough of a deterrent to keep whatever anima

FIRE STARTERS

THE SPARK OF LIFE

Humanity's oldest and most useful gear piece is fire. Virtually everything I am covering in this book are things you will buy and then utilize in wilderness adventure. This is for good reason. We can benefit greatly from the myriad of choices out there to make our trips more enjoyable. Fire is different, though. Fire is something you create from the environment. As with all things, be a good steward of natural resources and know the laws and regulations of the areas you travel. Some areas do not allow fires at all due to the sensitivity of the locale. Other areas have fire seasons in which you can and cannot build fires. Those regulations are in place for the safety and well-being of the environment. Now that we are clear on that, let's look and see what modern tools we can use for making fire and how to make fire itself. (Please note we will be covering cooking stoves and canisters in Chapter 7.)

I tell my students regularly that ego is the biggest obstacle to making fire. Remove your ego from the equation and look at the science of it. You can see where problems arise and come to a better answer if you are having difficulty. The science of fire building is simple. You need three things to make a fire, which most people refer to as the fire triangle: oxygen, heat and fuel.

One of the best things about the large interest in survival TV shows and equipment is that survivalists really like to spend a great deal of time on fire-building skills. Due to that, manufacturers have developed a multitude of various gear pieces that are great choices for all of us who venture into the wilderness. We'll cover each of these in detail in the following paragraphs.

The triangle of fire is the foundation of all things related to fire. If one aspect of it is askew, making fire will be more difficult.

DISPOSABLE BUTANE LIGHTERS

A disposable butane lighter is my most-recommended heat and ignition source. It is too affordable (approximately $1), usable and lightweight to not have one in your pocket and one in your pack as a backup. They seem like such simple little pieces of gear, but they are quite technical. You will notice that these types of lighters have liquid butane in them. Butane will remain a liquified gas if it stays under pressure and at room temperature. It is not this liquified gas that you burn when you utilize a butane lighter—it is the vapor coming from that liquid. When you flick your lighter on, the vapor at the top of the lighter burns off and the heat boils the top of the liquid. This then creates more vapor that passes through the lighter. The spark you see is created

Disposable butane lighters are inexpensive, lightweight and easy to pack. I carry one in my pocket and one in my pack as backup.

by a very small grinder (the part you rotate with your thumb) and a small ferrocerium rod in contact with and directly below it. When you remove your thumb from the button, the flame goes out. This closes the valve that allows the vapor to come out.

I imagine you are now saying, "Great, but why do I need to know all that?" Because there are many pitfalls when a lighter is your choice for starting a fire. You need to know what they are and how they are easily fixed.

MOISTURE

If the grinding wheel and the ferrocerium rod get wet, they will not work properly. I prefer to keep a lighter in my pocket just for ease of use and survival needs. I always have a backup in a waterproof container in my pack, particularly if I am on or near water, such as canoeing and kayaking trips. On those trips and in rainy conditions, I keep the lighter in a sealable sandwich bag in my pocket.

POSITIONING

Disposable lighters do not work well upside down. This is because the valve mechanism is in contact with the butane liquid and not the vapor. Not to mention, due to the placement of the button, it is easy to burn yourself when utilizing it at a steep angle.

COLD WEATHER

When temps are at or near freezing, disposable lighters do not work well. At this temperature, there is little to no vapor that comes off the liquid butane. You will sometimes be able to get a small but very short-lasting flame after shaking the lighter itself. This is a product of friction inside the lighter creating more vapor. A better solution is to keep your disposable lighter warm by keeping it close to your body. If you keep it stored in your pack during cold weather, it will take a few minutes of warming up from your body heat to ensure it works well.

VALVE FUNCTION

When the valve is released, the flame stops. Simple, right? Not so much when you are trying to build a fire. You will need to use fuel sources (which are covered later) to make fire building much easier.

NONDISPOSABLE BUTANE LIGHTERS

Zippo brand nondisposable butane lighters (about $15) were standard-issue gear for the U.S. Army, Navy, Air Force and Marines during World War II, and for very good reason. Many of the problems that occur with disposable lighters are solved with this type of lighter. This type utilizes a gas called naphtha, which is most commonly referred to as lighter fluid. The metal container houses a cotton pad that will receive several ounces of fuel. The wick that is connected to this cotton pad will also hold the gas for lighting. Much like disposable lighters, there is a grinding wheel and small ferrocerium rod that causes sparks. It is those sparks contacting the saturated wick that gives you a flame. There are important things to consider when choosing this style of lighter for your use.

WICK CONSTRUCTION

It is not the wick itself that catches flame. It is the gas saturated on it that does. The wick is supported and protected by wire mesh and will last you an incredibly long time.

CONTINUOUSLY BURNING FLAME

When it is lit and left on its own, this a nondisposable butane lighter that will burn until it runs out of fuel. Closing the top will starve it of oxygen and cause it to stop burning.

WINDPROOF

Zippo lighters are essentially windproof due to the design of the windscreen and a proper amount of fuel delivery. That is an asset when trying to get your stove lit for late-night hot chocolate on the trail or other such vital tasks.

HEARTINESS

Nondisposable butane lighters are nearly indestructible. They can take a lot of abuse. However, they are not waterproof.

FUEL EVAPORATION

Nondisposable butane lighters are not pressurized and the contents are therefore susceptible to air. The fuel in these lighters will evaporate over time. You can solve this problem by always filling up your lighter before each trip. I would also suggest keeping some sort of backup with you as well. That could be a disposable lighter, more fuel, matches or a ferrocerium rod.

MATCHES

All matches are not created equal. I am not a fan of taking matches into a wilderness. They are not waterproof (even most so-called waterproof ones). Most are also not windproof, are susceptible to breaking and are one-and-done. Most matches are a small stick or stiff paper with phosphorous on the end. There are three main types of matches to be aware of: safety matches, strike-anywhere matches and waterproof matches. I have noticed, however, that most of my students do carry matches, despite their disadvantages. With that in mind, you need to know the ins and outs of matches.

SAFETY MATCHES

Safety matches are the matches that are most readily available. They require you to utilize a striking surface usually provided for you on the container they come in. This surface is impregnated with chemicals to assist the chemical reaction of the match. Safety matches will have a solid-colored head on them.

STRIKE-ANYWHERE MATCHES

With strike-anywhere matches, as the name applies, all you need to strike these is a solid surface. You can note this type of matches because they will have a different colored tip at the end of the phosphorous. This tip, which is typically white, contains zinc oxide. The other chemicals in this tip are the same ones that you will find on the striking surface of most match boxes. This allows the user to have a match that is easier to strike nearly anywhere. It is more difficult to find this type of match because there are more extreme shipping and storage requirements on them. Many companies avoid those laws by just carrying safety matches.

WATERPROOF MATCHES

Waterproof matches most often will extend the phosphorous material farther down the length of the matchstick. The entire match will then be covered in a waterproof coating. This serves to make the matches harder to strike. The coating is also very thick and wears off even when just kept in your pack for later use.

➤ *(Right) Zippo lighters can be used hands-free and are nearly completely windproof, making them good choices in foul conditions.*

FERROCERIUM RODS

Although the ferrocerium rod was invented in the early 1900s, it was only recently that its widespread manufacture and use came about. Survivalists around the world have ferro rods on their bracelets, on their knife sheaths, in their packs and in their pockets. This is one "in style" piece of gear that I am a fan of. There are several metals that make up ferrocerium, and the combination will determine a rod's quality and cost. The hottest ferro rods I have ever used came from Firesteel. com. They are great choices and have a significant range of prices based on size.

Let's look closer at the types of ferro rods available.

MISCH METAL

Typically, but not always, misch metal ferro rods will have a higher amount of magnesium in them than others. Magnesium will reduce the temperature of the sparks coming off the ferro rod. Magnesium is also a softer metal, and rods with higher amounts of it will not last as long. This softness does however allow the user to scrape the metal off easily. I have found this to be beneficial for my students and me.

STANDARD

Standard ferro rods have a much lower concentration of magnesium and therefore put off hotter sparks. They are harder and more difficult for a beginner to strike. Most of the ferro rods manufactured in the United States are of this quality.

As I mentioned previously, the popularity of ferro rods has led to some interesting manufacturing innovations as well as some things you need to consider:

- **ONE-HANDED VERSIONS.** These devices are built inside a housing that holds both the ferro rod and scraper. By pushing the device, a spring assists with pressure so you can use them one-handed. As with all things, whenever there are more moving parts, the item is more susceptible to breaking.

- **INTEGRATED HANDLES.** Whistles, compasses and tinder boxes are all part of the handles in some ferro rods currently being manufactured. I do not consider these a go-to source for these tools, but they provide a backup to the better tool. They are a solution if you don't have the higher-quality counterparts packed away. An interesting tidbit I have learned after watching hundreds of students in my classes is that most of them have trouble using a ferro rod without a handle, rather than having poor technique. Get one with a good handle on it that you can grab in the palm of your hand. If you have a strong grip, you will not have this issue.

- **COATING.** When ferro rods are manufactured, they are often coated with a black protectant. This protectant should be stripped away to get good, hot sparks.

- **CORROSION.** Ferrocerium will deteriorate if it stays in contact with water. This is exponentially true with salt water. If salt of any source is left on a ferro rod, it will deteriorate it rapidly. Keep salt water, sweat and other sources of salt away from your rods. You can combat salt's effects by cleaning ferro rods after using them and coating them with clear polish.

HOW TO USE A FERROCERIUM ROD

- Remove any debris from the ferro rod and the scraper you will be using (the back of your knife works well).

- Grasp the ferro rod in your nondominant hand and place the tip toward the object you want to ignite. If you are wanting to ignite tinder, place the tip into the tinder source.

- Grasp your scraper and place it on the ferro rod close to your hand.

- Angle the scraper away from you and toward the tinder source. This will force the sparks to come off toward your target.

- If you are lighting a stove or similar piece of equipment, there is enough volatile fuel that one or two scrapes will get it ignited.

- If you are attempting to ignite forest materials for making a fire, it may take several scrapes to get it going. When doing this, I typically scrape vigorously and quickly to keep the tinder material hot. I scrape down the blade only, forcing the sparks to go into my tinder material.

Use a proper knife angle (as shown above) to push the sparks into the tinder material.

FUEL SOURCES

BUILD FIRES LIKE A BOSS

The second part of the fire triangle is the fuel source. This includes items from the environment as well as gear items you can purchase. If you are frugal with money, there are many variants of these you can make at home. I consider these sorts of things as "fire extenders." You have only two hands, so it is sometimes easier to light something that you know is going to hold a flame long enough for you to build the fire up around it. Please note the sidebar on how to make fire in the rain (page 132–133) as well as the sidebar on building a one-stick fire (page 31). Those two sidebars will help you build the fire. What I want to do here is show you what to buy so fire making can be much easier.

SOLKOA SURVIVAL SYSTEMS™ FASTFIRE™

In my experience, SOLKOA Survival Systems Fastfire (approximately $1 per cube) is the most reliable fire tinder available. These cubes burn easily when wet, can break apart easily, are lightweight, have a long shelf life, have a low flashpoint and are smokeless and odorless. The flame they produce is wind-resistant and when they are extinguished they are cool to the touch. This means you can use either the whole cube or a part of it to get a fire started, extinguish it, then use the remainder again later.

UST BRANDS WETFIRE™

Another great tinder material that burns well, UST Brands WetFire (approximately $1 per cube) has a medium flashpoint and can be extinguished easily. They are not immediately cool to the touch when you extinguish them.

ESBIT

Esbit brand cubes (approximately $0.50 per cube) are harder than those previously mentioned, which means that you need a scraper of some sort to get smaller pieces. This also makes them harder to ignite. The major downside to these fuel cubes is that they have a distinct odor that I do not find pleasant.

TRIOXANE

Trioxane fuel sticks (approximately $3 per bar) were standard-issue and were in great use for cooking in the Vietnam War era. They are rather unsafe to handle, so you should not have skin contact with them. They burn incredibly hot and longer than the other options listed here. They put off an incredibly strong odor when burning, but they are a more-affordable choice than other fire sources. Be aware that breathing in fumes from trioxane is harmful to your health.

Common fuel sources from left to right: Fastfire, Wetfire, Esbit, Trioxane, Coghlan's and über fire. The upper-right photo shows them unwrapped, and the bottom photo shows them lit.

In this table 1 is best and 7 is worst.

	COST	FLASHPOINT	ABILITY TO BURN WHEN WET	BURNING TEMPERATURE	DURATION
FASTFIRE	6	1	1	2	2
WETFIRE	5	2	2	3	5
ESBIT	4	7	5	4	3
TRIOXANE	3	5	4	1	4
COGHLAN'S	2	6	6	6	7
ÜBERFIRE	7	4	3	3	1
COTTON BALLS AND PETROLEUM JELLY	1	3	7	7	6

COGHLAN'S TINDER

Coghlan's brand of fire supplies is very budget-minded. Their fire cubes (approximately $0.50 per tinder) are good choices under good conditions. The cubes have a cotton base and accelerant infused in them. This makes it difficult to extinguish easily, and it is not cool to the touch immediately when it is put out.

ÜBERFIRE™

I came across Überfire (approximately $30 per 2-ounce [56-g] tin) while on a man-tracking course in Virginia. The person who shared it with me is a survival instructor for federal law enforcement. We burned a can of this starter for several minutes. Once it was snuffed out, it was ready to use several more times. He gave me a can and I bought a few more for me and the students in my classes.

COTTON BALLS

Cotton balls are great additions to your pack in the backcountry. Without anything added to them, they will burn for a short while. With fuel sources—such as petroleum jelly, alcohol, white gas, cooking oil or a similar substance—added they will last even longer. Ensure you have a leak-proof container to store these items in. Petroleum jelly quickly becomes a petroleum-liquid mess with only a small amount of heat. Another good thing to know about cotton balls is that they are not actually balls: they are cotton rolls. Find the end and unroll them for a long length of fire tinder.

Having a fire assists in staying warm, cooking food and providing a huge morale boost.

MAGNESIUM

Many ferrocerium rods come coupled with a large section of magnesium attached. Magnesium does not spark by striking but does burn very hot when it is ignited. It is easy to scrape some off into a ball about the size of a grape, then spark it with the ferro rod. It burns up very quickly, but it does burn when wet.

SURVIVAL SUPPLIES

Survivalists are very good at do-it-yourself fire starters. There are as many variants of these as there are pages in this book. I am going to list a few that I have seen in my classes that work well, mainly because I like budget-minded equipment:

- **DRYER LINT.** Rather than just throw it away, collect it for your next wilderness trip. The best dryer lint is that which comes from cotton clothing. Polyester lint mostly melts and doesn't provide a good tinder source for flame.

- **LIP BALM AND ANTIBIOTIC OINTMENT.** Many lip balms and antibiotic ointments have petroleum-based oils in them, which make them harmful to use on you but good to use for fire starting. They work best when they are spread and mixed with ignitable forest debris (e.g., wood shavings). The petroleum is the accelerant, and the natural material serves to hold the flame when starting.

- **WOOD SHAVINGS IN EGG CARTONS.** This is a Girl Scout favorite that works well. Collect wood shavings before your next campout. Place them in some egg cartons and cover with wax. Pull off a section for each fire you need to build. This is not very considerate of space in your pack, but it makes a great choice for car camping. I do like this idea because it is a nice way of getting kids involved in planning for outdoor adventure and then involving them safely in building the fire.

The table on the previous page lists some of the fuel sources we've covered along with the best choice (1) and the worst choice (7) for each application.

REAL-LIFE SKILLS: MAKING FIRE IN THE RAIN

Put Dad out back with a grill, lighter fluid and a lighter, and you will have a fire, even in the rain. Put that same dad out in the woods in the rain when he needs to make a fire for safety, warmth or cooking, and maybe not. Making fire in the rain is difficult for the average wilderness adventurer. I want to help you with that. Here are the basic steps you can follow so you can be the hero (or heroine) in the outdoors:

- When you source your materials, avoid picking them up off the ground. The ground holds moisture and makes it difficult for any material lying on it to get dry, even on a normal day. Source hanging material that gets plenty of air circulation and as much sunlight as possible. You can nearly always find dead branches hanging or leaning against trees. Finding a tree that has fallen over is bonus. Break off branches that are stuck up in the air from the dead tree.

- If there are any conifers (e.g., pine, cedar) in the area, look around and under them. Conifers have a resin in them that works as a fuel extender and is more flammable than the typical tree. They also keep their crown throughout the year and shed water very well. Any dead material under a conifer is going to be dryer than in other locations.

- As you gather materials and start the process of taking it to where you are going to build a fire, protect it from further moisture. I typically have a garbage bag for such things, or I use a tarp. Small stuff can be placed inside a rain jacket as you are walking around and gathering additional material.

- Once you have enough materials gathered, prepare the ground and your tinder materials to get the fire started. You should remove any standing moisture from the ground by raking it off. Build a good, dry platform to build your fire on with sticks you have gathered. Cover this so it doesn't get rained on. I call this a fire raft, because that is what it looks like.

- Prepare the small sticks by scraping all the bark from them. Bark will hold a significant amount of moisture and will shed much of it as well. This means that much of the wood inside the branch will be dry. I prepare enough materials in advance that I estimate the fire will be sizable and able to last half an hour without much assistance. Once it is going, I can go short distances to gather other materials. Another method is to gather all your materials for your purpose before starting to ignite the fire.

- Split larger sticks by batoning them with your knife (see the photo below). This also serves to get down into the heart of the branch, where it is more likely to be dry. Protect these materials from getting moisture on them as well.

- If you have a fire tinder accelerant (as we discussed earlier), get it out and have it ready. If not, make some feather sticks and small shavings to create a tinder bundle. The more edge you create on material, the easier the item is to ignite.

- I place my fuel source (see pages 128–130) or tinder bundle on the dry base. At this point I either hover over the setup so no more rain gets on it, or I get a companion to do it so I can focus on materials.

- I place my fuel source on the dry base I built. If I have plenty of small and dry tinder, I will add it as well, sparingly placing it on the main fuel source. This will help it get more oxygen. I then light my fuel source and watch it closely.

- If there is moisture, the fire may have difficulty lighting so I add oxygen by blowing on it or fanning it with any items I have available. This will increase the amount of heat.

- As I recognize that other material is being lit, I will continue to add materials and as the fire gets larger, I add larger materials.

- My goal is to have materials that are roughly the size of my wrist ignited and burning before I consider it a sustainable fire in the rain. I will continue to add materials to make the fire as large as I need it to be.

- In general, you should build a fire where it is sheltered from as much wind and rain as possible. Some wind is good to keep it going. Too much will make it more difficult to get started. Can there be too much rain? Yes, if you do not shelter the fire in any way. Very rarely does a downpour come straight down. You can easily shelter a fire by placing it near a rock, tree or other natural formation opposite the side of the prevailing winds.

Batoning gets to the dry portion of any woody stem.

CHAPTER 6
WATER AND HYDRATION

Water is one of the basic needs of survival of mankind and water can destroy it, too. That is the power of nature.

—Vikas Khanna

IN 2005, I TRAVELED FROM MY HOME IN KENTUCKY TO ATTEND A CLASS IN North Carolina. The mountains there, which might be considered hills by many, are of the same ecology as my home state. The class I was attending required me to literally live off the land with very minimal supplies for a week. I did have the benefit of being able to use a small poncho and a water bottle. On the first night, I was using them both to gather clean water for myself.

I had set the tarp over a sapling and allowed a wrinkle to run from the top to the bottom of it. This wrinkle served as a guttering system to run water directly into the water bottle I placed at the bottom of the tarp. Clean, drinkable water that I could drink without concern for contaminants is hard to find in the wilderness these days. Rainwater is clean, however, and I felt as if had I been gifted the extremely hard rain through the night.

Somewhere in the middle of the night I got a feeling "down there" that was a bit wet and eye-opening—literally. When I woke up to find that my bottom half was soaked, I had to turn on my head lamp to see what was going on. I then found myself eye to eye with a forest creature. In my sleep-deprived state, I wasn't sure if I was seeing accurately or if I was dreaming, so I rubbed my eyes and took another look. Sure enough, within one foot of my head under the tarp with me was a rabbit. He looked at me with a look that said, "Hey man, please let me stay a bit longer—it is raining really hard out there." I gave him a look that replied, "Yeah, I get it—you are welcome to hang out a while longer." So as not to startle my new bunk mate, I slowly readjusted my tarp and gear so I was no longer getting rained on and went back to sleep. When I woke up the next day, it had quit raining, my water bottle was overflowing with clean water and my little buddy had hoppity-hopped his way out into the wilderness.

CONTAINERS

CARRY IT WITH YOU AND IN YOU

It has been said before, and it's worth saying again: Approximately 60 percent of adult human bodies are made up of water. We need water, and lots of it, every day to ensure we function at peak efficiency. Consider these facts:

- Water is the primary component responsible for maintaining our pliable yet strong vascular system. Without water, our arteries and veins are overworked and cannot transport our blood properly.

- Water assists in taking the food we eat, breaking it down with our stomach acids and converting it into energy. Without it we are more sluggish and tired and less effective.

- Water and healthy fats are responsible for ensuring that our joints, including our spines, function properly.

- When we are even mildly dehydrated, we will experience dry mouth, headache, muscle aches, lack of sweating and more. Simply put, we cannot operate efficiently without water.

Trip planning is essential to maintaining a healthy level of hydration during wilderness adventuring. That is another reason why understanding how to utilize a map, a compass and a GPS system is critical to your overall enjoyment of your trip. Take the opportunity to preplan your trip so you will know how much water you will need to bring and when and where resupply options in the wilderness will be available to you. There is a sequence of methods of maintaining or obtaining water that I utilize, which is heavily dependent on what sort of trip I am taking.

Water bottles come in various configurations. Many people customize them with their favorite stickers.

The first thing you should determine is how much water you need. Just to stay alive, your body needs less than ½ gallon (1.9 L) of water per day. If you want to be a highly efficient and working machine, you will need more than 1 gallon (3.8 L) of water per day. If you add exertion through hiking, hunting, bushcrafting and so on, you could easily use 1 to 2 gallons (3.8 to 7.6 L) per day. Most of this would be for hydration, and some would be utilized for hygiene. It is estimated that 75 percent of Americans walk around at various levels of dehydration daily. I read those statistics for many years and scoffed at them because I felt I was okay and knew that I was not drinking that much water. I also had some significant spine and joint issues that I had attributed to farming, sports and heavy packs. I had a doctor who came to one of my classes and matter-of-factly stated that my issues were most likely due to dehydration. I committed to drinking 1 gallon (3.8 L) of water per day for a month. My life has been completely different ever since. Most of my joint and back issues were due to simply not having enough water in my body.

Before we dig into the strategies of procuring and cleaning water, I think we should start with the most common and easiest to way to get clean water: starting any trip with a water bottle. I have a water bottle with me nearly all of the time, whether I am in the wilderness or sitting at my computer writing. Not all water bottles are created equal, however, and you should consider the materials discussed in this chapter when choosing one for yourself.

My favorite bottle is a 27-ounce (810-ml) stainless steel bottle from Klean Kanteen (approximately $15). Like many other people's bottles, mine is covered in stickers from years of training with others and visiting places while teaching classes for Nature Reliance School. I prefer this style because in a survival situation, it is easy to boil water in, it is incredibly tough, the water flows easily through the spout and the common sport cap is built to be easily connected with a carabiner or cordage to my pack. For trips that last a weekend or longer, I also have a 40-ounce (1.2-L) Klean Kanteen bottle. This simply allows me to purify water less often. I do have others that I use as well, so let's dig into the options available to us.

STAINLESS STEEL

The reason I use stainless steel as my go-to is because I can carry water, lemonade, hot tea and virtually any other liquid and it will not be problematic in anyway. Klean Kanteen has become the king of water bottles. They make bottles in dozens of shapes, sizes and colors and with many kinds of tops. Some tops come off to expose the entire mouth of the bottle; others have a sport cap so you can drink without uncovering the bottle. I prefer the sport cap because of simple operator error: If I happen to drop my bottle while drinking, I don't lose all the contents with a sport cap. This seems unimportant, but once I have worked diligently to clean water in the wilderness I want to ensure I don't lose it.

PLASTIC

There are countless plastic water bottles available that range from inexpensive (and sometimes free) promotional bottles to the unopposed king of plastic bottles, Nalgene. I have several Nalgene bottles that I have used for many years. Despite the hardiness of stainless steel bottles, I do prefer the taste I get from my Nalgene bottles. The Nalgene 32-ounce (960-ml) wide mouth bottle (approximately $21) has been a best seller for nearly twenty years now. I actually do not prefer them, though.

My Kleen Kanteen bottle shown here has gone on as many trips as I have for nearly 10 years now.

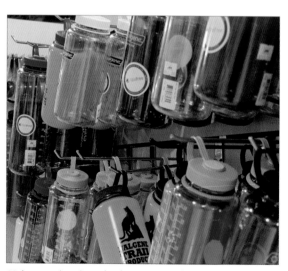

Nalgene makes plastic bottles in various shapes and sizes to suit any outdoorsperson.

I prefer the smallmouth bottles more. The narrower mouth makes the bottle a bit harder to clean but I like drinking from it better. Another big player in plastic bottles is CamelBak. Many of their bottles have straws in them so you don't have to turn your bottle up. Water-purifying companies, such as Sawyer and Aquamira (who makes the Aquamira Frontier Pro filter), also have their own branded bottles and partner with other brands to offer plastic bottles with integrated water purifiers in them as well.

GLASS

For regular wilderness use, you would think glass is the last material you would want. I thought the same thing until I purchased a CamelBak eddy® 0.7L bottle (approximately $16) with integrated straw. I do not use it for serious backcountry trips because it is heavy and more susceptible to breaking than other options available. I do, however, use it during short day trips and car camping. Glass is the only choice that I have mentioned thus far that does not leave me with an aftertaste of the bottle. Stainless steel gives a trace of metallic taste and plastics leave me with a slight plastic aftertaste. Glass does not do that, so I use it when I can. It is my preferred bottle at home as well.

INSULATED

The most common thing for people to carry nowadays is insulated bottles. These are not the large, bulky thermoses we have become accustomed to. These are come in shapes and sizes similar to typical water bottles. This allows you to keep hot things hot and cold things cold much longer than you can with a typical bottle. Insulated bottles are great for day hikes, picnics and similar trips (including trips high in the mountains, where you can get cool water and keep it that way). I have two from Klean Kanteen that are stainless steel.

Glass bottles, such as my CamelBak Eddy (shown here), are great for car camping, but probably too heavy to be worthwhile for backcountry hiking.

I prefer a water bottle with a small mouthpiece, as does my daughter (pictured here), since they are less likely to spill water.

ALUMINUM

Aluminum is the typical choice for promotional items and inexpensive models to gain market share. Aside from cost, aluminum bottles may be tempting because they are the lightest option available. But I avoid these at all costs. Aluminum has been linked to Alzheimer's disease. If you feel you must get an aluminum bottle, make sure you choose one that is plastic-lined to protect the liquids you are drinking from the aluminum. With that said, the best route is to simply avoid aluminum bottles.

In general, I prefer bottles that do not have large mouths on them, but that is definitely a matter of personal taste. I will detail in the final chapter some ways to get your family, particularly kids, involved in the outdoors but just know that water bottles are one of the keys. If you get your child their own special bottle that they can put their favorite stickers on, you will have a more healthfully hydrated child.

Also available are water bladders, which stay in your pack and have a long flexible straw for hands-free drinking. They are easy to use and carry. I have carried CamelBak systems of various sizes and functions for over twenty years now. I first started carrying them when I was mountain biking quite a bit. CamelBak dominates this market and they have bladders of every size, function and style you could possibly imagine.

FIELD AND HOME CARE OF WATER BOTTLES

In the field, the best way to take care of your bottles is to keep them close to you and not toss them around. There are any number of pouches, nylon handles and much more that you can get to personalize your carry method. At home, I run some water with bleach through the bottle and drinking spout, and then rinse with clean water. For bottles that have plastic O-rings, I will lubricate those with a food-grade oil (such as olive oil) from time to time just to ensure they stay pliable and to keep them from drying out.

PURIFIERS AND FILTERS

WHICH IS WHICH AND WHY IT'S IMPORTANT

If you are planning on spending just a portion of the day outdoors, your best strategy is to start the day well hydrated and start the hike with a 25- to 30-ounce (750- to 900-ml) bottle full of clean water (or a backpack-style water bladder). If you are hiking in extremely hot weather and are sweating profusely, you will obviously need more. Since I tend to be overkill on safety when it comes to outdoor adventuring, I carry a water filter straw with me as well—even on day hikes. My preferred choice is the Sawyer MINI squeeze system.

If you are staying overnight, you will want more water. There are a host of ways to do this.

CARRYING YOUR WATER IN

Some locations do not have water that you can filter and use; you will need to carry everything with you. You may also choose to do this if for some reason you believe the water in the area is suspect. For several years, I have contracted with a local nonprofit to offer environmental educational opportunities to U.S. military members and their family members. These camps are designed to assist the families in integrating with one another on a personal level after long periods of deployment overseas. The first two years I did this, we led the groups in rock climbing, rappelling, bushcraft and many more backcountry practices. We also hauled in all our water needs for at least twenty people. That is a lot of water to haul in for three-day adventures.

The Sawyer MINI squeeze system can clean up to 100,000 gallons (379,000 L) of water effectively, making it a lifetime purifier.

Each person carried their water in MSR Dromedary® bags and similar reservoirs. Dromedary bags are simple devices that hold personal amounts of water, topping off around 1 quart (1 L). Those bags are extremely hardy and withstood a lot of use. Since that time, the Platypus company has come to dominate that market with a range of reservoirs that you can use, such as water bladder systems, gravity-fed purifiers, carriage bags and more. I have two Platypus bags that I take on each class that I teach. They are used for emergency backups if something goes awry or we need some clean water quickly.

Pictured are a few options for water bags. They range in size from personal single-serving pouches, such as Renovo and Sawyer, to bladders, such as the red MSR.

One of my newest pieces of equipment, the Rapid Pure purifier may very well replace my Sawyer MINI in the near future.

CLEANING WATER AS YOU GO

You must understand two things before digging into water cleaners. The first is the different contaminants you might find in water (see the sidebar on page 145). The second is the different gear pieces you can get to clean water while you are away.

Words have meaning, especially when it comes to clean drinking water. To the uninitiated, it seems like *water purifier* and *water filter* mean the same thing. This is incorrect and the differences are important to your well-being.

WATER FILTER

A water filter is a device designed to remove waterborne protozoa (*Cryptosporidium* and *Giardia*) and bacteria (*E. coli* and Salmonella), but not viruses. For most backcountry trips in America, this will be just fine.

WATER PURIFIER

A water purifier is a device that will remove all three classes of microbes: protozoa, bacteria and viruses. I have used a Sawyer MINI squeeze system (approximately $18) for many years due to its affordability, size, weight and production of water. While writing this book I was introduced to Rapid Pure filters (approximately $45) that serve the same needs and are a bit easier to use. The volume of water they allow through the straw is more than the Sawyer MINI. Each device is different, and you should use one that has been third-party tested for accuracy. Viruses (norovirus and hepatitis A) in water are typically a result of human waste being present. This can happen in third-world countries and, unfortunately, in campgrounds anywhere. Some campgrounds in the United States are regulated heavily; others do not have has as much oversight. I never drink water from campground water spigots or fountains without cleaning the water first.

My Katadyn Hiker Pro has been used for hundreds of gallons of water with military, law-enforcement and other group classes.

WATER PUMP

Water pumps also filter water. They will have a handle to create pressure rather than requiring you to squeeze a bag. My favorite is the Katadyn Hiker Pro. This, and other pumps like it, have an intake tube that is placed in the water. The pump pulls water out and through the filter where it then leaves through an outtake hose and into a container. The Katadyn Hiker Pro also has connecters for all the most popular bottle sizes.

CHEMICAL TABLETS

Chemical tablets are purifying agents that, when placed in water, will purify it. Each tablet form is different, and you need to verify that a third-party tester has determined that it will clean the water. As an example, Aquatabs® will not purify *Cryptosporidium*. That is why I choose Aquamira tablets (approximately $10). Aquamira tablets use a chlorine dioxide formula. They do handle all three contaminants. Make sure you read the manufacturer's directions for use. Aquamira tablets, for example, take up to 30 minutes to kill *Giardia* and four hours to kill *Cryptosporidium*.

CHEMICAL DROPS

Chemical drops work the same way as chemical tablets. They require you to make the mixture in the field by combining drops from two different bottles. Although this system works, I think it is cumbersome to use and opt for the tablets instead. Drops and tablets both leave an odd taste in the water.

IODINE DROPS

Iodine is good at killing *Giardia* but does not kill *Cryptosporidium*.

UV LIGHT

UV light does not kill or otherwise remove the three main contaminants from the water. It does, however, make them inert. If you use a UV light and then drink the water, the inert contaminants will pass through your body without causing you any harm. Unless you prefilter the water, there will be suspended particulates in the water. You must have particulate-free, clear water for UV light options to work correctly. These particulates will cause the UV light to not pass through the water as it should. You will believe you have clean water when you do not.

METAL BOTTLE OR POT AND STOVE OR FIRE

The most tried-and-true method is boiling water in a metal bottle or pot over a stove or fire, because the three most-common waterborne contaminants cannot exist in boiling water. All you need to do is bring the water to a rolling boil and you will have clean water. There is a common belief that you need to boil the water for at least a minute (or more) to properly sanitize it. This is a myth and has been disproven in the laboratory. The myth was born out of the fact that water takes longer to boil at high altitude. Somehow, that fact got twisted and led people to believe you must let water boil for

➤ *(Right) Aquamira drops are good at purifying water and easy to pack and carry.*

	INTEGRATED PREFILTER?	REMOVES BACTERIAL CONTAMINANTS?	REMOVES VIRAL CONTAMINANTS?	GOOD FOR GROUP USE?	MANUAL PUMP?	BATTERIES REQUIRED?	HIGH-VOLUME OUTPUT?	CLEANS QUICKLY?
SQUEEZE SYSTEM	No	Yes	Yes	No	No	No	No	Yes
STRAW	No	Yes	Yes	No	No	No	No	No
PUMP	Yes	Yes	Yes	Yes	Yes	No	Yes	Yes
UV LIGHT	No	Yes	Yes	No	No	Yes	No	No
BOILING	No	Yes	Yes	Yes	No	No	Yes	No
GRAVITY-FED	Yes	Yes	Yes	Yes	No	No	Yes	No

longer to clean it. Science has shown that bacterial and viral contaminants cannot survive in water that is 212°F (100°C). Just know that boiling water does not clean all contaminants, particularly chemical ones. However, it does provide you with a visual reference for killing or inactivating the most common ones you could face in a wilderness environment.

Boiling water is also a good choice for silty or other sediment-infused water choices. When you boil the water, the sediment will settle to the bottom of your container. You can also avoid this altogether by using a prefilter before placing the water in your container. This is another good way to use your handy bandana that I suggest you have with you always.

Check out the sidebar on the next page to understand the common contaminants of water in the wilderness. I originally wrote this for my book *Extreme Wilderness Survival*; it is good info and well worth understanding before we visually break down all the various uses and tools for cleaning water.

The table above will help you to understand the various ways you can clean water. In the rows, I have listed the various ways or devices you can use to clean water. In the columns, I have listed the important items of consideration. I put an *X* in that column if that device can accomplish the task listed.

FIELD AND HOME CARE OF WATER PURIFIERS

In the field, I remove all the water I can when I use purifiers. They can break if they freeze, so in cold weather I go overboard by blowing out all the water I can and also shaking it vigorously. Anytime I use purifiers on a trip, I will run bleach through them when I get home. I then rinse them with clean water. If the purifier is removable, I will sometimes boil it instead of bleaching it. Regular bleaching can break down the filters and make them more susceptible to breaking or deteriorating.

WATERBORNE CONTAMINANTS

There are four main sources of waterborne threats that pose a problem when they make their way into the human body:

1. **PROTOZOAN.** These are the most-common contaminants. *Giardia* and *Cryptosporidium* are the biggest culprits. Symptoms are diarrhea, stomach cramps, weight loss (in longer-term problems) and severe fatigue. The incubation period (how long they take to start causing problems after entering the body) is quite varied. *Giardia* typically takes over a week to two weeks. *Cryptosporidium* can cause issues within a few days.

2. **VIRAL.** Viruses sometimes transmitted through unclean water include rotavirus, enterovirus and hepatitis A. You will notice a fever, fatigue, diarrhea, nausea and vomiting. Incubation times vary greatly and are dependent on the virus. Some set up as quickly as one day; others may take a full month.

3. **BACTERIAL.** Bacterial contaminants are more common than the others. Bacteria, such as Salmonella and *E. coli*, can trigger diarrhea, pain in your abdomen, nausea and vomiting. Depending on your health and the number of bacteria, you can start experiencing problems from one day up to two weeks after taking them in.

4. **CHEMICAL.** There is no standard understanding of how chemical contaminants will affect us. Their origins are incredibly broad (e.g., agricultural runoff, industrial waste and human waste runoff).

A metal container that you can boil water in, heat food in and eat out of is an incredibly important tool in the backcountry.

Water tablets are a lightweight option for carrying a water purifier with you in the backcountry.

CHAPTER 7
FOOD

A crude meal, no doubt, but the best of all sauces is hunger.

—Edward Abbey, *Desert Solitaire*

I AM NOT SURE WHY, BUT SOME OF MY MOST VIVID MEMORIES OF EATING WHILE in the outdoors have come from deer hunting trips. I could literally write you a book on the stories of deer hunting camp food that occurred in Owen County and Henry County, Kentucky. There are two distinct stories that come from the Owen County hunts that are memorable because they cover both ends of the spectrum of eating in the outdoors. In the late 1980s, Owen County had a population of just under 10,000 people spread out over 354 square miles (917 square km)—not a whole lot of people for a large area. What Owen County does have a lot of is white-tailed deer. My dad knew a gentleman whose father had a large farm there, much of which was wooded and was home to a lot of deer. We were pleased that he gave us an opportunity to hunt there. It was there that my dad and the natural world started teaching me about deer hunting.

The first of my stories occurred one day when my dad and I had come out from the hunt to warm up by moving around a bit and getting some food in our bellies. My dad had brought a classic Coleman camp stove and we set it up on the tailgate of his truck. We also had a classic brand of canned beef stew as our chosen delicacy for lunch. We got the stove going, opened the can and set it on the stove to warm. While waiting, we turned our backs to the stove to try to spot some deer on the hillside opposite us. A few hundred yards away we were pleased to watch as two deer came across the hillside and jumped a fence. A third deer came by a few moments later and crawled under the fence. That is out of the ordinary for a deer, and I believe it's part of the reason I can still see those deer in my mind 30 years later.

What is also nearly as vivid in my memory is the sound and then the sight of the beef stew spewing out of the can and all over the place. My dad and I had gotten a unique show with the deer and had forgotten about the beef stew. My dad did his best. He sprang into action, trying to save it. It was to no avail, though. The stew had already made its way to places that made it inedible. Have you ever had one of those moments where you are in shock over something very simple and cannot believe it has happened? This was one of those times. My dad and I looked at each other in disbelief. My hunger and desire for warmth was going to come from somewhere else than that beef stew.

I do not intend on leaving you disheartened, though.

My dad and I took another hunting trip to that same farm. We were deer hunting when out of nowhere came what we in Kentucky lovingly refer to as a gulley washer storm. Translated: lots and lots of rain. It was a miserable hunt, to say the least. My dad and I were doing our best to wait it out while sitting in the cab of his truck. I was cold, wet and hungry. Although those three things build character, which I am grateful to have, they don't make a teenage boy very happy in the moment. It was raining so hard that we could not see the front of the truck. Out of nowhere, like a mirage in the night, came the landowner. He had with him two warm and juicy hamburgers. I suppose he felt sorry for us sitting out in his barn lot while he was inside enjoying dinner. Remember that moment of disbelief I mentioned in the story above? Well, that same feeling came back. However, it was on the opposite end of the spectrum this time. Simply put, that was the best hamburger I have ever had in my 48 years of life.

FOOD CHOICES

DETERMINING WHAT IS BEST FOR YOUR NEEDS AND MORALE

There are a lot of food choices available, and we should know how they work for us and how they will satisfy our needs (and a few of our wants). I taught a wilderness safety and survival class many years ago in which one of the students was an employee at a fruit-packing plant. Specifically, he put grapes into boxes for shipment out to grocery stores. If the fruit doesn't meet a time allotment for shipment, it cannot be shipped and must be discarded or taken home by the employees. At that class we had a pavilion and several tables on which to do coursework. The student set out several boxes full of grapes for everyone to share. We all thought they were delicious. When I say *we*, I mean the students in class and the ten raccoons that found the grapes in the middle of the night. I woke to a disturbance, turned my headlamp on and was met by the growl and hiss of several raccoons. Needless to say, we let the racoons have the grapes after that. Your food choices must satisfy your needs and keep the animals away. Let's look at some good options.

FREEZE-DRIED AND DEHYDRATED FOODS

If you are new to the outdoor lifestyle, you will be amazed at the various freeze-dried and dehydrated options available. They offer great taste, which can prove to be a nice morale boost in the field. I am a big fan of Mountain House Spaghetti with Meat Sauce (approximately $8). This brand tends to be a bit pricey, which adds up when you are planning a multiday trip. However, Mountain House meals are very easy to prepare. Just add hot water and you have a hot meal in about ten minutes.

Mountain House meals have a been a staple on backcountry trips for me. Don't forget the Raspberry Crumble dessert.

It can be confusing to figure out which food is freeze-dried and which is dehydrated. Since they make up a large portion of our choices, let's break them down a bit more.

FREEZE-DRIED FOODS

The process of manufacturing a freeze-dried meal is more expensive and therefore that cost is passed on to the consumer. It is my opinion that sometimes this is worth it. The process for freeze-drying removes 98 to 99 percent of the moisture content in the food. Freeze-drying also retains a high percentage of the vitamins and minerals in the food.

DEHYDRATED FOODS

The process for dehydration is less expensive. There are even very affordable options to do it at home. Dehydration only removes about 90 percent of the moisture content in the food. This is an issue only when you want to store food for long periods of time. For the typical outdoorsperson interested in creating palatable, easy-to-carry food sources, this is the way to go in my opinion. You can make your own meal choices at home. It can be time-consuming, though. If you do not want to invest the amount of time (it varies with the quality of your dehydrator), you can easily purchase dehydrated meals from your local outdoor store.

Dry Foods

Noodles, rice and similar choices are great because they are light and take up little space in your gear.

Canned Foods

Remember my first backpacking trip that I mentioned in Chapter 1? I carried canned foods and paid the price because they were so heavy and bulky. I do think canned foods are a good choice for car campers. One big advantage of canned food is that small animals, like raccoons, and big animals, like bears, cannot smell through cans. This, if nothing else, makes them a good choice.

Drink Mixes

Drink mixes are a great way to get extra calories, increase morale and add a little bit of pep to your step. I don't use these exclusively; of course, water is healthier.

Drink mixes come in two main types. The first type is powdered drink mixes that you simply pour into your favorite water container and shake. The second type is squeezable liquids. For outdoor use, I prefer the powders from Vitalyte. For liquids (I use them regularly on camping trips), I prefer the liquids from MiO. In cold weather, I love hot chocolate, hands down. Warm liquids provide comfort against the cold as well as a morale boost; my first choice is hot chocolate, but maybe it's tea or coffee for you. Each of these come in caffeinated and decaffeinated versions.

Finally, do not confuse drink mixes with protein workout drinks or similar products. The mixes we've covered here are for the electrolytes or morale boost more than anything else.

Spices

I am a big fan of taking my favorite spices to add to various meals (Himalayan pink salt is my favorite). Spices are most useful when cooking food that you bring from home or wild game you harvest in the field. The meals already prepped for you, such as backpacker meals, contain a large amount of sodium, so adding more is not warranted.

Meals-Ready-to-Eat

I am fortunate to train numerous active and discharged military personnel. Nearly all of them despise the thought of eating meals-ready-to-eat (MREs), mostly because they had to eat them for lengthy periods of time with no other choices. For the rest of us, MREs can be a good choice. They come with a primary protein, plenty of carbs, spices, a dessert and have their own cooking device that requires you to supply only water. MREs are heavy and not good choices for backpackers. But for those who are on a camping trip or in a class like I teach at Nature Reliance School, they can save a lot of packing headaches with a complete meal and stove in one neat package.

CAMP FOOD

By *camp food*, I mean bring it all. Car camping, glamping, whatever your flavor is, go ahead and take it all with you, whatever you eat at home. Get a good cooler, a good camp stove (I will show you mine shortly) and a good outdoor cook set. You will make some mistakes, learn some lessons and get better at it as you continue to go outside. Even on car-camping trips, I like to take a few backpacker meals so I can try new things over the fire. If things go south (maybe you've burned a few meals like me), then you have a backup meal plan. However, what will probably happen is you will find you do well out there and enjoy cooking outside. A common thing overheard at campfire mealtime is, "Food just seems to taste better out here." That is so very true.

CALORIC NEEDS

STAY FUELED AND READY FOR ADVENTURE

Food can be a huge downer or a huge morale booster, depending on how well you plan. I want to help you find the gear and food that will assist you in having a wonderful time while eating in the wilderness. It has been said by many that backpackers pack their fears. One of the biggest fears is not having enough food. Much like we did in Chapter 5 on fire, we need to look at this issue as science and take the subjective emotion out of the equation.

The first thing we must do is understand the role food plays in keeping our bodies working at peak efficiency. I need to consume a minimum of 2,500 calories per day to function, and I divide these between protein and carbs in such a way that I don't make my body do overtime to process the calories. Please bear in mind that I am not a typical backpacker putting lots of miles in anymore—I spend more time studying nature and equipment or assisting my students than anything else. Therefore, I don't burn a lot of calories. I will detail some calculations for backpackers and share how I divide the 2,500 calories between carbs and protein a bit later.

I avoid most processed foods. Simply because they taste good, I do have an MRE or a backpacker meal on occasion to break up the monotony. I considered proper caloric intake from two approaches to come up with a good sense on caloric planning for outdoor adventure. The first set of requirements I considered was that of your typical backpacker. I queried several backpacking friends and the staff at the stores in my area to see what most of them considered an adequate number of calories. Nearly every single one of them agreed with me that 2,500 calories was the standard most people should aim for when planning for food. This assumes the person has little exertion. Serious hiking and backpacking involve lots of exertion and will therefore require more calories.

I also looked at the vast amount of research from the U.S. military and its nutrition needs for basic training. I did this because while members of the military are often engaged in lots of physical exercise, they also do other work and a whole lot of "hurry up and wait." This means a lot of anaerobic exercise throughout very long days. The calorie count suggested for them was 2,400 calories per day. You can see why I think it is safe to assume that those are good numbers to start with. Let's use 2,500 calories, because it is an easy number to remember. The question lies in how to best use those calories for our purposes.

We must first give attention to various aspects of our trip and put them up against our need for food.

EXERTION

You need to estimate the number of calories you think you will be burning during the activity you will be engaged in. A good way to go about getting an estimate is to get a heart rate monitor and fitness app. These will allow you to input your personal data—such as your age, weight and fitness level—and monitor yourself as you walk. I am not suggesting you do this every time. If you are new to outdoor activities you may surprise yourself at how much (or little) you burn. Getting this estimate will then help you preplan your activities and meals to support them.

TRIP LENGTH

Knowing how long you plan to be out and planning for contingencies is paramount. Preplanning your route with the aid of topography maps will help tremendously. This allows you to see what portions of a trip will involve high levels of exertion. For high-intensity days, you may want to have another 500 calories in reserve. It is not the norm anymore, but on a rare occasion I will be engaged in outdoor activities for two or three weeks at time because I have back-to-back classes or events I am guiding. I have noticed that once my body starts to dig heavily into fat reserves due to malnourishment, I have a strong desire to eat. Upon further investigation with dieticians, I have determined this is natural. It is the way our bodies give us an alert message, as if to say, "You *need* to eat." It is easy in this stage to overeat. Recognize that it is coming and you can deal with it accordingly.

SPACE

I like to carry food that takes up as little space as possible. One way to do this is to carry foods that can all go in one bag and then get out only what you need for various meals. Food such as rice, beans, oatmeal and noodles are easy ways to carry one large container with lots of food that covers several meals.

MORALE

It is best to view food as fuel for your body and to not eat for fun. I must say, though, that having a special treat of some sort with your food will increase your overall morale. You can increase the enjoyment factor of your meal by packing some honey packets or a shaker with various seasonings in it. Each of these take up minimal space and weight in your gear but can add much to your well-being.

NUTRITION

You will need carbohydrates for energy and protein to help your muscles recover from fatigue and breakdown. A good thing to consider is the glycemic index (GI) of various foods. You can do a quick Internet search to see the GI of the foods you prefer. Foods with a low GI (55 or less) are more slowly digested, absorbed and metabolized. These are the foods that I like to take with me on trips. Foods that have a high GI are basically metabolized in a short period of time and your body will want to eat again. The most common high-GI food eaten on the trail is oatmeal. It is also easy to pack and prepare. Any brand of trail bars are good choices for this as well (I am fond of CLIF Bars®).

WATER AVAILABILITY

Some meals will need to be rehydrated before consumption. You need to factor in that water if you are carrying it or know where water sources are along your trip.

PREPARATION

Obviously, prepping food in the wilderness is nothing like prepping it at home. For starters, there is typically no type of flat surface for you to work on other than the ground. To keep things simple, I like eating one main meal when I stop to rest for the night and "grazing" during the day.

You need to stay fueled to see more beautiful scenery in the outdoors.

MEAL PLANNING

WILDERNESS ADVENTURING IS HARD (SO PLAN AHEAD)

Now that we have a good understanding of the various food choices available and our basic caloric needs, let's take a look at how best to keep ourselves fueled for adventure. I will break down how I handle a basic day. I did an incredible amount of research on this topic for my first book and even more for this one. I am a fan of making things simple, and that research boiled down to two schools of thought:

1. Determine how many calories you will burn per day and pack that many calories.

2. Determine how many meals and how often you want to eat and pack that amount of food.

Removing all emotion from the equation, I believe the first option is a more accurate way of getting what you need. The second option is the one that will most likely give you better morale. While your body is an engine and you can think of food as being the energy you need to keep it running, you must also consider that your mind-set and how you view the activity you are doing can also overcome some, but not all, deficiencies. I am going to offer you suggestions here that offer a hybrid of both of these options.

If you are an average adult, your caloric burn will equal approximately 25 calories per pound (450 g) of body weight for strenuous activity. This would include backpacking with a heavy pack in rough terrain. For the sake of discussion, let's assume that you weigh 180 pounds (81 kg), you are moderately fit and you are hiking 8 hours per day. This means you need to budget about 4,500 calories to meet your needs.

Those are the basics of the physical aspect of your needs, but in the backcountry you must also consider a multitude of other factors, such as the following:

NUTRITION

If you seek only to make your mind-set happy, you will forego proper nutrition and that is not going to work. You must have some complex carbohydrates and proteins that give you both fuel and material to help your muscles heal from the strenuous activity of hiking. The most common form of this carbohydrate-protein combination comes in good old raisins and peanuts, mostly commonly referred to as GORP (see the sidebar on page 154 for my favorite recipe), and marketed in stores as trail mix. GORP provides both the carbs and proteins you need to keep going. I have had multiday trips in which I have existed on nothing more than this. That is incredibly boring and gets old. Not to mention it takes up considerable space in your pack and if you put it in one bag, it is easy to overeat when you are hungry.

TRASH AND WASTE

Although trail bars and such are great, they can create a problem for packing. If I am going on multiday trips, I will remove the packaging and put all of my bars in a resealable bag. This cuts down on waste tremendously.

CALORIES

Experienced backpackers understand that a hiking trip is not the time to go into a weight-loss program. A large number of beginners do, though, so avoid this pitfall. You need to have proper nutrition and energy, and calories will provide those for you. If you are not already working out regularly, weight loss will come naturally with so much strenuous activity.

WATER

Since many premade backpacker meals require water, you will need to carry out some good planning to make sure you have plenty for hydration, meal preparation and hygiene. So do not let this slip through the cracks of preplanning. Here is a list of my favorite brands of premade meals that require the addition of water:

- **MOUNTAIN HOUSE:** These meals have been a staple at Nature Reliance School for classes and my family outings for many, many years. They combine tasty food with affordability more than other options. You can pick up an entrée for around $8 that the package says is two servings. That is for you sitting at home, watching TV. For you out on the trail, that is one serving you will enjoy and need. There are a variety of meals offered but most come in at the 600-calorie-per-bag range. For dessert, the Mountain House Raspberry Crumble is also great. My kids still talk about some great trips out hiking and eating Raspberry Crumble as a treat a decade later.

- **BACKPACKER'S PANTRY:** This brand comes in as a close second as my favorite. Backpacker's Pantry's foods are about the same price as Mountain House's offerings. They also have some incredibly good choices that are out of the normal food you would consider for backpacking. Case in point: The pad thai is great. I go back and forth between Mountain House and Backpacker's Pantry based solely on my taste buds at the time I am packing. Backpacker's Pantry also comes in at the 600-calorie (or more) range. As an example, the pad thai that I love is obviously heavy on the noodles—it has nearly 900 calories in one bag.

- **COLEMAN:** These meals are one of the less-expensive meal offerings at around $5. Don't let that dissuade you from finding a meal choice that you prefer. They have a nice variety as well (Cheesy Tomato Pasta is my favorite). With all due respect, they did have one meal choice that was unfit to eat, the Mountain Man Stew. As I was doing research for this chapter, I queried Coleman about it and they said I was not the only one who felt that way so they removed it from their lineup. With that said, I have had about five of their meals and they were all tasty and satisfying. I love it when companies listen to customer feedback and aim to please.

Organic choices are becoming more popular as well. Backpacker's Pantry offers some, as does Outdoor Herbivore. If organic food choices are important in your planning, know that you have premade choices. Or you can dehydrate your own at home. Both options will make tasty and healthy meals.

It will serve you well to get some ideas about how the actual meals should be laid out. I have a strategy to stretch out my energy needs along with my other trail tasks.

BREAKFAST

Breakfast usually takes up about 30 percent of my calorie intake for the day. I like breakfast to be simple so that I can clean my camp and get onto the trail or start other tasks at hand. Instant oatmeal, granola, dry cereals and dried fruits are my favorite choices. Although I do not like eating a heavy breakfast in the wilderness, many of my students do. Mountain House makes some good breakfast choices that my students really enjoy, particularly the biscuits and gravy, bacon and eggs and similar dehydrated choices. One of my good friends likes to take pancake batter along with some spreadable jellies for a nice breakfast treat.

LUNCH AND SNACKS

Lunch and snacks take up approximately 20 to 30 percent of my caloric intake for the day. If I am doing a long-weekend or weeklong class, I prefer to eat energy bars and GORP+ (see the sidebar below) throughout the day, rather than stopping and setting up a stove to make a big meal. I do like to take a long break during lunch to rest and take care of my hygiene needs. Eating some grazing-friendly foods is a way that I can meet all of those goals.

DINNER

Dinner usually takes up approximately 50 percent of my caloric intake for the day. Everyone needs goals to accomplish hard tasks, and this is one for me. I enjoy saving a nice meal for dinnertime. After I get my camp set up and I get ready to go to bed, I then set about making dinner: Sometimes I prepare a dehydrated meal that has great taste, or sometimes I even bring instant mashed potatoes and packaged chicken breast for a very hearty meal. Either way, I do what I can to reward my hard work with a nice meal at night.

GORP+

Certainly, the traditional GORP will keep you nourished. What about your taste buds? You don't want to leave them blowing in the wind, do you? You could easily include your favorite treats (e.g., yogurt-covered raisins, pretzels and so on) to make a GORP mixture specific to you—what I call GORP+. A word of warning, though: If you don't want your GORP+ to disappear unexpectedly, do not let your trail mates know you have it. Here is my recipe for GORP+.

- 1 (28-oz [794-g]) jar peanut butter

- 1 (12-oz [448-ml]) jar natural honey

- 1 (12-oz [340 g]) box Cheerios

- 3 cups (241 g) rolled oats

- Raisins, dried cranberries or candy-coated chocolate pieces, to taste

Preheat the oven to 350°F (177°C). In a medium saucepan over medium-high heat, combine the peanut butter and honey. Cook until they can be combined thoroughly. Stir in the Cheerios and oats until they are coated evenly with the peanut butter mixture. Lightly spray a large baking sheet with oil. Spread the mixture on the baking sheet. Bake for approximately 10 minutes, until the oats and Cheerios are golden brown on top. Remove the baking sheet from the oven, stir the mixture and place it back in the oven. Bake 10 minutes, until the mixture is golden brown throughout. Remove the baking sheet from the oven and allow the mixture to cool to room temperature. Place it in a sealable container. Add the raisins and other mix-ins, and stir gently to combine.

▶ *(Right) Backpacker's Pantry and Mountain House are common and have great-tasting options for short-term trips.*

STOVES AND FUEL

BECOME A WILDERNESS CHEF

I thoroughly enjoy cooking over a campfire. In some areas it is not feasible, legal or beneficial to the environment to do so. In that situation, we have a variety of cookstoves. I have several of them and have come to appreciate two. For ease of use I have an older Jetboil cup system, which has since been replaced with the Jetboil Zip (approximately $80). The components of this system nest together nicely and are lightweight. I most often use this system to heat water to prepare backpacker meals or hydrate noodles. I have also used it often to warm up some water for hot cocoa on many cool campouts. My other favorite stove is a MSR Whisperlite International (approximately $100). It is a multifuel stove that takes a bit more time and effort to utilize. Once I learned that, it became a pleasure to use. When I am planning a trip and can take only one stove, it is always the MSR Whisperlite International.

There are five types of stoves that we need to know are out there.

LIQUID FUEL STOVES

My beloved MSR Whisperlite International is a liquid-fuel stove. You have two distinct parts to this stove setup: The first part is the burner, the second is the fuel canister. Most liquid-fuel stoves run most efficiently on white gas. The reason that I prefer the MSR Whisperlite International is because it runs on several different fuels, including white gas, kerosene and unleaded automobile fuel.

CANISTER STOVES

My Jetboil is an example of a canister stove. Canister stoves work like your backyard grill, just in miniature form. They have a burner that screws into a fuel canister. These fuel canisters typically run on a mix of isobutane and propane.

ALTERNATIVE FUEL STOVES

Alternative fuel stoves are powered by fuels such as pellets or tablets. There is a growing collection of these coming more readily available; I see them regularly in classes. Almost always, when we have mealtime, most of my students and I have prepared food, eaten and are ready to move on while students with these types of stoves are still getting their food warmed up. I find them to be inefficient time wasters. If all you have is time, then they are an okay choice. Sometimes being in the outdoors is like that. You are on no one's clock.

WOOD-BURNING STOVES

Wood-burning stoves represent a growing segment of outdoor stoves. They utilize woody material from your environment. BioLite makes one now that converts energy from the fire into stored energy in a battery. That battery can then be used to power a cell phone or other small device. Other wood burners provide an apparatus that holds wood in place and allows you to put a pot on top of it easily. A very popular version of this is a Kelly Kettle® Basic Kit (approximately $114 for the Scout version). I wrote Kelly Kettle about these stoves as I researched this topic. They were kind enough to send me one to test, which I have done at three different classes. It works like a champ, albeit a bit slower than gas-fuel alternatives. To be clear, I am not saying it is a bad thing—just be cognizant that you will need extra time to prepare your meals or boil water if you are using this type of stove.

CAR-CAMPING STOVES

Just like the food mentioned on page 149, you can bring as big a stove as you want. I see people in campgrounds at times who bring the grill from the back deck of the house. I think this is a bit overkill, but I am also

Stanley Cooking Cup with foldable stove.

Kelly Kettle® wood-burning stoves are descendants of similar Irish fisherman stoves. Their unique design is easy to use with wood as a fuel source.

supportive of anyone that wants to get outside more, even if it means bringing the propane grill. With that said, I have a favorite Coleman (approximately $90) camp stove that uniquely packs away for storage, is easy to set up and is a very stable platform to cook on (see photo on the next page).

Listed here will be the specifications you should determine when buying a stove for your use. I have also put together a table following these specs on page 159 that will assist you in purchasing your first or next stove. Before consulting the table, though, read through the following items carefully, as they will help you understand it:

- **AVERAGE TIME TO BOIL WATER.** Since most people will utilize stoves to boil water for food prep, this is important to know. In the table following this list, the fastest option got a 1, the slowest a 5.

- **BURN TIME.** This is vital to calculate during preplanning. You should know how long the typical fuel canister will last. The longest-running items a 1 if you are in the wilderness and wood is plentiful, while items bearing a 5 run out the quickest.

- **BACKPACKING.** How easy is a particular stove to use on a backpacking trip? Items with a 1 are the easiest.

- **COLD WEATHER.** This refers to a stove's effectiveness in cold weather. Please note that all isobutane, propane and mixtures of the two will not be effective during cold weather (see the sidebar on page 161 for a story about cold weather and stoves). In my table, 1 is the best to use in cold weather for quick and high heat.

- **EASY TO USE.** I see my students, many of them beginners, utilizing all manner of stoves. This is my opinion based upon those observations. I have labeled the stoves from easiest to use (1) to hardest to use (5).

- **WEIGHT.** If you are camping, the weight of the stove is not an issue—pack it up and bring it. If you are carrying your stove on your back, this is an issue. Options bearing a 1 are the lightest, while the ones with a 5 are the heaviest. I chose wood as 1, because you don't carry it with you. You just get it at your location.

	AVERAGE TIME TO BOIL WATER	BURN TIME	BACKPACKING	COLD WEATHER	EASY TO USE	WEIGHT
LIQUID FUEL	2	3	2	1	3	3
CANISTER	1	5	1	5	2	2
ALTERNATIVE FUEL	5	4	3	3	5	4
WOOD-BURNING	4	1	4	2	4	1
CAR CAMPING	3	2	5	4	1	5

- **IGNITION SOURCE.** Most canister stoves will light with a piezo-style igniter, like the ones found on backyard grills. Other stove choices will often need an ignition source, such as a lighter or a ferro rod. I did not include this in the chart because it needs no further explanation.

As I said earlier, my all-time favorite stove is the MSR Whisperlite International. It burns hot, it packs up small, it is easy to use, it uses multiple fuel sources and it works well in cold temperatures. What is not to like, right? The only slight drawback is the ability to get it lit easily and safely. This is remedied with just a slight amount of practice (see the sidebar on page 160 for my easy steps to guide you).

While the things we've discussed so far comprise the nuts and bolts of stoves, I have many more things to share based on my own personal experiences and the hundreds of people who have been through our classes. Here are a few:

- **Always choose a level surface when setting up any stove.** Your stove will work more efficiently on a level surface, and it is much safer.

- **Do not use canister stoves between your legs while sitting on the ground.** This mistake is more common than you'd think. What people don't realize is that there have been a large number of accidents in which boiling water has spilled over into the users' laps. That is a very painful injury and could prove to be deadly if you are far from help.

- *Never* **use a stove inside a tent, hammock or any other enclosed space.** Excess fuel could ignite and be a terrible fire hazard. Carbon monoxide poisoning occurs when natural gas fuels do not burn efficiently. This can easily kill you.

- **Canister stoves do not work well in cold weather, but you can overcome this by warming the canister itself up.** *Do not* do this with a fire. Place a canister in your jacket so it warms with body heat. You can rotate it in your jacket to get it more uniformly warmed. Alternatively, you can place it in your sleeping bag to warm as well.

- **When using liquid-fuel stoves, always know the recommended number of pumps to create the correct pressure to push the gas out.** Realize that it will almost always bleed off through time. As you continue to use it, there will be less fuel and you will need more pumps.

- **Use a filter to strain your white gas before a trip.** Over time, white gas degrades and leaves sediment in the container. White gas should be clear and not cloudy or colored. If it is not clear, discard it appropriately and get fresh. Old gas will clog your stove and sometimes make it unusable.

- **Some stove manufacturers provide you with a windscreen, which looks like a thick piece of aluminum foil.** They are very valuable to the overall setup of your stove—they will help the burner to burn the gas in a more-uniform fashion, which helps it warm your water and food more uniformly.

◄ *(Left) A folding stove, such as the Coleman shown here, is a great choice for camping and glamping trips. It uses propane as a fuel source.*

LIGHTING AN MSR WHISPERLITE INTERNATIONAL STOVE

- Unfold the burner supports and take the childproof top off the fuel bottle.

- Place the pump into the fuel bottle and tighten it with your hands only, not with any extra tools. Also, do not overtighten it. You will know if you've overtightened if the O-ring is compressed after opening when you are finished using the stove.

- Ensure the valve is turned clockwise to the Off position (remember the old saying, "Righty-tighty, lefty-loosey").

- Place the fuel line into the pump apparatus. Ensure the locking arm is in place. This will keep the burner from coming loose during operation.

- Pump the bottle up with pressure. The number of pumps will be determined by how much liquid fuel is in the bottle. A good starting point is twenty pumps to the bottle. You will feel the pump getting harder to push as it builds up an adequate amount of pressure.

- The next step is to prime the burner with fuel. This is the step that confuses people and causes problems. All you want to do at this point is allow enough fuel out of the bottle to start to fill the primer pan. You will see the wick beginning to get saturated as well.

- As soon as you see the wick getting saturated, turn the fuel completely off.

- Light the fuel in the pan and you will see an orange-red flame coming from the pan and wick. This step is done to warm up the burner to get it prepped to light.

- Once you notice that fuel is beginning to run out and the flame is getting small, the burner is warmed up and ready to be used.

- Slowly turn the valve on so the flame will get more fuel. You will notice the flame starting to get hotter, turning bluer (i.e., hotter) and actually making an audible hiss. These are all good things. Once you see these things occurring, go ahead and open the valve to your desired setting.

FIELD AND HOME CARE OF STOVES

The stoves that I utilize come with a maintenance kit (which can also be purchased separately). Get one of these kits and keep it with your stove. Once per year I replace the removable seals and O-rings on my stoves.

I also keep extra in my stove supplies so I can do this in the field if the need arises. Soot can build up on gas burners as well as cooking supplies. These items are cleaned each time I get home. If the buildup is problematic in the field, I will use sand from a creek as a scouring pad to clean off pots and pans.

LEARNING ABOUT STOVES IN THE COLD

I played an insignificant role in this story, but it is worth retelling. Two of my good friends, who shall remain nameless (you will understand why shortly), asked me to provide them with a shuttle service for a short weekend hike a few years ago. Their intention was for me to drop them off at a campground, which was closed for the season and which also served as a trailhead into the Red River Gorge Geological Area. They were going to hike Friday night and all day Saturday, then I was to pick them up Sunday evening. It wasn't a long hike at all. They were going to hike, explore and just enjoy the sights and sounds of that wonderful area. As the weekend drew near, the weather forecast became more and more foreboding. I did my best to talk them out of it, but they were determined.

When I dropped them off, it was raining so hard I had a difficult time driving. They had a planned location to be at that night, so they put on their rain suits, hoisted up their backpacks and headed off into the pouring rain. I went back home and slept in my warm bed. It's worth noting that while one of them had a cell phone, he had no service in the area to get in touch with me. Upon arriving at their location for the night, they dug into their packs to set up their tent to get out of the rain, only to find that their tent was soaking wet inside one of the packs and each of them was carrying nearly soaking wet sleeping bags and pads. This was partially due to the fact that they did not have a good setup to keep the contents of their packs dry (note that I cover how to keep everything in your pack dry in Chapter 4). In a very smart move, they swallowed their pride a bit and headed back to the campground. They were fortunate enough to find that one of the campground toilets was unlocked. This provided them with a shelter from the rain. It also provided them with a concrete floor, one smelly seat with a hole in it, and no heat of any sort.

Deciding to make the best of the trip, they correctly determined there was enough ventilation to allow them a use a cookstove to warm some water and put together a backpacker meal. The only problem was that they had stored their stoves in their packs and it was so cold that the isobutane mix would not flow, making their stoves useless. They did not have enough experience to know why they were not working, so they did not warm them up. They chose to eat the meals dry. Because the food was dry, it did not take up much space in their hungry bellies, so they each ate two meals. They then filled themselves up with water. The water then helped expand the backpacker meals in their stomachs to unexpected proportions. The result was two bloated young men—in the dark, sleeping on concrete with wet pads and sleeping bags, all in the odoriferous environment of a campground toilet—taking turns purging the backpacker meals on their seat with a hole in it.

I had a sneaking suspicion something might turn them back, so I went back a day early to see if they were around. I found my two friends, packed them up, got them some local grub and took them home.

That, my friend, is what I like to call experience.

CHAPTER 8
PACKS

I like the city. I like the concrete. I like big business. I like being a CEO of my own company and having a lot of responsibilities. At the same time, when I can go off with a backpack or off on a surfboard or even off on a run somewhere in the woods—that's where I'm really happy.

—Matthew McConaughey

CAN YOU PLEASE STAND BY FOR A MOMENT WHILE I GO THROUGH MY GEAR checklist? Sleeping bags, check. Backpacker meals, check. Stuffed animal, check. Dog food, check. Watermelon, check.

I am not certain it went like that, but there was one trip I took in which I looked like a Sherpa about to climb Mount Everest. I had everything on that small checklist and a whole lot more. It was the first overnight backpacking trip that my young family and I were going to take together. I wanted to make sure that my wife, daughter, son, dog and I had what we needed to enjoy our time out.

I packed a pack that had all manner of bed pads, sleeping bags and other gear in it so everyone could stay warm and comfy. We got to our location and my daughter immediately started playing in the woods with sticks, leaves and just about everything else. You know, like little girls do. My son immediately started digging in a hole next to a rock. You know, like little boys do. Shortly thereafter, my son found a piece of an arrowhead, then another, then another. We immediately got him to quit digging because it became obvious that he was on top of an old Native American artifact find. Those are protected and should never be disturbed. My wife decided she was going to have the kids sleep with her for safety and warmth. You know, like moms do. She unzipped one sleeping bag and placed it on a bed of leaves, and placed the others on top. At the same time, I found a nice flat rock, set up my camp stove and commenced heating up water. Everyone had brought their favorite backpacker meal for the night. We were all very excited to have brought the last of the watermelons we had raised in the garden for a nice dessert. Just as a backup, we had also brought a Mountain House Raspberry Crumble for dessert as well. You know, just in case.

After we had finished our dinner, it was time to dig into the watermelon I had hauled the 3 or 4 miles (5 or 6 km) back in the woods, along with the camp stove, fuel, sleeping bags, blankets, a few toys and so on. Much to our dismay, the watermelon was nearly rotten inside and had a strong, fermented smell to it. I disposed of it away from camp and settled back into camp for raspberry crumble and bedtime.

We all went to bed under a beautiful night sky. Everything was perfect.

CHOOSING A PACK

LIGHTEN THE LOAD

Trips like the one my family took are memorable because, while each of us had varying degrees of comfort, if you ask any of us about it, we all remember it. Can we put a price on making memories? For many of us, all it takes is buying a pack and some essential gear and going outside with it. In this chapter, I am going to help you find your first or next backpack.

Name any kind of wilderness travel, and I have most likely done it while wearing a pack: backpacking, day hiking, fishing, hunting, man tracking, orienteering and family picnics. Many years ago, I started designing a pack system that would meet my needs. There were simply some things that I felt were missing in the pack systems available. What I wanted was a system that would provide the following:

- **MODULARITY.** For years I had big packs, small packs, day packs and more. I wanted a system that was modular but allowed the individual pieces to integrate well with one another.

- **TOUGHNESS.** The trend in pack materials is to develop lighter materials. Sometimes the packs I was utilizing and researching were light but simply did not hold up to the abuse of someone that was off-trail as much as on-trail.

- **LIGHTNESS.** The opposite end of that scale is that I did not want to deal with a heavy pack—I just wanted one that was tough enough to withstand some hard use. I wanted something in the middle.

- **AFFORDABILITY.** By coming out with newer and different designs, companies had to recoup their costs in research and development. This meant that many of the packs were simply not affordable.

Picking your first pack is made easy by shopping at a reputable store and getting sized and fitted properly.

After coming up with several designs that suited me, as well as gaining feedback from dozens of friends and students, I was all set to start developing the pack system with a more serious focus. It was then through some more research that I came across Hill People Gear products (an excellent pack of theirs is the Umlindi, approximately $220). It was then that I abandoned my idea of a new pack system, because they had already developed one that was better than I had designed. I jumped right into their products and have not been disappointed since.

HILL PEOPLE GEAR PACK SYSTEM

To begin, we must understand why Hill People Gear created their pack system. It was designed by the company after its owners served as professional smoke jumpers. Smoke jumpers are the brave men and women who go into the backcountry to put out fires. They needed a system that was comfortable, easy to maneuver in and easy change up quickly based on their mission. They created a system to meet those needs as well as the needs of many interested in regular outdoor travel.

After decades of wilderness travel, I have chosen Hill People Gear (Umlindi) packs as my go-to source due to their great modularity.

The Tarapocket extends the volume of the pack and is easily removed for shorter day hikes.

The harness system of any pack should be there for stabilization, not weight bearing.

The hip belts on Hill People Gear packs are easily removed and replaced to meet the needs of various hiking needs. Remember that your hip belt should carry the majority of your pack's weight.

The butt pack integrates like the many other parts. I keep survival supplies here so I can easily take them with me on trips away from a base camp.

The beauty of this system is that it is built around a harness system that is slightly different from other packs of similar size. The top of the harness rides slightly lower on the shoulders so that weight is distributed more evenly across the back. The main cargo pocket can easily be removed from the harness system with little effort. The harness can then carry small pockets for things like a water bladder or simple safety supplies. The hip belt is innovative in that it is attached by velcro fasteners and is also rubberized to maintain grip on the portion it is married to. It also comes out easily without the need to slide through a sleeve. This allows me to keep the items I want on the hip belt, without having to remove them just to get the hip belt off.

I also have a butt pack that I use as a lid for my pack. It can be easily removed and placed on the hip belt. This allows me to be in the backcountry, take my main pack off and make camp. I then take the hip belt off and attach the lid, which carries my must-have safety and survival supplies. It is easy to explore, fish or do some nature study.

Another product by Hill People Gear is the Kit Bag. They are lightweight, slim packs that you wear on your chest. They have a four-point harness system with mesh on the back. I wear this item each time I go out. It is incredibly comfortable and keeps all the small items I might want or need within easy reach.

In my opinion, Hill People Gear's products are some of the most innovative, and they are at the forefront of general packing gear. I see similar innovations in only a few hiking systems. Each time I share this type of system with others, they say something along the line of, "That system makes so much sense." This gives me reason to believe this is the way to go for the future. With that said, many of my friends and students—and maybe you—do not need this type of packing system. One simple pack may meet your needs, much like various ones met my needs for many years. Therefore, I am going to share with you the ins and outs, pieces and parts and pros and cons of various packs and all that goes into making them do what they do.

I will cover packs and how to wear them comfortably. Big packs, little packs, modular-system packs and the various accessories that can be used in concert with them. One of the biggest issues that keeps people from returning to a wilderness area for enjoyment is their lack of comfort while they were there. Two things make most people uncomfortable during wilderness travel: the first is a pack not utilized correctly; the second is an improper sleeping setup (see page 118 for my solution to this second issue).

Tactical Tailor makes great, lightweight packs that I have used on many tactical trips.

Aluminum stays, as seen in my son's Eberlestock pack, offer the stability to haul heavy loads.

At the time of this writing, I have consistently been rucking (day hiking for exercise) five or six days per week for well over a year. This purpose has been twofold: The first was to get outside for exercise; the second was to test packs, loads, methods and so much more. I have spent a lifetime with a pack on my back, but it has been in these last few months that I have taken the time to diversify what and how I am carrying gear daily. I wanted to educate myself on things that I do not normally carry with me that others do. I have had the good fortune of being a gear reviewer for several years now, so I have access to a large assortment of packs. I have been given the opportunity to review backpacking packs such as Osprey, military-style packs such as Eberlestock and Tactical Tailor, along with handmade gear by The Hidden Woodsmen.

The items I've mentioned here are not even one-tenth of the packs that I have tested, used and passed on to students to use and give feedback on. With so many packs available, you need to understand the basics and how they work. To say that no two packs are the same is an understatement. However, there are categories we can break them into to help us understand them better.

UNFRAMED PACKS

Think of unframed packs as your typical, everyday backpack or bookbag. There is no rigidity to them and they can easily be wadded up and stowed away. Unframed packs make good gym, student or computer bags. They make a poor choice for wilderness travel with 25 pounds (5 kg) or more. This type of pack has two straps and a bag attached to them—not much else. This means your shoulders alone are going to be carrying the brunt of the weight. That is never a good idea. For serious and comfortable travel, you will want a pack that has a frame and other modular pieces.

FRAMED PACKS

Framed packs can be further divided into those that have internal frames and those that have external frames. External frame packs are not nearly as common as they once were. External frame packs have a frame that fits the torso and a pack built around or on the frame. As technology and materials advanced, internal frames came about, which were lighter, stronger and less cumbersome.

The most important aspect of framed packs is the way they transfer weight to a stronger and more-durable part of your body, namely your hips and core. Framed packs will be worn with a hip belt and shoulder straps, whereas a pack without rigidity to it weighs heavily on the shoulders. Your shoulders do not carry that sort of weight well. A framed pack connects to the biggest muscles in your body: your glutes, quads and obliques. When worn properly, the pack will rest on this portion of your torso and the shoulder straps are simply there to keep it stable and in concert with your body, not bouncing around or away from it.

The frames that give these packs their strength can be made of two distinctly different materials: plastic and aluminum. Plastic comes in the form of a sheet that is slightly pliable so you can mold it to your body shape and size, or it comes premolded in an acceptable body shape for most people. Many of the premolded versions also come as an insert and in varying sizes so you can customize the fit. Some plastic inserts are pliable enough that they mold to your body without memory at all. These types of packs work exceptionally well.

Packs come in a wide range of sizes, colors and uses. They make wilderness travel safer and more manageable.

Aluminum comes in two different forms. Most often you will find long, slender aluminum stays that insert into pockets directly behind the straps of your pack. Since aluminum can be bent with little work, they can be formed to your specific body shape and size as well. A word of caution when doing so: Bending aluminum too sharply or several times will weaken it. Many outdoor stores have staff that will help you and make sure it is professionally measured and bent to maintain your comfort and the viability of the stay itself. Less often you will find tubular aluminum that helps support even internal frame packs. These tubes are found on the borderline of your pack. My body shape is stocky and broad and I simply cannot find a pack of this style that does not make me uncomfortable. Someone with a smaller frame will be more likely find these to their liking.

PACK SIZE

People often ask me how much someone can carry in their pack. The answer to that question is totally subjective to the individual. I can say with certainty that above 25 pounds (5 kg), I prefer a pack that has a hip belt and has some form of rigidity to it. There was one pack that I carried on my daily rucks that had shoulder straps and a hip belt but no aluminum or plastic stays. I was carrying 30 pounds (14 kg) of sand in it. It felt like I was doing my best Luke Skywalker impression with a wild Yoda riding on my back. It was very uncomfortable. I went with another pack that had virtually the same setup plus a rigid, plastic sheeting and it rode much more comfortably.

ACCESSORIES

WHAT ARE ALL THOSE STRAPS FOR?

A good sternum strap helps to ensure the shoulder harness stays in place.

Compression straps on packs are good for storing items you may want to grab in a hurry such as an extra layer or rain gear.

One of the most confusing aspects of packs for those that are new to using them is all the straps that are on them. When used properly, the various straps, loops, buckles and more serve vital roles to the comfort and usability you experience while carrying and living out of a pack.

These accessories found on the pack and other aspects will literally make or break you when wearing one. Following are several things that you should look for and consider:

STERNUM STRAP

A sternum strap packs a punch when it comes to comfort and stability. Depending on your torso size, you may find that the shoulder straps want to slide out and away from your shoulder and chest area. A sternum strap prevents this from happening and keeps the pack against your torso.

MOLLE webbing on packs allow you to easily customize your pack or bag to meet the needs of yourself, team or group.

Zippered panels on the top of a pack make small items easily accessible.

COMPRESSION STRAPS

Compression straps go horizontally around the main body of the pack. They serve to compress the contents of the pack down and into the pack itself. They will help keep items from bouncing around, tighten the load on your torso, hold gear that you may need quick access to and can serve to secure a rain cover to the pack.

MOLLE AND PALS STRAPS

Modular Lightweight Load-Bearing Equipment (MOLLE) and Pouch Attachment Ladder System (PALS) straps are webbing that are stitched tightly to portions of packs, most often to hip belts. These systems were originally designed for use in the military. They provide the user the ability to attach a large range of pouches and other gear to a base pack, allowing military personnel to build a pack that is specific to their unit or mission. Some backpacking models will have similar webbing on them, allowing the civilian market to customize packs as well. Various pouches can be attached to meet your needs (e.g., to the hip belt to hold a camera, phone, extra water, first aid kit, sidearm and many more items).

ZIPPED PANELS

You will often find zipped panels on the top pocket of your packs. These offer you the ability to grab small, essential items without ever taking the pack off. Many hikers I know keep a map case in this pocket that holds their map and baseplate compass. They can then reach the pocket easily and regularly check to make sure they know where they are. These pockets also make a great place to store energy bars and other snacks. I can tell you from experience that when you are hiking and you come around the bend to see a nice, big hill you need to climb, being able to reach up and grab an energy bar is fantastic.

A tool loop can be used to secure a small axe, shovel or other tools you may need on trips.

HIP BELTS

As you are looking for packs, do not choose one that has a one-size-fits-all hip belt. They simply do not work in that manner. Good-quality packs will have hip belts that can be removed and exchanged. With the wide range of body shapes and sizes, this is an absolute must. The basic cargo area of pack does not need to change between someone that is large and stocky and someone that is thin, but the hip belt most certainly does.

TOOL LOOP

One of the most misunderstood design features of a pack is the tool loop found on the bottom of many packs. I have seen quite an array of items clipped onto this loop. Water bottles, carabiners, gloves, camp shoes and more have been placed in this location. What this does is place an item in the back of the pack, which will then cause a weight shift when it swings. Although these small items do not seem like much, that small amount of weight swinging can cause stress on your lower back. This loop should be used for tools like an axe, shovel or similar item. You place the handle of the item you want to carry into the loop and then twist it until it is upside down in the loop. You can then secure the handle with a compression strap. This will adequately secure the tool for easy use. This also means that a tool does not have to be compacted or made to fit inside the pack itself.

EXPANDABLE MESH POCKETS

Avoid expandable mesh pockets whenever you can. They are a great idea, but function poorly over the long run. Mesh pockets are often on the sides of a pack near the bottom. Many are built this way to make it easy to stow a water bottle. The mesh allows any possible condensation on the bottle to evaporate more easily. These pockets are also often used to stow small items easily, such as your camp shoes, gloves, hat and so on, all for the same reason. These items are likely to also have forest debris along with moisture. It would be better to strap them to your pack than depend on the mesh pocket. The elastic in every expandable mesh pocket I have ever used has given out. At that point, I cut them off since they are of no use. I suggest you avoid them no matter what the marketing says about them.

MESH BACK PANEL

One of the more innovative aspects of the newer packs I enjoy greatly is an integrated yet suspended back panel. One sales representative referred to these as a back trampoline, which I thought was a nice way of looking at them. Rather than the main cargo area of the pack resting directly on your back, it rests against this back trampoline. This is great because it offers you ventilation. They also prove to be comfortable. One user told me that they feel that the pack is unstable while using one of this type. He said it felt like it was bouncing on his back. While that is a concern I believe you should be aware of, I do think this can be corrected by wearing the pack straps and hip belt properly.

OTHER POCKETS

We will discuss other pockets later, but backpackers are very fussy when it comes to whether pockets are helpful. I get it: Any weight that is not needed is a bad thing for a backpacker. The adage that "ounces add up to pounds" is also true. But I do think you must take into consideration the efficiency as well. Having multiple pockets gives you the ability to organize your pack more efficiently. Why go digging into your main cargo compartment for your hat when you can just stow it away in a pocket for easy access?

SLEEVES

I have two packs that have sleeves on the sides. The sleeves are made by simply adding a piece of fabric and sewing it onto the cargo area on the sides only, leaving the top and bottom. This creates a great place to store your trekking poles, a small axe or any other rigid piece of equipment that is too long to place in the cargo area itself. The sleeve will serve to keep it close to the cargo area. Compression straps and pockets on the bottom

of the pack will ensure that it stays secure and doesn't slide out. For two years, I worked as chain man on an engineering crew for a natural gas utility company. I carried a pack on the job that held stakes, ribbon and other gear. I sewed sleeves onto the pack; they gave me the ability to carry my engineering equipment and bush axe so I could clear the way for the civil engineers' transit shots.

TOP COVERS

As I mentioned earlier, many packs come with a small top lid that can be removed. This is one of my favorite features of packs made today. Typically, I keep my must-have survival supplies in that top lid. The lid pocket then serves as an over-the-shoulder or butt pack whenever I set up camp. Underneath this lid, you will find various closures. Some are zippers, others have drawstring closures, while still others have their own flap that buckles down. I have had various tops and don't believe that one kind outperforms another. Please choose the one you like the best. However, keep this in mind: Moisture falls from the sky. Whatever is on top of your pack will be responsible for shedding a large amount of rain if you are out in it. Look closely and ensure your top will do this for you. If it has a zipper, make sure it has as storm flap over it to protect it from rain. If it is drawstring, it will impossible to close it tightly enough to keep out all the rain. Ensure that the flap covering the top covers it completely. Otherwise, when you cinch the drawstring, you will create channels for rain to run into your main cargo area.

> ➤ *(Right) One good option for rain protection is to have a waterproof liner bag and a rain cover. This ensures your gear stays dry.*

CRAIG'S TOP TEN USES FOR A TRASH BAG

A trash bag can be an indispensable piece of equipment in the outdoors. I typically use one as a pack liner and have another one folded in my bag of survival supplies. I use it for a lot more than survival. A trash bag can serve as many things, including the following:

1. **WATER COLLECTOR.** Dig a hole in the ground and line it with a garbage bag, or place it at the end of your rainfly or tarp to catch rainwater. Rain is clean water and can be used for drinking or hygiene.

2. **BERRY CONTAINER.** Set up camp and then go back to that nice meadow you saw the blueberries in. Use your garbage bag to collect them.

3. **RAIN JACKET.** Cut holes in the bottom for your head and in the sides for your arms. It will make a nice impromptu rain jacket when you have forgotten yours.

4. **SIT PAD.** My favorite use for a trash bag is to keep my bottom from being uncomfortably wet. For example, if I sit down to rest or eat lunch and the area is wet, I can put a bag down and keep the moisture from soaking into my clothing.

5. **FIREWOOD PROTECTOR.** If it is raining and I process wet forest materials into dry ones, I can store them in a garbage bag until I am ready to use them. I can also lay it over my wood pile to keep rain and dew from getting my firewood wet overnight if I am staying in the same location multiple nights.

6. **WATERPROOF BED BARRIER.** I can lay a trash bag down on the ground underneath my tent or sleeping pad to keep moisture from soaking into my sleep system. I can also slip it over a sleeping pad to do the same.

7. **STINK BARRIER.** Hiking often makes for stinky feet. This can be problematic inside a tent or hammock. You can place your stinky boots and socks in a bag overnight so they do not run your traveling companion (or you) out into the woods.

8. **TRANSPIRATION BAG.** A trash bag can be an easy way to gather clean water in a survival situation. Place a clear garbage bag over nontoxic green plant life (e.g., leaves on a tree branch). Tie off the bag on the branch and wait. Condensation will come off the leaves and gather at the bottom of the bag.

9. **FIRST AID COVERING.** If you need to cover a wound so that forest debris does not get in it, cover it with a portion of a trash bag or a whole trash bag. Just remove it often so the wound site can get air to it as well.

10. **PILLOW.** Stuff it with clothes from your pack at night and use it as a pillow. Much like a rain jacket, there are better choices, but this allows you to carry minimal equipment and use it for multiple purposes.

PACK COVERS AND LINERS

I am lumping pack covers and liners together because they both serve to protect your gear from rain and debris. I have used many different pack covers. Most are made with elastic and often have a buckle, loop or similar way to fasten to the top of your pack. They then cover your pack, serving to keep the falling rain away from the main cargo area. However, they do not keep rain from running down your back and on that portion of your pack. The back trampoline does this minimally because the pack does not actually rest against your back—it is suspended from it.

A pack liner is a waterproof barrier that goes on the inside of your bag to keep your contents dry. You can purchase specialty liners that are sprayed or impregnated with silicone or similar waterproofing. Personally, I think a garbage bags works well for this and it costs much, much less. You have the bonus of having another trash bag in your supplies to use for various survival purposes (see the sidebar on the opposite page).

STUFF SACKS

Stuff sacks are small bags primarily made for efficiency and the organization of your pack contents. I have some of these that are also waterproof as well. I use the waterproof stuff sacks specifically for my bedding. I do *not* enjoy sleeping in a wet bed. Therefore, I take extra precaution to ensure it stays dry by keeping it in a dry bag in my pack. I like to organize my gear in color-coded bags so I can efficiently find the specific gear I need when I dig into my pack. For example, I keep all my cooking supplies in a red bag, because it represents fire. My toiletries are in a yellow bag and so on.

Stuff sacks of various color and sizing allow you to organize gear pieces so you can find them easily.

Well, there you have it. A lifetime of experience in packs. I love them and cannot get enough of them. I certainly have my favorites, but my intention is to help you find your favorite. Without a doubt, it is worth it to spend a bit extra on a pack. For extended time outdoors it will make your life so much easier.

HOW TO PACK A PACK

MORE THAN OPENING IT UP AND SHOVING IT IN

Nature Reliance School collaborates with Rodney Vanzant of Iron Sight Defense to teach a class on tactical survival. One of the hallmarks of the class is that we always start class with taking a ruck straight up a hill. This serves to force people, including me, to consider what is important and what is not important. If you are new to rucking gear up a hill, it is at about midpoint up the hill that you seriously reconsider what you have brought. During our first of many of these events several years ago, a gentleman who is now a good friend brought a condominium-size tent with him. It was intended to sleep him and one other person. I estimated that tent would sleep twenty people (not really, but you get my point). Not only that, but he had portions of it strapped to the top and sides of his pack, which were shaking about and shifting weight the whole time. It was a great opportunity for him to learn a lesson and continue outdoor travels without the need for such gear. I do not want you to make that same mistake. I am going to teach you how to fill your pack in such a way that it is efficient and does not leave you with a permanent limp.

Now that we have a much better understanding of gear and what we need, I want to focus our attention now on how to carry it all. There is a systematic way of carrying gear. I developed this protocol after many trips carrying packs. I have spent years backpacking and enjoying all the wilderness has to offer. I have paddled hundreds of miles on rivers. Although I don't engage

The location where you carry items in your pack can make or break a long hike. For example, you do not want heavy items at the top of your pack. See the illustration on page 177 for the best spots to carry heavy and light items.

in long trips anymore, I still ruck for exercise several times a week. Depending on my mood, I will crank out 20 miles (32 km) or more each week carrying packs of various sizes and weights. What I am saying is that I know a thing or two about packing packs. For years, after many trips teaching classes for Nature Reliance School, Tracy Trimble (another instructor with our organization) and I would lay our gear out in three piles: stuff we used, stuff we didn't use and stuff that we didn't use but still must carry (e.g., a first aid kit). It was easy to see the patterns and recognize what things we only thought we needed but in truth did not. By doing this, we developed a kit that contained our needs and a few wants while still being reasonable to carry.

I have also queried my good friend Tali Hunt, who leads backpacking trips all over the country. Additionally, I also have several friends who are professionals when it comes to gear. J&H Lanmark Store, Canoe Kentucky and Mike's Hike and Bike are all businesses in my area that have been most helpful as I've researched and tested the latest gear available. Since they engage in lots of backpacking trips each year, their help was invaluable. I suggest using the following list to help you with your next trek. Pack your pack from bottom to top in the following manner so your gear is easily accessible and allows you to move as freely as possible without risking injury:

- **BOTTOM:** Big and bulky gear that you will need only when you stop and make camp.
- **MIDBACK:** Heavy items that need to stay close to your core.
- **TOP:** Bulky yet lightweight gear that you may need to access quickly and efficiently.
- **POCKETS AND LASHING:** Small yet essential items you may need to access quickly.

I prefer to roll my gear and place it in my pack like I am stacking firewood rather than in columns along the vertical length of the pack. This makes it easy to find and get to items if they are needed, even when those items are in the bottom of the pack. Let's look at these areas of the pack in more detail.

BOTTOM

The bottom of your pack should hold things you do not need until making your camp. Since rain comes from the top down and most packs are waterproof or water-resistant on the bottom, placing the following in the bottom is wise:

- Sleeping system (e.g., tent, hammock)
- Sleeping bag
- Sleep-clothing layers like long underwear
- Socks and other camp footwear

MIDBACK

The midback portion of your pack is where you will pack your heavier gear that you will not need during the meat of your trek. Having these heavier items at your midback helps to stabilize the load. Since the following items are heavy, they tend to move around during movement—use other items in your gear to wrap them up so they do not move as much:

- Cook stove and cooking kit (ensure your liquid-fuel canister is tight)
- Main food source
- Extra water
- Tent (If your tent is heavy compared to other items you are carrying, this is a great place for it; you may spread the tent out to include putting the poles on the outside, which will more evenly distribute the weight.)

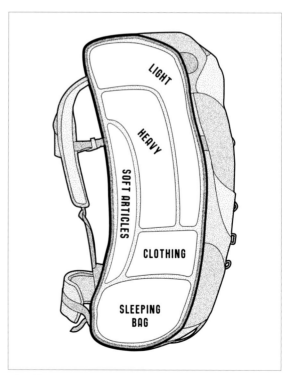

This illustration offers you the best method to carry gear so it carries well on your body and does not move about too much.

HOW TO PUT ON A PACK

Let's keep your back healthy so you can keep getting out for wilderness adventure! Reverse the left and right hands if you are left-handed.

1. Loosen the hip and shoulder straps.

2. Grab the right strap with your right hand and the top loop (if available) with your left hand.

3. Bend the knee of your right leg to form a platform to rest your pack.

4. Squat as much as you can so you can use your legs to lift the pack to your right leg. Place the bottom of the pack on your leg, with the straps facing you.

5. Pull the pack up and onto your right shoulder as you bend over. Stabilize your body by keeping your feet spread.

6. Place the left shoulder strap onto your shoulder.

7. Stay bent over (keeping weight off your shoulders) and tighten the hip belt. The pack should rest on your hips via the hip belt.

8. Pull the shoulder straps tight, then the sternum strap if you have one.

9. Stand up slowly to verify the pack is secured to you.

10. Do a basic range-of-motion check so you can be aware of any adjustments that need to be made.

When putting on a pack, grasp it tightly and bring it to your leg to rest. Then move it up to your shoulder. This extra step ensures you protect your back from injury when lifting a heavy load.

TOP

The top of your pack should carry the items that you will use along the trek and need to get to readily:

- Layers for core body temp, such as fleece or insulated gear
- Water purification gear
- Toiletries (make sure you bring items that are not hard on the environment)
- Tarp, bothy bag or similar emergency shelter

POCKETS AND LASHING

You may remember from Chapter 3 that I recommend the following to stay on your body at all times in the wilderness: knife, compass, IFAK, predator defense and signal panel (such as bandana). Everything else goes in pockets and lashing. Pockets and lashing can secure items that do not fit into the pack or need to be utilized quickly:

- Tent poles
- Sleeping pad
- Trekking poles
- Rain jacket
- Water bottle
- Snack items for energy

Now that we have all these items nicely arranged in our pack, how do we go about putting the pack on without hurting ourselves? Many thanks to the U.S. military veterans that have shared this method with me. Many methods require you to put your pack on one strap at a time. When the pack is heavy, this can cause strain to various portions of your spine. Check out the sidebar on the previous page for the steps that both my military friends *and* my chiropractor suggest. This should help save your back from getting injured while putting your pack on or taking it off.

FIELD AND HOME CARE FOR PACKS

There is nothing worse than a squeaky pack. Each step you take can be an annoyance. Duct tape is good to have around to act as a buffer for pieces that squeak when they rub together. It also serves to temporarily hold broken buckle pieces together. Paracord is also a great field tool to fasten broken pack straps. Straps and buckles would need to be replaced when you get home. I ran one pack for several years whose main waist belt buckle was held together with duct tape. I loved that pack and could not find a suitable replacement buckle. You can also empty your packs and spray them off with a hose after a trip (particularly the back, waist belt and shoulder straps). On excessively hot trips when sweat soaks them, I will wash them with soap and water as well to get out all the salt and smell.

CHAPTER 9
SPECIALTY GEAR

Wilderness is not a luxury but a necessity of the human spirit.

—Edward Abbey

FOR THOSE WHO ARE NEW TO BACKPACKING, I AM GOING TO LET YOU IN ON [A] little secret. When you go on a trip with other people who are new to such trips, there will be a lot of questions: "Did you bring extra clothes?"; "How much does your pack weigh?"; "Can I try your backpacker meal?" Three of my friends and I took a trip like that many years ago. One of my friends and I were experienced, the other two people were not. Those two had bought a lot of new equipment for the trip and were excited to get to the woods and try it out. We all met at the house of one of the inexperienced guys, threw our packs on top of his in the truck and headed out.

When we got to our destination, we began tying up boots and situating clothes and putting on packs. I had started grabbing the packs out of the truck and handing them out when I came to the one on the bottom of the pile, the one belonging to my friend who had driven us. As I started tugging on it, I thought it was stuck on something underneath because I could not move it. I started to pick it up when I discovered it was not stuck on anything at all, but rather it was so heavy that I was having difficulty moving it. Now keep in mind I am no Mr. Olympia, but I am a woodsman with the brawn of a Kentucky farm boy. I asked the obligatory question: "What in the world do you have in that pack?" My friend answered, "Nothing I don't need." I thought to myself, "This is going to be a good day of lessons learned."

We all got our packs on and, fortunately, headed downhill from the trailhead. (Had we needed to go uphill, I am afraid my friend would have not taken the first step.) We were a bit surprised because the trail was crisscrossed with downed trees uprooted by a recent storm. This had forced us to climb over, crawl under and walk around many of these trees to get down the hill. My friend was struggling, to say the least. At one point he simply could not get up after sitting down, was overheating, and we worried that he was having heart issues (he wasn't). I then asked him how much his pack weighed, which I should have done before we started. He told me it weighed 130 pounds (59 kg)! We were only about fifteen minutes into our hike, so I made the determination to go back to the vehicle and dump some of his load at the vehicle. This was not for him to learn lessons just on his own, but for me and the other experienced fella to show him a new way. He was in so much distress that I carried my pack and his pack back up the hill.

When we got to the top of the hill, we discovered this newbie (I say that lovingly) was carrying three Duraflame logs, a complete camping-style cook set, several flashlights, enough food to feed the four of us for a week, a hardback book and several other odds and ends that I have purposely chosen to forget. My experienced friend and I removed about 70 pounds (32 kg) of his gear, assured him we would take care of him so he did not have to worry and set out hiking again. The one-night stay in the woods turned out perfectly for each of us. lessons were learned by all and we are better for it now.

HUNTING

ACQUIRING YOUR OWN FOOD SOURCE

There are some specialty items that I think should be considered to either enhance or change the pace of your outdoor adventuring. Some of these are useful on every single trip (e.g., hygiene items) while others are more specific to a particular activity (e.g., paddling or mountain biking).

In our modern times, a larger number of people are returning to more self-reliant behavior. These are not prepper fanatics wearing tinfoil hats. These are people who simply want to take care of their needs more so than they have in the past. Many of those people are delving into hunting, either as total beginners or experienced woodsmen. Hunting has many benefits:

- Hunting provides you opportunities for 100 percent organic meat sources. No additives, no steroids or added growth hormones. Wild game is the ultimate free-range meat.

- Hunting provides increased conservation opportunities for wildlife. By harvesting in accordance with game regulations, hunters play a vital role in the overall health and continuance of wild animals.

- Hunting allows you to spend plenty of time afield, enjoying the natural world. You will often see things you simply would not see without dedicated time hunting. This means you can see things that are wilder and more unaffected by human encroachment. Most hunters have a close relationship to nature and what it can teach them.

- Hunting brings you the confidence and satisfaction of providing food for the table. It literally encourages a "field-to-fork" mind-set.

Learning to hunt can provide many hours afield and a 100 percent organic meat source to the table.

I grew up hunting, so I come to the subject very naturally and with lots of experience. There is a table on page 185 that has a list of the top ten game animals hunted in North America. I have successfully hunted each of them except for bear and elk. This section is not intended for those that already spend a great deal of time hunting. It is intended for those who are interested in hunting but really have no idea how to begin. I am going to share the fundamentals to get you started.

TYPES OF GAME

A major goal in all hunting endeavors should be to have effective, quick kills. The alternative should never be the goal. I believe you should spend plenty of time afield observing and studying wildlife with a mentor if at all possible. Different types of animals present specific challenges. For our purposes here, I am dividing huntable wild game into two categories:

1. **MAMMALS.** Mammals include large game—such as elk, bear and deer—as well as small game animals, such as rabbits and squirrels.

2. **BIRDS.** These game animals can fly, and most that you are likely to hunt dwell primarily on the ground. Wild turkey, grouse, quail and pheasant are examples.

TYPES OF WEAPONS

I would love to give you my favorite weapon to hunt with, but I simply can't do it. I love all types of hunting, and each type requires its own weapon for safe and efficient use. Not to mention that we must abide by the all-important game laws to continue to be good stewards of our natural resources. With that said, for big game hunting (e.g., white-tailed deer in my area), I enjoy the efficiency of my Ruger® M77 chambered in .243 (approximately $500). My dad, son and I have harvested well over 100 deer with this and similar rifles and enjoy effective hunts with it. My shotgun of choice is an Ithaca 20-gauge (approximately $330) for small game such as squirrels, rabbits, quail and grouse. These are primarily my go-to choices because they are guns that were given to me by my parents. That is typical of certain "family guns"—guns that were either handed down through generations or were gifted new to people that hold special meaning. There are many other guns that I have used at different times for the same reasons. An honorable mention is my "sweet sixteen" Savage side-by-side double barrel, which I use for grouse and similarly sized upland game birds. I also was gifted a camouflage Henry 12-gauge that I use exclusively for hunting turkey, which happens to be my favorite animal

to hunt. They are incredibly observant animals, which makes it a challenge to get one. One reason I can is that my 12-gauge allows me to reach out a bit farther than my 20-gauge.

I realize some of this may sound foreign to you, so I want to offer you some fundamentals in weapons that can be used for hunting.

SHOTGUNS

A shotgun uses a large quantity of shot (i.e., small pellets of lead, copper or steel). When you fire the weapon, the shot leaves the gun in a pattern resembling a cone. Determining the size is easy. The most common gauges for hunting are 12 and 20. The gauge measurement is taken by determining how many lead balls you can make of equal diameter to the gun barrel out of 1 pound (450 g) of lead. For example, the term *20-gauge* means you can make 20 lead balls that are the same diameter as the gun barrel out of 1 pound (450 g) of lead. Shotguns "break down" and allow cartridges to be placed in them. Others, referred to as double-barreled, have two barrels that you can break down to load with cartridges. Others are pump shotguns, which means you manually move a grip handle after you shoot. This handle moves an internal mechanism that cycles in another cartridge. Other shotguns are semiautomatic.

RIFLES

When you fire a rifle, one projectile comes out of the barrel and goes toward the intended target. The projectile is a certain caliber. I mentioned my .243 earlier. The term *.243* denotes the caliber and represents the diameter of the projectile and also the internal bore of the rifle's barrel.

Rifles come in many different forms. Some break down in order for you to put in a cartridge, others have a bolt that pulls back to open a magazine that is permanently in the weapon and others require you to place rounds in a removable magazine and place that in the weapon when you want to fire it.

MUZZLELOADERS

A muzzleloader (or black powder) is a specific type of shotgun or rifle that uses black powder or its equivalent as the propellant that moves the lead round out of the barrel.

BOWS

A bow is simply a device that propels an arrow instead of a round. There are many different types of bows that can be used for hunting, and they are worth considering:

- **COMPOUND BOWS.** This is the most modern bow that I will share here. It utilizes a pully, cable and cam system to give the user a significant "let off." This means that about mid-draw, the amount of weight you are pulling back significantly decreases so you can hold it back and ready to fire more easily. The modern compounds have advanced sights and other attachments to make them more accurate. Matthews and Hoyt brands make some excellent compound bows that many of my fellow hunters use.

- **CROSSBOWS.** Crossbows are bows that look more like a typical gun. They have a stock and a small bow that is perpendicular to it. They shoot much shorter arrows called bolts. They are often outfitted with scopes and are utilized much like guns. This makes them very accurate and easy to use.

- **RECURVE BOWS.** This is my preferred choice of bow and one that I have harvested several deer and small game with, including a wild turkey. Recurves have limbs that curve away from the archer when they are unstrung. This allows the bow to have more energy than a comparable longbow but not as much energy as a compound or crossbow. Most recurve users shoot "instinctively," which means they do not have sights and similar assistance built into the bow. This requires the archer to spend a great deal of time developing their skill to shoot accurately. I have been using a PSE Blackhawk for nearly twenty years now.

- **LONGBOWS.** Longbows are more primitive in their making and use. Longbows also require the shooter to shoot instinctively and therefore will require a large amount of practice. I made one longbow many years ago that I used on only a few hunts before breaking it. I have many friends who make their own bows and use them with great success. There is much pride in building your own bow and utilizing it to put food on the table.

Small game hunting with a .22 rifle is a great way to begin, and continue, the conservation practice of hunting.

JEFF COOPER'S FOUR RULES OF GUN SAFETY

Jeff Cooper was a United States marine and is regarded as one of the twentieth century's leading small arms experts. Here are his four rules for gun safety:

1. Treat all guns as if they are loaded.

2. Never point a gun at anything you are not willing to destroy.

3. Keep your finger off the trigger until your sights are on the target and you have made the decision to shoot.

4. Be sure of your target and what lies beyond it.

	STARTER WEAPON	WEAPON SIZE	HELPFUL HINTS
BEAR	Rifle then bow	.308 or bigger	Know their food sources and hunt near those.
DEER	Rifle then bow	.243 or bigger	Most active at daybreak and sunset; hunt during the mating season in the fall.
DOVE	Shotgun	20-gauge	Are attracted to seed plants, such as foxtails and sunflowers.
ELK	Rifle then bow	.308 or bigger	Most active at daybreak and sunset; hunt during the mating season in the fall.
GROUSE	Shotgun	20-gauge	Very fast and hard to hunt; good choice to use bird dogs on.
PHEASANT	Shotgun	12-gauge	Good choice to use bird dogs on.
QUAIL	Shotgun	20-gauge or smaller	Often come up together in a small covey; be ready for multiple shots.
RABBIT	Shotgun	20-gauge	Likes lots of overgrown areas away from predators.
SQUIRREL	Shotgun then rifle	20-gauge	Hunt near the trees that they frequent.
TURKEY	Shotgun then bow	12-gauge	Hunt in the spring during their mating season; use calls to bring them in.
DUCK	Shotgun	12-gauge	Hunt during migration periods.

WEAPON CYCLING MECHANISMS

Weapon cycling refers to the method by which you get another cartridge into the weapon. Cycling your weapon efficiently is something all hunters should be skilled at:

- **BREAKDOWN.** This type of weapon opens at the breech (where the barrel and handle meet). You place cartridges in it individually. Double-barreled weapons are those in which you place cartridges as a pair.

- **BOLT.** This type of weapon has a handle that you maneuver to open the areas in which cartridges are placed. Once you shoot, you will need to cycle the bolt to remove the spent cartridge and replace it with another.

- **SEMIAUTOMATIC.** This is the type of weapon that uses the blowback from one shell being fired to push back the slide and cycle another cartridge in the weapon.

I share all that with you to give you some basics. The table on the previous page will be helpful to you as you get started. It lists the top ten most common species hunted in North America and offers hints on each. There are several things to keep in mind as you start to hunt. Your area's fish and game department will be most helpful to get you started. These departments are often called natural resources, fish and game, game and fisheries or wildlife conservation. They will be easy to find and get feedback from. Keep in mind that game seasons are there to assist in the overall health of the game animal. Always follow game laws and follow the four rules of gun safety (see the sidebar on the previous page).

In the table, you will see a choice or type of weapon to use. This is only a suggestion; you can hunt wild game with a variety of weapons. Once you get started, you will find what works best for you in your season. Most states have laws that have longer seasons for bows than guns. That is one good reason to get a bow and begin your practice. I have also included a short note on each species to give you a leg up on getting food on the table. I hope it helps!

Finally, for hunting there are some general ideas that will help in harvesting all species:

- Wild game mammals can scent humans very well. Be careful with anything that has an odor. Wash your clothes with unscented soaps and store them with some wilderness debris (I use cedar shavings). This way I smell like the woods when I go out. There are also a large amount of scent-blocking soaps and clothing choices that serve to "extinguish" odors before they drift off into the wilderness.

- When attempting to hide, camouflage is beneficial but not required. Just do what you can to blend in with the environment, hide in the shadows and put vegetation between you and the game you are hunting. The key to all camouflage is to make as little noise and movement as possible. Both are quick ways to bring game animals' attention your direction.

- Practice with new weapons on a gun range many times before going hunting. If you borrow a weapon to get started, make sure you take the time to shoot it before going.

- Respect the animals. Do all you can to make clean and quick kills.

PADDLING

GETTING AROUND ON THE WATER

The distance from the confluence of the North Fork and South Fork of Elkhorn Creek near Frankfort, Kentucky, to the creek's end meet-up point with the Kentucky River is only slightly more than 18 miles (29 km). I cannot begin to share with you all the stories I have about the creek and my paddling adventures on it. Maybe I can share those with you in another book someday. A few that come to mind here include how I caught my largest smallmouth bass on the creek (I weighed it during the trip at just shy of 5 pounds [2 kg]); how, many years ago, my girlfriend (now my wife) and I would enjoy a day of paddling on the Elkhorn, pulling up on sandbars to hang out, eat a snack and jump into the deep holes for some fun; and how I would take my kids paddling and exploring the creek, a nonstop learning adventure.

I love to paddle. Canoe, kayak, stand-up paddleboards—it doesn't matter, I enjoy it all. Some of the greatest trips I have ever had in a wilderness setting were primarily spent in a canoe or kayak. Paddling sports, particularly kayak fishing, has exponentially grown in popularity since the 1980s. Modern kayaks were being manufactured in the 1950s. The materials and processes have grown tremendously since that time, but some paddling boats still contain subpar materials in them and should be avoided.

Like most technical skills, it would serve you well to get some paddling training before going all out and buying the equipment you may need. What I will do here is get you a good reference point to start. This will allow you to have an informed conversation with your preferred boat suppliers.

Paddling trips offer the adventurer an easy way to haul a lot of gear to far away places in a wilderness.

There are several questions to ask before starting your paddling adventures: What is your primary reason for paddling? What type of waterway appeals to you? Do you like the idea of being on a lake, a meandering creek or river or a wild river? Determining that will help determine the best boat for you.

My preferred brand of kayak is Jackson Kayaks. For canoes, I love the beauty and history of Old Town. Both brands have superior manufacturing processes that I feel are worth the extra money you will spend on them.

I recommend one particular aspect of these boats that you should look for when it comes to finding a good "ship" to paddle about. Rotomolding is the process by which quality kayaks and canoes are made. You can think of this process as being a hollow mold in which plastic is inserted. The mold with plastic is then inserted into a huge oven that rotates it so ensure the plastic is spread evenly throughout the boat. This makes a boat that paddles smoothly and responsively. The other options available will make weak points in the boat, which will prevent the boat from functioning smoothly. Jackson Kayaks (approximately $700 to $1,300) and Old Town (approximately $700 to $1,600) both use rotomolded processes to avoid such problems.

Here are some points to keep in mind when determining if a flatwater (lake) boat is the right choice for you:

- **LONGER IS BETTER.** Length will help the boat track well. This will serve to keep you going where you want to go and add stability to the boat.

- **SITTING INSIDE.** Canoes are set up so you sit down in them. With kayaks, you have the option of sitting inside or on top. Sitting inside lowers your center of gravity and therefore bolsters your stability.

- **SITTING ON TOP.** A lot of fisherman prefer to sit on top. This allows you to maneuver easier to bring in that lunker as well as easier access to gear.

If you prefer the idea of heading downstream on a meandering creek or river, here are some points to keep in mind:

- **A SMOOTH WATERWAY IS LIKE A LAKE.** If the waterway is more flatwater, think of it much like a lake and look at the preceding points.

- **RIPPLES.** If you will encounter a ripple or two, which means you are nearing the bottom of the waterway, get a boat with some rocker to it (see the sidebar on page 190).

- **INSTABILITY.** Moving water and a ripple or two will mean your trip will be a bit more unstable. Choose a boat that is bit wider to help with stability.

If you are an adrenaline junkie and want to hit some gnarly rapids, there are many things to consider. The first thing is that you should never engage in whitewater paddling without first training or traveling with experienced paddlers. There are many things that can go wrong, and an experienced paddler can help you avoid most of them. Once you are trained to face the challenge of rapids, you'll need the following:

- **LOTS OF ROCKER.** The more rocker you have, the less likely the boat is to dig into rocks. More rocker also means much more maneuverability.

- **SHORTER LENGTH.** For maneuverability, you want a much shorter boat to make those quick turns through the rapid and into an eddy to catch your breath before hitting the next big one.

- **LOWER CENTER OF GRAVITY.** Sit lower. The lower you are, the better your center of gravity. I have also found that I can feel the water much better when I am sitting closer to it. This is vital to making your way through aggressive sections of rivers.

- **SKIRT.** You will want one. Getting splashed is a guaranteed aspect of fast-water paddling. You will want something to shed it away from you and the inside of your boat.

➤ *(Right) Canoes and kayaks come in many configurations that meet your needs for adventure, fishing and fun.*

COMMON PADDLING TERMS YOU NEED TO KNOW

- **TRACKING:** The ability of a canoe or kayak to stay on course while it is moving. A boat that has good tracking will stay on course despite outside influences, such as crosswinds and sweep paddle strokes (i.e., strokes that are used to turn the boat in place).

- **RUN:** To paddle through a waterway, particularly in faster rapids.

- **ROCKER:** The curve of the bottom profile (keel line) from the bow to the stern.

- **CLASS I TO CLASS VI RAPIDS:** The classification system for moving water. It is technically referred to as the International Scale of River Difficulty. It was created by American Whitewater. This provides a good summary of the difficulty and skills required to run a river:

  - **Class I, Easy.** Fast-moving ripples and small waves. Risk to swimmers is slight, and self-rescue is easy.

  - **Class II, Novice.** Straightforward rapids, with clear channels and occasional maneuvering.

  - **Class III, Intermediate.** Rapids with moderate, irregular waves that can swamp a canoe. Complex maneuvering in rapids is likely.

  - **Class IV, Advanced.** Intense and powerful but predictable rapids. Rapids may require "must make" moves to avoid dangerous hazards. Risk of injury is moderately high and self-rescue is difficult.

  - **Class V, Expert.** Extremely long, obstructed or violent rapids. Proper equipment, extensive experience and practiced rescue skills are essential.

  - **Class VI, Extreme and Exploratory Rapids.** These rapids exemplify the extremes of difficulty, unpredictability and danger. Often rescue would be impossible for even expert paddlers. These rapids should be undertaken only by those with extensive experience and scouting of rapids whenever possible.

- **SKIRT:** The covering over the cockpit that connects the paddler's torso to the boat. It is in place to keep water from swamping the boat. Skirts are designed to be removed easily in case the paddler needs to remove themselves from the boat in an emergency.

Life jackets are an imperative piece of equipment for paddlers. Verify you have Coast Guard–approved flotation by looking for the label pictured on the right.

LIFE JACKETS

Life jackets are a must-have feature in all paddling sports. I wear a NRS Chinook (approximately $90). Even the best paddlers are surprised from time to time, and they are either thrown in or they fall into the water. Modern equipment has come a very long way in recent years to make jackets much more comfortable. Many life jackets are designed for various sports in mind. Whitewater jackets are very smooth, without items on them to hang up on waterway obstacles. Fishing vests have plenty of pockets on them to keep gear handy. Regular paddling vests are made so your arms are not restricted. They have a pocket or two for essentials and many have vents on the back to help rid you of some heat. There are even emergency vests that are used in a minimalist approach to safety. Worn similarly to a scarf, these vests are activated by CO_2. Some have a pull tab on them so if you fall in, you can quickly pull the release and the vest will inflate rapidly. Others are activated by water. This is a nice option to have if you fall in and are unconscious for any reason. It will inflate for you without your needing to do anything.

PADDLES

One of the common themes you have most likely noticed in this book is that manufacturers have good, better and best versions of their equipment. This fact became more apparent to me than anything else as I was preparing to write this book. I have been paddling for the better part of 30 years and during that time I have had the same two paddles. One is a classic wood paddle and the other is a nylon that is equivalent in size and shape. It had been many years since I had picked up any other paddle. I was very pleasantly surprised at what technology is now available. I did some testing with several different paddles on a survival event that I co-taught while writing this book. I was happy with the innovations in materials and with how stable the take-apart kayak paddles are. There is no give in all the newer models, and they all performed very well. With that in mind, the materials make or break paddles. Here is what you need to know:

- **GOOD:** Nylon material makes a very affordable and hearty paddle. Wood is also a good choice. My experience is that the basic wood paddles do not stand up to the elements in the same manner as the other options. I have a couple of wood paddles that I have owned for over 30 years. Having received virtually no maintenance, they are splitting and losing their usefulness. My nylon paddles (approximately $50) of the same age have a few scratches but are basically as usable as the day I bought them.

- **BETTER:** Fiberglass paddles (approximately $150) are stronger, but they have some give against rocks.

- **BEST:** Carbon paddles (approximately $150 to $200) are surprisingly lightweight but incredibly strong at the same time.

As you would imagine, each of those choices increases in price as you move up in quality. The carbon paddle that I utilized in a test session surprised me by how light and strong it was. I was almost as equally shocked by the fact that it cost nearly a third of the price of a whole boat! You get what you pay for with paddles, though. Find one that meets your budget.

A good paddle can save you energy and strength on long paddling trips. The best paddles currently on the market are made of carbon, shown here. They are lightweight, yet incredibly strong.

MOUNTAIN BIKING

SINGLE-TRACK YOUR WAY INTO AND OUT OF THE WILDERNESS

My mountain biking experience was short lived. It was not because I did not enjoy it. It was because I enjoyed it too much. I got into mountain biking in my early twenties and fell in love with it. It was a fantastic way for me to add some thrill to my life and do so in the outdoors—a good combination, I believe. As I have said before, I believe it is good for us to do dangerous things at times, to take some risks, to not be complacent—but to do so with contingency plans and safety nets in place that keep those risks from going too far. For some reason, I thoroughly enjoyed the hard work of pedaling up the side of a mountain for the sole purpose of going down the other side as fast as I could. The results were dislocated shoulders, a hurt back, sprained and nearly-broken wrists and a mangled bike several times over. You see, although I loved mountain biking, I was not very good at it. I did not take the time to learn how to do it correctly and safely (big mistake). With all that said, if it even slightly interests you, you should try it. My son now does it and I am considering doing it again both on my own and with him. It has been a long while since I engaged in single-track excursions, so I went and chatted with Mike Hale at Mike's Hike and Bike here in Kentucky. I wanted to find out what had changed and what I needed to know after a twenty-year absence. I am going to share with you what that discussion and research has shown me.

There are some must-haves when you want to engage in mountain biking. There are also a few other items that I personally think from my experience you should have as well. As for the must-haves, you will need a bike, helmet and repair kit.

Mountain bikes are durable for riding and incredibly lightweight for carrying through unridable areas.

MOUNTAIN BIKES

Wow, mountain bikes have come a long way in only twenty years. Back then, I was riding a Giant (approximately $1,000 to $2,400 today). There are some things you should know about mountain bikes when purchasing one, the first of which is: *Do not* go to your typical big-box sporting goods store and get one. Most bikes are made in China and they simply do not have the same quality control standards that premium bike manufacturers have. When I first got started, I did exactly what I told you not to do. I bought what I thought was a decent bike at a big-box store and took it for a ride the next day. I literally broke it in half during that ride. I know what you are thinking—no, it was not operator error on my part. I chose a relatively hilly, but not steep, ride that went over dirt single-track with a few rocky crossings. After crossing a rocky section of the trail, the whole front of the bike came apart at the welds. That is not a good thing, especially when you are riding the bike when it happens.

Another reason you should avoid big-box-store bikes is that the clear majority of them are put together by someone who most likely does not ride bikes and is an assembler of goods, not just bikes. That is why I would rather spend my money for a bike that is assembled by someone who rides bikes and is working in a small, privately owned outdoor store or bike shop. Those kinds of people are passionate about such things on a level bordering nerdiness (I say that lovingly and with respect). In other words, I want to buy a bike from someone who can answer any question I could possibly come up with about bikes. Here are some of the things to look for when you walk into a bike shop:

- **ASK ABOUT THE MATERIALS THE BIKE IS MADE OF.** To make strong bikes that are lightweight, you will want something that is made of aluminum, titanium, chromoly or carbon fiber. You will find a lot of bikes that are made of steel because it is the least expensive metal to build them with, but steel is too heavy to utilize in a good bike.

- **COMPONENTS SHOULD NOT HAVE A LOT OF WIGGLE TO THEM.** This is especially true of the gears. You should put any bike you are considering purchasing up on a rack and pedal it (with your hands or feet, depending on the type of rack) and change gears. You want the gears to change smoothly and not have any play in them. One of the things that regularly occurs on less expensive mountain bikes is that the chain will fall off due to wiggle. I also know this from the experience I had with the less expensive bike I owned.

- **GEOMETRY OF THE BIKE IS IMPORTANT,** and you should know what you want to do with your bike before purchasing it. Since I am discussing this in a wilderness gear book, I will forego all the important aspects of road biking. For wilderness use, you will want to get a mountain bike or a hybrid that will do trail and road riding. Aggressive trail bikes will have an aggressive geometry to them, meaning the head-tube angle is around 72° to 73°.

- **TUNE-UPS WILL BE NECESSARY.** If you purchase from a small bike shop, you will almost always get a tune-up (or multiple ones) thrown in for free. They will also most often talk to you about your bike. A recent example is my son's bike: After his third day of riding it, he crashed and the gear shifter got hung in a tree, which ripped the covering off and loosened it enough that it was not going to work properly moving forward. We took it to the shop and told them what had happened. They fixed it at no charge and got him riding again. As Mike told me during our interview, "If you are not crashing, you are not riding hard enough." On a mountain bike, it happens. It shouldn't happen as much as I was doing it, but it happens. In those cases, it is good to have a tune-up at least once per year—twice or more regularly if you ride a lot every week.

HELMETS

A helmet is a must-have for any cyclist. If you do not put one on for mountain biking, you are downright foolish. This is also another component of outdoor gear that you should spend as much on as your budget allows. Cheap helmets are made with spray foam and the shell is nothing more than tape on top of it. A more expensive helmet is going to be have a lot of features that are important:

Spend the extra money and get a good fit on your mountain bike helmet. Your life may very well depend upon it.

- **The foam is formed so that it has crush zones.** This helps to spread the force out over a larger surface area rather than it being localized.

- **Quality helmets will have a removable pad set.** This is vital to ensuring a helmet fits your head properly. You can have a great helmet, but if it does not fit properly, it might not give you appropriate coverage. You want your helmet down on the front of your head and not riding high.

- **Quality helmets will have a better occipital protector.** This serves to protect the back of your head and give the helmet stability.

- **Quality helmets will offer better airflow.** These helmets are designed in such a way as to provide maximum protection and airflow. You are going to sweat. Good airflow will help to dry you out, so the sweat doesn't fall in your eyes excessively.

- **The helmet and support system are not necessarily one-size-fits-all,** which is a good thing. You want a helmet that is sized correctly and at the same time has a great suspension system in it that can adjust for the variances of your individual head.

Helmets should be replaced after seven years or one good fall on it. I have tried on a bunch of excellent helmets that fit wonderfully. The brands were Giro, Kali, Lazer and the higher-end Bell helmets (approximately $100 and up).

REPAIR KITS

The last thing you want while mountain biking is to have an issue several miles out on a trail and no means to fix it, forcing you to push your bike back to your vehicle. That is why a repair kit is also a must-have. You should include the following items in your repair kit:

- **SPARE INNERTUBE.** Patch kits are not as effective as simply replacing the tube altogether and getting home.

- **SOMETHING TO INFLATE TIRES.** You can carry small pumps or cartridges designed to inflate them quickly.

- **MULTI-TOOLS.** There are also multi-tools that are specifically made for mountain biking. You will want one of these to change tires, put chains back together or make similar repairs.

Those are what I would consider the must-haves. When I asked Mike what else he considered essential for those wanting to get into mountain biking, he gave me the list you see in the sidebar on the next page. Great advice from someone who has biked his entire life and now teaches people the pros and cons of mountain biking gear.

Mountain biking is a fun and exciting way to add some miles to your outdoor travels. If you want a grueling workout, then find some hills. If you want a pleasurable ride in lots of beauty, find some flat ground. Either terrain offers a fun way to get away from the crowds.

TEN ESSENTIALS OF MOUNTAIN BIKING, BY MIKE HALE OF MIKE'S HIKE AND BIKE

You will notice that there are eleven. Mike is like that, always going above and beyond people's expectations:

1. **FOOD.** It is best to carry some sort of lightweight, high-calorie food—such as granola bars or trail mix—even if you plan on being out for only a couple of hours.

2. **HYDRATION AND WATER PURIFICATION.** Figure on drinking at least 1 quart (950 ml) of water every 2 hours. It is a good idea to bring along some way to purify water just in case you must be out longer than anticipated.

3. **TRAIL MAP AND COMPASS.** This does you very little good if you don't have at least some basic knowledge of how to use it. Get a book or take a class. This skill will help keep you from getting lost and give you the ability to get out quickly if everything goes wrong.

4. **FIRST AID KIT.** A simple one with some gauze pads, tape, a compression bandage and some antibiotic ointment is all you really need, but bring whatever makes you feel confident.

5. **LIGHTER.** A lighter (and perhaps a fire starter if you are in wet country) can be a lifesaver in a lot of situations.

6. **LIGHT.** Having one that attaches to your head or handlebars is best, but it does not really matter whether it is a headlamp, flashlight or even just a tiny LED—it is always a good idea since it can help you find the trail, work as a signal device or just let you explore a little bit more.

7. **TOOL KIT, SMALL REPAIR PARTS AND TIRE REPAIR KIT.** A small tool with multiple Allen wrenches, a chain tool, and a T25 torx wrench is necessary. You might also want to have a quick chain link, a shock pump, a few feet of duct tape and some zip ties along for trailside repairs. A spare inner tube patch kit (even if you ride tubeless), tire levers and some sort of inflation device are necessary.

8. **EMERGENCY SHELTER.** A thermal blanket, small tarp, poncho or even just a large, heavy trash bag will work great as emergency shelter in case you get stranded or injured and must wait for rescue.

9. **KNIFE.** Does this really need an explanation? Your knife does not have to be a gigantic, sword-size survival one; a small pocketknife is probably sufficient for almost all situations.

10. **WHISTLE.** Just bring one. They don't weigh much and you can use it to signal others in your party or to help summon emergency aid. The sound of a whistle can carry for well over a mile, even in bad weather!

11. **TOILET PAPER.** Several feet of this in a plastic bag might not really be an essential, but it can sure improve your quality of life (and it can work as emergency material for starting a fire).

LIGHT, ULTRALIGHT, STUPID-LIGHT

OUNCES EQUAL POUNDS

I think the classifications of light, ultralight and "stupid-light" are worth mentioning because folks that engage in activities calling for minimalist gear are truly pushing the envelope on the idea of minimalist adventuring. I am not sure who, if anyone exactly, coined these phrases. The order in which I have them listed is a progressively more minimalist approach to outdoor adventuring. It seems that the key to going light is really simple: Take a hard, analytical look at your gear and consider if there is a lighter way of designing it or putting it together. Many ultralight folks even purchase rolls of material and make their own packs and completely remove all things they consider wasteful. I want to give you a few highlights so you can consider if this is the right way for you as well. I must offer a few words of caution. Do not go so far into ultralight activities that you do not have a safety net. Before you venture out, ensure you have some backup plans—including communication gear—to help preserve your safety and survival should you need it.

Ultralight is a good way to stretch your know-how and what you are comfortable with. It definitely makes your pack lighter.

MATERIALS

Dyneema® Composite Fabric (commonly known as Cuben fiber), Pertex® nylon and Ventum nylon are all various types of materials that ultralight folks are using for bags, packs and other gear. Cuben fiber is the one that seems to get the most attention and is more widely available. I have seen several Cuben fiber tarps being used by students in my classes. They hold up and shed water incredibly well.

TENTS

Besides the materials used to make a tent, the overall strategy here is to get a tent that you can set up using trekking poles. This allows you to go about without carrying tent poles that serve only that purpose. Many ultralighters will choose tents that are mesh with a good rainfly. This keeps the insects and rain off them.

RAINFLY OR TARP

To venture out even more minimally, just take a rainfly and no tent at all. I do a number of safety and survival classes with just a rainfly. It is easy to set up a strong shelter. You will need to have good situational awareness and observe the prevailing weather patterns when doing this, so you don't get hit with rain or worse. You should also know what the insects are like where you are as well. If you have an aversion to having insects on you, then this is not for you. I have slept out like this many times and with even less. Just expect to be woken up during the night by insects crawling on you.

BIVY SACKS

An even lighter methodology is to go with a bivy sack. I have also done this on a number of occasions and this is very common for our students who are current or former military personnel. I have slept in heavy rain with a bivy sack several times. If you keep everything buttoned and zipped properly, it works well. You should also spray this, and all similar gear, with waterproofing material as I suggested earlier.

SLEEPING BAG

I have a good friend who is an ultralighter who approached the sleeping bag situation by actually cutting off the mummy hood and only utilizing a wicking cap at night. They now make sleeping bags where you don't have to cut off the hood, but it could save you a few ounces.

SLEEPING PAD

The easiest way to save ounces here is to choose a half-length or three-quarter-length pad. Take it a step further by using an air pad rather closed-cell foam. By doing so you run the risk of losing comfort, particularly insulation, from the knees down. You can solve this by using leaf litter in a forested landscape or your pack.

FOOD

I shared the most effective and lightweight food source in Chapter 7. Most people who go ultralight make much of their own dehydrated food and package it as well. A vacuum sealer at home makes food sources small and manageable in the pack and fresh when it is time to whip up some dinner.

If the weather is warm enough and there is no concern for insects or snakes, you can save a lot of weight by bringing only a rainfly as shelter to protect against rain.

NATURE STUDY

LEARN HOW TO READ THE ENVIRONMENT

I have mentioned several times throughout this book that I often engage in nature study. Some of the things that I find interesting are edible and medicinal plants, tree identification and all things tracking. If you are a kindred spirit in such endeavors, are a wildlife manager, an environmental educator, a biologist or just simply enjoy nature because it is cool, you may want to pick up some supplies to help your study. The following are my favorites.

RITE IN THE RAIN

Rite in the Rain has been producing quality products for nearly 100 years. They created paper products, pens and notebooks that are essentially waterproof, as you could guess by their name. I have crates full of run-of-the-mill notebooks, which contain my field notes. Many of them were washed out or hard to read due to rain, sweat or other forms of moisture. Once I was introduced to Rite in the Rain products, those problems went away. I prefer their ring-binder style over the other offerings. The ring binder allows me to keep my same notebook and cover together and just add and remove paper when needed. I can also offer you another good tidbit to help: if you get an earth tone or camouflage binder like I have, attach a bright piece of cordage to it. This makes it easier to find when you lay it down in an effort to spot the coyote whose tracks you have been drawing.

For nature study, Rite in the Rain notebooks are a must-have as they allow you to continue writing in poor weather conditions.

A good ruler allows you to capture information for your own knowledge or share it on social media for identification purposes.

The Hidden Woodsmen line of packs are great for short hikes. This over-the-shoulder bag carries all my nature study books and notebooks.

EVIDENCE RULER

You do not have to be a detective to utilize or have one of these rulers. They make a great addition to notebook supplies. You can easily take great photos that are indexed properly. This will help you share the photo on social media to help get a positive ID if you are seeking it. It is also a great tool to use in concert with your favorite naturalist ID book, such as the Peterson Field Guides.

NOTEBOOK COVER

Rite in the Rain has some great notebook covers of their own, but I carry one made from Tactical Tailor. It is made to also carry a few extra supplies, like a ruler, a compass, map tools, pens and pencils. I also carry a Fresnel lens now that my eyesight is getting a bit cloudier.

BOOKBAG

I have a bookbag made by The Hidden Woodsmen called the Haversack (approximately $75) that I keep all my nature guides and notebooks in. It is easy to grab it and go to the woods for whatever I want to engage in.

HYGIENE

LEARN HOW NOT TO BE OFFENSIVE TO YOURSELF AND OTHERS

Being smelly, sweaty and chafed are all simply part of being outdoors on extended trips, right? Not necessarily. As I tell my students and have told you here, the two big reasons that people do not enjoy spending time in the outdoors overnight are a poor sleeping arrangement, which equates to no rest, and poor food choices, which lowers morale. Rounding out the top three complaints would be the issues that arise with poor hygiene. In addition to a big dose of common sense, there are some simple gear pieces that we can get to help us. I cannot offer you the proper mind-set and gear to have you smelling and looking like you are heading to prom in the backcountry. But I can help you to be more comfortable and clean so you don't offend yourself, your friends and the wildlife.

The first thing you need to remember is that backcountry adventure, even glamping in a campground, is not the same as being at home. Sweating is a natural occurrence and should be expected. As a matter of fact, if you are adventuring in hot weather or are engaging in physical exertion (like backpacking), you *want* sweat. Sweating is your body's way of cooling down. I tell my students that it is nature's little air conditioner that we carry around with us all the time (see the sidebar on page 202).

As I write this, I have just returned from teaching my three-day Scout/Tracker course. In this course, my students study how to move through a wilderness and remain unseen. They are also taught how to read tracks on the ground and gather information. In short, this means they are walking in, crawling through and lying in a wilderness area. This class was done in near –90°F (32°C) temperatures during the day with high humidity and no modern shower facilities at night. That is a perfect recipe for noxious students. Following are some simple things I recommended to them that you can do in a situation where you are exerting yourself.

CLEAN YOURSELF WITH WATER

During most adventuring, cleaning up with water will be done at night. I recommend you do this as often as your schedule allows. Specifically, on backpacking trips, I always did this—at a minimum—around lunchtime and at night before going to sleep. Whenever possible, use your land-navigation skills to recognize areas where you will be around water. Use those opportunities to stop and clean the sensitive areas of your body, such as your armpits, genitals and feet. These areas will hold a lot of moisture and bacteria. If these areas remain unchecked, the bacteria will grow and your outdoor friends and family may begin to wonder if a skunk is in the area. I have said it many times: During simple outdoor fun and in survival training, a bandana is a wonderful piece of equipment. You can get to a water source, soak the bandana then utilize it as a washcloth to clean these sensitive areas of your body. If you do this at midday, you can avoid a lot of buildup, which helps prevent friction and other issues. Also take the time to soak the bandana when you are finished to remove as much bacteria as you can from the bandana so it will not become too odoriferous. You can do this easily without soap.

THE SCIENCE AND STRATEGY OF SWEATING

Sweating is a natural process that helps your body deal with higher temperatures. When you engage in physical exertion (and severe mental duress), you will sweat. Your brain sends a signal to your sweat glands to pump fluids out to moisten your skin. These fluids then evaporate, and this evaporation removes heat from your skin's surface and you cool off. Here are some hints to help you sweat efficiently and healthily:

- In humid conditions, it is hard for the water to quickly evaporate. Your body will work harder to cool you off, which causes you to get hotter. Be careful in humid temperatures and recognize when your temperature is rising. If you become overheated, you must stop your activity level and get out of the sun whenever possible.

- Studies show that even a 2 percent drop in body weight from sweat can negatively affect your overall performance during any physical activity.

- It may seem counterintuitive, but one way to regulate sweat is to drink more water before an activity. If you are dehydrated, your body will work harder to function properly. This means you will heat up more and use up more water. If you are hydrated, your body can function optimally.

- Your sweat will not smell as bad if you stay hydrated. Much like they do in your urine, toxins come out of your body through the sweating process. If you sweat regularly and often, the toxins come out over time rather than all at once.

- When you are sweating, you should replace electrolytes, the most important of which is sodium. I typically use naturally occurring Himalayan pink salt rather than salt manufactured in a lab. This natural salt has a vast array of minerals and other compounds that we need, whereas normal table salt is nothing more than the chemical compound of sodium chloride.

- Another good choice for electrolyte replenishment is Vitalyte drink mixes. Vitalyte makes great sports drinks that do not contain as much sugar and other problematic substances that are not good for us in the wilderness.

At night, I do an all-over cleaning with water, soap and the same bandana. If the weather allows, I will then wear some light shorts, a T-shirt, camp shoes and nothing else to allow plenty of air circulation. In cold weather, I focus only on cleaning my sensitive areas. (None of us will sweat as much in cold weather as we do in hot conditions, but we still need to sweat. It is a sign that we are hydrated well. If you are exerting yourself and not sweating, that is a sign of dehydration and you need to correct it.) If it is extremely cold, I will at the very least wipe these areas off as best I can with my cold-weather gear on, or in my sleeping bag. This allows me to stay warm and remove the offensive sweat and bacteria. Just be safe to not introduce any more water to the inside of your cold-weather gear than you must. This makes it work inefficiently and maintaining your core body temperature is more important to your safety than your hygiene.

UTILIZE WIPES

There are numerous brands of wipes on the market. Many of these will offer you some antibacterial qualities. I prefer the ones that have been made specifically for outdoor use. I have used Coleman Bio Wipes on more trips than I can count. They are my preferred choice because they are biodegradable, have antibacterial qualities and are inexpensive. As I mentioned earlier, I utilize a bandana and water for basic cleanliness but for bathroom breaks, I use these types of wipes.

AVOID CHAFING

It is a sad day in the woods when a trip is uncomfortable or gets derailed completely due to chafing. Chafing most often occurs on or around your genitals or thighs. This is a sensitive area of your body, so when it experiences a fair amount of rubbing in a moisture-rich environment, it gets chafed and painful. You can avoid chafing in several ways. The main thing to avoid is cotton underwear. As we discussed earlier, cotton holds moisture and therefore it is problematic in cold weather and can lead to chafing. I have had two approaches to this problem and both work well for me. The first is to wear polyester-based underwear with boxer-style legs. This allows the rubbing to occur on the legs of the undergarment rather than the skin of my legs.

One thing to look for when purchasing underwear is how the crotch is sewed. If it is sewed in such a way that the individual portions bunch up at the crotch with lots of thread and overlap, you will most likely get some chafing due to that portion rubbing you. Avoid this at all costs. It seems to me that the inexpensive models of undergarments do this regularly and the more expensive models, such as Under Armour and ExOfficio, do not.

Therefore, I can easily recommend either of those for your use. There are several products you can use to help keep moisture from occurring in and around your sensitive areas. I do not use antiperspirant deodorant because in the long run, I want my body to sweat; I do not want to chemically prevent it from doing that. If you choose to use antiperspirant, you can also use it on your legs to accomplish the same goal. There is also a product used with great success by many backpackers called Body Glide. This does two things to benefit you. It has a lubricant in it to make it easier for your legs to rub without chafing, and it also has zinc oxide in it to prevent moisture. Another more inexpensive solution is to put a light coat of petroleum jelly on your legs. This also serves to lubricate the area as well. Yet another solution is to utilize cornstarch powder. Since I use it most often on my feet, I will discuss it in detail in the following section.

TAKE CARE OF YOUR FEET

I have yet to meet a backpacker that has not had issues with their feet at some point during their adventuring. When moving about, our feet are going to be involved up to the point we sit down and take a break. This means they get a lot of wear and tear. There are not as many sweat glands in the feet, which helps keep the amount of moisture down. However, due to our need to keep our feet protected, they are nearly completely encapsulated by socks and shoes. This same protection can cause issues that will need to be resolved. As we discussed in Chapter 4, I am a big proponent of socks manufactured with merino wool. For many years now, my go-to source for these has been Smartwool. Smartwool has a great blend of merino wool, nylon and elastane that makes their socks great for wicking moisture and retaining their shape and function.

This is the sort of beauty that's best seen in person. This location is overlooking Cave Run Lake in Bath County, Kentucky.

I was recently introduced to Darn Tough socks. They are the first company that I know of to offer a lifetime guarantee on their socks. I have been wearing them for a few months now on my rucks, and they certainly live up to their name. What is not to love about that sort of guarantee? Please remember that I have a lot of detailed information on socks in the discussion of Tier 1 clothing in Chapter 4 (pages 82–83). I feel the two-sock system is nearly a necessity of you are a serious backpacker. This is another one of those things I was doing 30 years ago before it was so cool. Now that my emphasis on outdoor adventure has changed a bit, I do not utilize the two-sock setup any longer.

There are several things you can do beyond these simple basics to help take care of your feet:

- **Have moleskin, duct tape or similar available.** If you are new to backpacking, you will most likely wear some blisters on your feet until you get them toughened up a bit. Being 12 to 20 miles (19 to 32 km) into a hike is not the time to get a blister and not have a solution for fixing it. Most adhesive bandages do not have glue on them to handle the rigors of a backpacker's feet. Moleskin or duct tape most certainly do. Clean your blisters as best you can with water and let them dry before covering them with the moleskin or duct tape. You can make the removal process more comfortable if you place a gauze on the wound first. I soak the covering for quite a while before removing it. It is best to do this soak in warm, soapy water. The will help lessen the amount of adhesive stuck to your skin. Just be advised that some dead skin will attach to the adhesive and will likely rip your skin as you remove it. The soaking makes the removal process less painful.

- **Use medicated foot powder.** I queried a large segment of my students about their footcare and many stated that they utilize powder such as GOLD BOND®. I have not had much luck with powders unless they were primarily made of cornstarch. I do want to offer them here, because even though they don't seem to work for my feet, they most assuredly work for many other folks. My simple queries told me that they too mostly utilized cornstarch-based powders.

- **Use lubricants.** Lubricant is another great choice for many, but lubricant does not work for me. The thought is you can employ the lubricant to limit friction inside of the sock and boot. My experience with lubricant is that it makes my feet feel slippery. I do not care for that while trekking through the wilderness.

HOW TO POOP IN THE WOODS

The modern toilet is a wonderful thing, right? Modern sewage systems are great for removing waste from the areas we live, work and recreate in. That same toilet is one we take for granted when we go outdoors and need to do our business. In this step-by-step guide, I want to help you poo, stay clean while doing it and make sure it is environmentally friendly all at the same time.

- First and foremost, the most environmentally sound way to take care of this is to bag your poop and pack it out. This is also a requirement on some federal and state natural areas. Have small, individual sealable bags that you turn inside out. Use the bag as a hand cover to pick up your waste and then turn it right-side out. Seal it up. You can then keep odor and leakage possibilities down by putting the individual bags into one larger bag.

- Choose a spot where you can squat comfortably. You may want to grab a tree for support and lean back when doing this if you lack hip flexibility like I do. Do not sit across a log as if it were a toilet like they do in the cartoons. That never works out well.

- Verify you are not near a water source. You should distance yourself a minimum of 200 feet (61 m) from any water source and trail area.

- Once you have chosen a spot where you can squat comfortably, dig a hole for the poop to go into. This is often referred to as a cat hole. Make sure you pile the dirt up from the hole next to it. I use a pocket trowel when I can afford the weight and a digging stick from the environment when I can't. The hole should be about 8 inches (20 cm) deep. This keeps it away from most critters and doesn't allow it to go into the water table easily, yet keeps it near enough to the surface that it will decompose more rapidly.

- Do your business in the hole. If possible, carry your waste paper out. If not, then please make sure it is unscented, biodegradable paper made for such purposes. Regular paper from your bathroom at home is not a good choice. You can also use nontoxic leaves. I stay on the lookout for mullein on my travels and pick it up for bathroom purposes when I see it. It is soft and pliable.

- Scoop the dirt from the hole onto the waste and fill the hole back in. I mix in some forest leaf debris with the dirt to aid in decomposition.

- Cover the top with normal forest debris, which will help the spot return to normal.

- If you are in an area that is covered in rocks and cannot dig into the earth, the best solution is to simply spread the waste as thinly as possible on a rock. Place the rock in direct sunlight. The UV rays of the sun will break the waste down rather quickly. I would like to emphasize that packing your waste out in this situation is best. However, spreading it thinly on a rock is a best-case setup in a situation where you must leave it.

- Finally, use some hand sanitizer or water and soap to clean your hands. It is easy to get caught up in the moment of being rugged in the outdoors and forget that clean hands are the key to remaining illness-free in the backcountry.

FAMILY OUTDOORS

START 'EM YOUNG

According to Dave Barry, "Camping is nature's way of promoting the motel business." It is certainly a cute quote, but one that I disagree with wholeheartedly. He did not have me as a teacher. My mission at Nature Reliance School has always been to get more people outside. Sometimes we offer a certain topic that appeals to our students' desire for training; other times we appeal to their need to be safe. Another thing I have always attempted to do is encourage and assist families in getting outside together. While this entire book is a resource primarily for adults, I also want to make a few recommendations for those who have children.

If you have children who are too small to walk on their own, do not feel as if you have a few years before you can venture out again. There are several gear items that will assist you in getting outside with your kiddos. This is another area where I feel you should spend some extra money. When my children were little, my wife and I regularly carried them in backpack carriers. We had inexpensive versions and one that was costlier. We purchased only one that was expensive because it lasted until we no longer needed it and it wore very comfortably. That was many years ago, but I still look at these from time to time and lament that we did not have back then what is available now. Osprey™ (approximately $250) is one such carrier. These things are bombproof and carry all the essentials, including a fantastic suspension system for the kiddo. They will include sunshades, places for toys, diapers and cleaning products. Since my wife breastfed both our children, she also had a front carrier. She preferred the backpack carrier, although it was less convenient for nursing. A front carrier caused too much strain on her back. I carried our kids in the front carrier a few times as well and had the same experience. We both felt the backpack was the way to go.

Just because you are a new parent doesn't mean your outdoor days are over. Get a child carrier and bring the kids along.

For children who can walk on their own, I can give you the best piece of advice in the world to get them, and keep them, interested in the outdoors: Get them a water bladder and pack system for it. CamelBak has literally hundreds of products for you to choose from. The nice thing is that many of the water bladder packs made for adults can work as a main backpack for a small child. They are typically small enough for an adult to carry water, keys and a wallet, yet they are sizable enough that when a child wears them, they feel like they are the big kids. In my experience with my children, as well as teaching hundreds of others, one thing has rung true: kids are drawn to water. I personally believe it is because we naturally understand our need for it. Whatever the reason, having a backpack with what appears to a be a very long bendy straw attached to it is golden.

Other gear for the kiddos should include items that will bridge the gap between their life at home and life outside. If you take all electronics from kids and expect

CamelBak's water bladders are great choices for both adults and kids to carry water and stay hydrated. Kids love them.

them to enjoy being outside, they rarely will. They need to have some familiarity or they will feel too far out of place. I recommend you allow them some familiar toys or gadgets to bridge the gap. It was nearly twenty years ago, but I can distinctly remember my daughter traipsing out through the woods with her "snuggle cuddles" (stuffed animals) tucked under her arm to go play in the woods. Snuggle cuddles got a bit dirty from time to time, but my daughter enjoyed herself immensely. Another example is how I first taught my son to still-hunt for deer. He was very energetic, so sitting in a tree stand at an early age would have been a miserable experience for him. I bought a blind and a chair. He took his mobile video game and a two-way radio with him into the blind. I could call him on the radio when the animals were approaching. It allowed me to stay close to him, keep him confident and at the same time give him some familiarity with his regular gadgets. This allowed me the opportunity to teach him things (via radio) about what was going on around him outside the blind. He is now the main provider of

Helping kids to enjoy being outside ensures the next generation will preserve the great outdoors.

venison for our dinner table because of it. See the sidebar on the next page for some of my favorite games to help kids get used to being outdoors.

MY FAVORITE WILDERNESS GAMES FOR KIDS

SCAVENGER HUNT. Most everyone knows some variation of this one, so it is an easy one to replicate in the wilderness. In this game, you offer a list of items that kids are supposed to find from their environment. If it safe, they can go off and do it on their own. If it is not safe, you can do it right along with them. I prefer to use this game to also teach some stewardship and conservation. Therefore, I do not recommend they pick or cut anything that is alive. Here is a sample list of simple items you can find in a wilderness setting:

- A leaf that is rounded on the end

- A leaf that is pointy on the end

- A nut

- A hole in the ground (ask them what they think lives there)

- A smooth rock

- A rough rock

- A piece of bark that has fallen from a tree

- A dead branch that looks like something else (let them use their imagination here; they will find a branch that looks like a dog, a pencil or something they are familiar with)

- Something they could build a fire with

* See photo on page 207 (right column, top).

ROPE MAZE. This is a great game to do in any city park or at a campground. All you need for this game is a rope and bunch of trees. Tie one end of the rope to a tree with two half-hitches. Then weave the rope around other trees in a maze pattern. The more the rope passes on, under and around itself, the better. Ensure the other end is several feet away from the start. Blindfold those that want to be involved (this could sometimes include adults). Place their hand on the rope at the start and tell them they cannot remove their hand and must slide it along the rope until they come to the end. You can tie an object at the end like a stick, ball or other recognizable object to make sure they know they have completed the game. Being blindfolded, even as part of a game, is nearly always frightening. The rope maze game allows kids to overcome a small amount of fear or apprehension to accomplish a task. This mental programming helps them overcome fears in a simple and protected way. They can then use that newfound courage to be outside more and not be afraid. * See photo on page 207 (right column, bottom).

MEET A TREE. This game is much like the rope maze in that it starts with children gathered around a tree and blindfolded. It is best done in a park or forest where there are several trees. This allows you to spread the children out so they each have their own tree. Once you give the word to go, the child will feel the tree. I encourage them to develop a picture in their mind with questions like "Is the bark smooth?", "Is it rough?", "Is the bark deep or shallow?", "Does it feel like where the tree meets the ground?" I then tell the children to keep their blindfolds on while I move them somewhere else. Once all the children are moved I then tell them to take their blindfolds off and go find their tree. This offers the child the ability to recognize different aspects of a tree they may have otherwise ignored. It is rare for them to not be able to recognize a tree after being blindfolded. This will open their eyes a bit more to what they are seeing when they look at a wilderness.

ELECTRONICS

BALANCE IS KEY

Most of us want to get into the wilderness to unplug and get away from technology and all that goes along with it. The idealist in me is the same way. I regularly go to the woods to get away and leave everything but a few essentials somewhere else. The realist in me is the one who wrote this book. I must admit there are times when modern technology is quite handy and useful. I want to share a few electronic items with you here. You should consider whether these offer something useful to your supplies.

GPS

I love my Garmin Foretrex® 401 (approximately $150) and have no issues with it. In the past I have also used a Delorme Earthmate as well. (Delorme is now owned by Garmin, and I believe this will only serve to make products from both companies better.) I prefer the Foretrex over the Earthmate due to its small size and ease of use. I wear mine on my chest kit or wrist on a regular basis when I am going cross-country, during man tracking and as quality control using maps for terrain association. As I mentioned in Chapter 3, a GPS and a map are great combo for easy land navigation use.

GPS units come in various sizes. Here my daughter is using the Garmin Foretrex 401.

CELL PHONE

I do have apps that I use on my phone during outdoor fun. Most of them are plant identification tools. Although I prefer a good book in my hands, there is no mistaking how easy it is to carry numerous resources with you on a cell phone or a tablet. (Another good reason is because this book is also available on Kindle!)

The other obvious thing is that cameras are everywhere now. Although I prefer people getting out and experiencing nature firsthand, I also enjoy others getting to see some of the stuff that gets captured with a camera, which they might not have seen otherwise.

Handheld radios—both ham systems, such as the one shown, and less-expensive family radios—are good for safety and fun.

RADIO

When my children were young, we did not let them out of our sight when we went to the wilderness. They did not know that, though. We gave them radios so they could, on occasion, adventure on their own (at least they thought they were on their own). They kept in radio contact with us, which added a "cool factor" to their trips. I had a set of the basic Motorola family radios (approximately $100). I always ensured they had lanyards and were attached to my kids' packs so they would not get lost. I have now gotten my ham radio license and use my portable Yaesu for a host of different uses: for class communication between instructors, for use during SAR training, for better communications in the event of a disaster. Most ham radios have National Oceanic and Atmospheric Administration weather channels as well.

BATTERY POWER

For non-backpacking adventures, I carry an Anker brand battery backup device. Once charged, it can provide enough power to charge my cell phone ten times. For those adventures where I know I will need extra or backup power but am carrying my gear on my back, I have a Goal Zero Switch 10. It provides a flexible solar cell that I can recharge the batteries in the field. I do this often on trips during which I am teaching.

LOCATOR BEACONS

I have had my eye on these for quite some time but have not bought one yet. When I do it is going to be the SPOT personal tracker (approximately $75). With one of these devices, you can use satellite technology to let others know you are okay or if you need assistance. Locator beacons are a great choice for those who want to push the envelope on trips—even solo ones—and still have some method to be in contact with help if it is needed.

TIME TO KICK YOU OUT OF THE NEST

I told you early on that my whole purpose in writing this book was to assist you in getting outside more. I sincerely hope that you have gained more knowledge on how to select gear that will suit your needs and a lot of your wants.

What am I going to be doing now, you ask? I am swapping this keyboard for a daypack, and I am heading out into a wilderness. Do you want to know why?

Well, it's because I hope to see you on—or off—the trail!

APPENDIX: RESOURCES

Of all the paths you take in life, make sure a few of them are dirt.

—John Muir

I am confident I have put together one of the most researched and experiential guides ever published on the topic of gear. To cover every single facet of detail would make an encyclopedia of books rather than one book. So here is a listing of the brands I have mentioned, their most current websites (as of this writing) and an overview of the products they carry.

CHAPTER 2: ESSENTIAL TOOLS		
NAME	**WEBSITE**	**PRODUCTS**
BEAVER BILL FORGING WORKS	beaverbill.com	fixed and folding knives, axes, tomahawks
BRIGHT FOREST FORGE	brightforestforge.com	fixed knives, axes
BUCK KNIVES	buckknives.com	fixed and folding knives
COLUMBIA RIVER KNIFE AND TOOL®	crkt.com	knives, axes, general outdoor gear
GERBER	gerbergear.com	knives, shovels, multi-tools, general outdoor gear
GRÄNSFORS BRUK	gransforsbruk.com/en/	axes
HUSQVARNA	husqvarna.com	axes
LEATHERMAN	leatherman.com	multi-tools
L.T. WRIGHT HANDCRAFTED KNIVES	ltwrightknives.com	knives, outdoor gear
MORAKNIV	morakniv.se/en/	knives, fire starters
ULTIMATE SURVIVAL TIPS	ultimatesurvivaltips.com	knives, survival guides
WANDER TACTICAL RESEARCH TEAM	wandertactical.com	fixed and folding knives

CHAPTER 3: MAINTAINING YOUR PERSONAL SAFETY

NAME	WEBSITE	PRODUCTS
CAMMENGA	cammenga.com	compasses
COMET	comet-marine.com	first aid supplies
COUNTER ASSAULT	counterassault.com	aerial, ground and water signaling devices
DELORME MAPPING SOFTWARE	delorme.com	bear spray
FOX 40 WHISTLES	fox40world.com	GPS, mapping software
GAIA	gaia.com	whistles mapping software
GARMIN	garmin.com	bear spray
IMMINENT THREAT SOLUTIONS	itstactical.com	GPS, mapping software
ISRAELI FIRST AID	israelifirstaid.com	first aid supplies
MAPPING SUPPORT	mappingsupport.com	first aid supplies
MYTOPO	mytopo.com	mapping software
NATIONAL GEOGRAPHIC MAPS	natgeomaps.com	mapping software
NORTH AMERICAN RESCUE	narescue.com	maps, mapping software
SARTOPO	sartopo.com	mapping website
SWAT-T™	swattourniquet.com	first aid supplies
TACTICALGEAR.COM	tacticalgear.com	tactical and general outdoor gear
TACTICAL MEDICAL SOLUTIONS	tacmedsolutions.com	first aid supplies
U.S. GEOLOGICAL SURVEY	usgs.gov	maps, mapping website

CHAPTER 4: SHELTER		
NAME	WEBSITE	PRODUCTS
5.11 TACTICAL	511tactical.com	clothing, packs
ARC'TERYX	arcteryx.com	clothing, packs
ASBELL WOOL	gfredasbell.com	wool clothing, bow supplies
ASOLO	asolo.com	boots, shoes, outdoor clothing
BIG AGNES	bigagnes.com	tents, sleeping pads and bags
CABELA'S	cabelas.com	wide range of outdoor gear
CARHARTT	carhartt.com	outdoor clothing, packs
CATOMA	catomaoutdoor.com	tents, sleeping bags
CHACO	chacos.com	outdoor sandals
COLUMBIA	columbia.com	clothing, footwear, packs
CROCS	crocs.com	outdoor sandals
DANNER	danner.com	footwear
DARN TOUGH	darntough.com	socks
DREAM HAMMOCK	dreamhammock.com	hammocks
FIRSTSPEAR	first-spear.com	tactical and general outdoor gear
FROGG TOGGS	froggtoggs.com	rain gear
HENNESSY HAMMOCK	hennessyhammock.com	hammocks
KEEN	keenfootwear.com	footwear
KLYMIT	klymit.com	sleeping pads
LOWA	lowaboots.com	footwear
MERRELL	merrell.com	footwear
MOUNTAIN HARDWEAR	mountainhardwear.com	clothing, climbing gear
OUTDOOR RESEARCH	outdoorresearch.com	wide range of outdoor gear
POLARTEC	polartec.com	clothing, gloves, hats

(Continued)

CHAPTER 4: SHELTER (CONTINUED)

NAME	WEBSITE	PRODUCTS
REI	rei.com	wide range of outdoor gear
SALOMON	salomon.com	boots, shoes, outdoor clothing
SMARTWOOL	smartwool.com	wool clothing
SNUGPAK	snugpak.com	packs, bags, sleeping bags, tents
TETON SPORTS	tetonsports.com	wide range of outdoor gear
THERM-A-REST	thermarest.com	sleeping pads
UNDER ARMOUR	underarmour.com	wide range of outdoor clothing
VASQUE	vasque.com	footwear
WILDERNESS INNOVATION	wildernessinnovation.com	tarps, insulated ponchos

CHAPTER 5: FIRE

NAME	WEBSITE	PRODUCTS
BIC® LIGHTERS	flickyourbic.com	lighters
BIOLITE	bioliteenergy.com	compact wood burning camp stoves
COGHLAN'S	coghlans.com	fire tinder, inexpensive outdoor camping supplies
COLEMAN	coleman.com	wide range of outdoor gear
ESBIT	esbit.de/en/	fire tinder, stoves
FIRESTEEL	firesteel.com	ferrorcerium rods
SOLKOA FASTFIRE	solkoa.com	fire tinder
ÜBERFIRE	topsknives.com	fire tinder
WETFIRE	ustbrands.com	fire tinder
ZIPPO	zippo.com	lighters

CHAPTER 6: WATER AND HYDRATION

NAME	WEBSITE	PRODUCTS
AQUAMIRA	aquamira.com	water filters, purifiers and drops
CAMELBAK	camelbak.com	water bladders and packs
KATADYN	katadyn.com	water purifier
KLEAN KANTEEN	kleankanteen.com	water bottles
MIO	makeitmio.com	drink enhancers
NALGENE	nalgene.com	water bottles
RAPIDPURE	rapidpure.net	water purifier

CHAPTER 7: FOOD

NAME	WEBSITE	PRODUCTS
BACKPACKER'S PANTRY	backpackerspantry.com	backpacking meals
JETBOIL	jetboil.com	camp and backpacking stoves
KELLY KETTLE	kellykettleusa.com	wood burning camp stoves
MOUNTAIN HOUSE	mountainhouse.com	backpacking meals
MSR	msrgear.com	wide range of outdoor gear
SNOW PEAK	snowpeak.com	backpacking stoves, cups, bowls

CHAPTER 8: PACKS

NAME	WEBSITE	PRODUCTS
BODY GLIDE	bodyglide.com	anti-chafing first aid supplies
EBERLESTOCK	eberlestock.com	packs
HILL PEOPLE GEAR	hillpeoplegear.com	packs, sling bags
KELTY	kelty.com	packs, chest kits
OSPREY	ospreypacks.com	wide range of outdoor gear
S.O.TECH	sotechtactical.com	packs
TACTICAL TAILOR	tacticaltailor.com	tactical packs and chest rigs
THE HIDDEN WOODSMEN	thehiddenwoodsmen.com	chest rigs, packs, tactical gear

CHAPTER 9: SPECIALTY GEAR		
NAME	**WEBSITE**	**PRODUCTS**
BELL	bellhelmets.com	mountain biking helmets
EVIDENT	shopevident.com	forensic nature study supplies
GIANT	giant-bicycles.com	mountain bikes and gear
GIRO	giro.com	biking helmets
ITHACA GUN COMPANY	ithacagun.com	shotguns
JACKSON KAYAK	jacksonkayak.com	kayaks and canoes
KALI	kaliprotectives.com	biking helmets
LAZER	lazerhelmets.com	biking helmets
MOTOROLA	motorola.com	two-way radios
NRS	nrs.com	paddling gear
OLD TOWN	oldtowncanoe.com	kayaks and canoes
PETZL	petzl.com	climbing gear, headlamps
PSE	pse-archery.com	archery supplies
RITE IN THE RAIN	riteintherain.com	waterproof notebooks and pens
RUGER	ruger-firearms.com	rifles, shotguns, firearms supplies
SAVAGE	savagearms.com	survival bows
SPOT	findmespot.com	rifles, shotguns, firearms supplies
STREAMLIGHT	streamlight.com	locator beacon
SURVIVAL ARCHERY SYSTEMS	survivalarcherysystems.com	high quality flashlights
SUUNTO	suunto.com	land navigation supplies
TRADITIONS PERFORMANCE FIREARMS	traditionsfirearms.com	muzzleloading supplies
YAESU	yaesu.com	two-way radios

ACKNOWLEDGMENTS

Gratitude can transform common days into thanksgivings, turn routine jobs into joy, and change ordinary opportunities into blessings.

—William Arthur Ward

Many thanks once again go out to Will Kiester, Sarah Monroe and everyone else at Page Street Publishing: Will, for his vision and professionalism in putting out a quality product, and Sarah as an editor, for her wonderful oversight and developmental editing of this book from start to finish. Nichole Kraft of Paper Weight Editing has once again assisted you, the reader, by helping the grammar and structure of my work.

A big thank you goes out to Jennifer, my wife, as well as Lily and Zane, my wonderful kids. They have patiently listened to the endless tales of outdoor pursuits I experienced before I met them, and they have always supported me as we have enjoyed, and sometimes endured, scores of others together as a family. Many lessons have been learned by all of us along the way, not the least of which is thankfulness: I am forever grateful that I have been blessed to have them in my life. I must also give a huge shout-out of thanks to my wife for her excellent photography in this book!

I have said it many times, but it bears repeating: My mom and dad gave me a life where I was encouraged to spend more time in campgrounds than playgrounds. On some of those trips we drug along a camper filled to the gills with stuff. Other times my dad and I had not much more than a couple of pack baskets with minimal gear.

Numerous staff members at J&H Lanmark Store in Lexington, Kentucky, were incredibly helpful in offering me insights into the latest trends, materials and uses of outdoor gear. That research is spread throughout the whole of this book and I could not be more thankful for it. Chris Howard of Canoe Kentucky in Frankfort, Kentucky, was generous in sharing knowledge on all things related to paddling. Mike Hale of Mike's Hike and Bike was most helpful (and quite funny and engaging) when I was doing research on the latest equipment available to mountain bikers.

(Continued)

ACKNOWLEDGMENTS (CONT.)

I am forever trying to find ways of helping others with their mind-set, skills, tactics and gear in the outdoors. Being safe has always been at the forefront of my pursuits. Tracy Trimble, Chad and Tiffany Conway, Aaron Stamper, Alex Hyrzca and John May are all dedicated SAR volunteers. I have queried each of them at some point during the writing of this book about ways I can help people be safer in the outdoors. Mike Poynter and Ken Galbreith were incredibly forthcoming with tactical-related gear questions. Both men have decades in law enforcement and military direct action.

Doug Meyer, a fantastic primitive technologist and tireless researcher, offered me understanding and wisdom in the section in Chapter 1 titled "Historical Giants: Knowledge Weighs Nothing." He also gifted me the beautiful flint knapped knife that you see on page 19.

Brian Eury and his beautiful wife, Stacy, once again basically let me treat their remote cabin as my own as I wrote this book. The view from the front porch of that cabin and Brian and Stacy's friendship are gifts from my Creator that I cherish.

Last and certainly not least, I want to thank the thousands of students of Nature Reliance School who have trusted me with their outdoor pursuits. Whether it was in a hands-on class, in a workshop or through YouTube, I have done my best to teach and train you to the best of my ability while at the same time intently listening to, watching and learning from you so I can grow my own understanding of mind-set, skills, tactics and gear. Thanks to each of you!

ABOUT THE AUTHOR

Craig Caudill, the author of *Extreme Wilderness Survival*, began his outdoor experience while growing up backpacking, exploring, hunting and fishing in the woods of Kentucky. He has actively pursued experiential knowledge of all things related to wilderness recreation and living. He regularly teaches corporations, government agencies, universities and the public sector in these methods as a means of safety and team building. He is a professional gear reviewer and provides insight and research for outdoor gear manufacturers. He has been featured on the TV shows *Kentucky Afield* and *Kentucky Life*, and he has been interviewed on news segments to share outdoor skills and insights on gear. His written work has been featured in *Self-Reliance Illustrated*, *Wilderness Way*, *American Frontiersman*, *RECOIL* and *American Survival Guide*. He has a very active blog and guest blogs for numerous websites. He has active YouTube and Patreon channels in which he provides gear reviews and education on all things outdoors. His website can be found at www.naturereliance.org.

INDEX